Wall St N.York

Painted by N.Calyo, N.York

ACHICOLA.

Outposts on the Gulf

William Warren Rogers

with love To Claire
from Claire

We love our first
evening at the new
Melrose. Fondly, Katie

Outposts on the Gulf
Saint George Island and Apalachicola from
Early Exploration to World War II

William Warren Rogers

UNIVERSITY PRESSES OF FLORIDA
University of West Florida Press
Pensacola

Second printing, 1987

Library of Congress Cataloging in Publication Data
Rogers, William Warren.
Outposts on the Gulf.

Blbliography: v. 1, p.
Includes index.
Contents: [1] From early exploration to World
War II.
1. Apalachicola (Fla.)—History. 2. Saint George
Island (Fla.) — History. I. Title.
F319.A62R63   1986   975.9'91   85-17802
ISBN 0-8130-0832-8 (v. 1)

UNIVERSITY PRESSES OF FLORIDA is the central agency for scholarly publishing of the State of Florida's university system, producing books selected for publication by the faculty editorial committees of Florida's nine public universities: Florida A&M University (Tallahassee), Florida Atlantic University (Boca Raton), Florida International University (Miami), Florida State University (Tallahassee), University of Central Florida (Orlando), University of Florida (Gainesville), University of North Florida (Jacksonville), University of South Florida (Tampa), University of West Florida (Pensacola).

ORDERS for books published by member presses of University Presses of Florida should be addressed to University Presses of Florida, 15 NW 15th Street, Gainesville FL 32603.

Endleaves: By the late 1820s, Apalachicola was becoming a busy port. Goods from the hinterland of Florida, Georgia, and Alabama were shipped to the port and transshipped to domestic and foreign markets. Imported products were sent up the Apalachicola, Chattahoochee, and Flint rivers to inland towns and landings. The port's bustling activity is seen in this lithograph/painting done in 1837.
APALACHICOLA HISTORICAL SOCIETY

This book is for two remarkable women:
Alice Hodges and Audrey Roux

Contents

Contents

Illustrations

ILLUSTRATIONS

The *Crescent City* mail and supplies boat
Apalachicola's first train arrives, 1907
Whist, c. 1890
Promotional map of Popham's lands and oyster bottoms
William Lee Popham
"Bird's-eye view of Apalachicola, c. 1906
The William Lee Popham family

Acknowledgments

A NUMBER of people—privately, professionally, intentionally, gratuitously, and sometimes unexpectedly (responding out of innate courtesy)—greatly aided me in writing this book. One true pleasure of research in Southern history is to work in county courthouses, and I wish to thank staff and personnel at the following courthouses in Georgia: Decatur County, Bainbridge; Henry County, McDonough; and Muscogee County, Columbus. I am equally indebted to similar officials at Florida courthouses in Calhoun County, Bristol; Leon County, Tallahassee; Gadsden County, Quincy; and Franklin County, Apalachicola. Much of my research was conducted in Franklin County, and I am grateful to the following people there: Robert L. Howell, former circuit clerk of the county, and employees in his office including Renee Shivers, Marcia Johnson, Nita Hicks, Barbara Schoelles, and Nedra Jefferson. Other officials there whom I wish to thank are Corey Henriksen, John James, Jr., and Walter N. Creekmore.

Unexpected sources of valuable material turned up in municipal libraries. Staff members gave generous assistance at the Apalachicola Public Library; Haydon Burns Public Library, Jacksonville, Florida; Southwest Georgia Regional Public Library, Bainbridge (especially Ruth Marshall); Thomasville (Georgia) Public Library; and Atlanta Public Library.

The book could not have been written without professional aid at the Library of Congress, Washington, D.C.; British Museum, London; Florida State University Library, Tallahassee; University of West Florida Library, Pensacola; Florida Department of Archives, History, and Records Management, Tallahassee; Georgia Department of Archives and History, Atlanta; and Alabama Department of Archives and History, Montgomery.

I extend sincere thanks to Gene Brown and John Stocks (who got me started on the book), Kathy Jackson Willis, Dr. William Warren Rogers, Jr., Sarah Ball Proctor, Palmer Proctor, Dr. Burke Vanderhill, Dr. Robert M. Ingle, Mary Louise Ellis, and Juanita Whiddon. I am equally appreciative of help from Dr. Dorothy Dodd, Mary McRory, Barbara Miller Mattick, Opal Frye, Shirley Fogle, Hazel Richards, Joan Morris, Denise Mosconis, Mary Kay Rudolph-Schonweiler, Dena Snodgrass, Dr. Edward Keuchel, Leo Hanze, Patricia Paul, Barbara Fisher, Joe Evans, Phyllis Holzenberg, George Chappell, Pearl Marshall, Marianne Donnell, John Lee, Dr. Douglas Helms (who helped far beyond any superficial "obligations" of a former student), Dr. William S. Coker, and Herbert and Rebecca Brown.

Members of the family of William Lee Popham were cooperative and supplied vital information. I wish to thank his son, William Lee Parker, as well as Arthur C. Popham, Claire Tillman Stanton, and R. R. Popham.

Dr. James P. Jones, chairperson of the History Department, Florida State University, has supported my work, while colleagues such as Dr. John H. Moore, whose work in the Old South is related to mine, and Dr. Ralph V. Turner, whose research in medieval history is not, have always been ready to listen and willing both to praise and to point out error. I am particularly aware of my debt to Mr. James A. Servies, director of libraries, University of West Florida, and director of the University of West Florida Press. For twenty years I have leaned heavily on the advice of two colleagues: Dr. Bawa S. Singh (traveling companion, expert on the history of India, and talented photographer) and Dr. Jerrell H. Shofner, distinguished scholar of Florida history, who read the manuscript and made many helpful corrections and suggestions.

ACKNOWLEDGMENTS

My wife, Miriam, as always, has listened and been patient. Death on a dangling participle, she has also convinced me that an eternity of unrelieved hellfire awaits those who split infinitives. All of these expressions of appreciation are insufficient, and where I fall short in this book, it is solely my fault.

Introduction

THIS book is the first volume of a proposed two-volume work on the history of Saint George Island and Apalachicola, Florida. Of the many people who had an impact on the island and the town, William Lee Popham was the most important. Popham did not make an appearance until the twentieth century, but after that he dominated affairs—completely of Saint George Island and mostly of Apalachicola—through the 1930s.

Originally my intent was to trace the history of Saint George Island and its various owners, then to shift the focus to the era after World War II when the island was developed. By the 1970s it had become the center of bitter political, economic, social, ecological, and emotional struggles. Arrayed in combat were environmentalists, bent on preserving a pristine island, and their allies—certain politicians and people of the seafood industry—determined to protect Apalachicola Bay from pollution and eventual disaster. Their opponents were developers, who also had political support; they wished to convert the island into a place of people, beach homes, condominiums, and the accompanying restaurants, motels, and businesses. Thus would jobs and capital flow into an impoverished county. Each side would muster formidable arguments for its point of view.

Unexpectedly, a different approach emerged as carefully constructed writing plans were abandoned. At least the order and direction changed. The history of Apalachicola had also to be written. Then it became clear that the story of the two places made little sense unless the development of the entire area was considered. So much material was found that for reasons exceeding convenience and including space, time, and logic, this book ends in 1941. In the early sections Apalachicola dominates the story, but gradually Saint George Island becomes more and more important. By the twentieth century William Lee Popham is so central that the last chapters recount his controversial career.

Geographic details pervade this book.* Saint George Island is a narrow barrier island that stretches for thirty miles or more—seeing it in 1693, a Spanish sailor, Milán Tapia, observed, "its width is slight, in places about a pistol-shot's distance from one side to the other."[1] The island lies two to three miles off the arching mainland of Florida's Gulf coast. Waves from the Gulf of Mexico roll onto broad white beaches, which yield to large dunes covered with sea oats and other coastal vegetation. Beyond the abrupt hills of sand lie pine and palmetto forests, groves of scrub oaks, and small hammocks of live oaks and cedars that grow in the porous soil. The bay shoreline faces the mainland and is indented with wide tidal marshes. In its entirety Saint George Island contains approximately 5,895 acres.

The island's western third has historically been called Little Saint George Island (1,856 acres). It was physically divided from the larger, eastern portion by a passage known as New Inlet or West Gap. Their division was caused by periodic hurricanes, although as time passed silt filled in the gap and the islands became one. Little Saint George Island acquired a permanent separation in 1957 when the United States Army Corps of Engineers opened a passage from the Gulf to the bay. The purpose was to shorten the

* So difficult is it to establish the "correct" spelling of geographical place-names that a U.S. Board of Geographic Names adjudicates disputes brought to it when it can. Over the years treated in this history, the forms "St." and "Saint" have been used with equal frequency. Since modern readers expect consistency, we will use "Saint" in all instances where there is no decision by the U.S. Board of Geographic Names on record, even silently expanding the abbreviated form sometimes used in our source documents.

1. Irving A. Leonard, *Spanish Approach to Pensacola, 1689–1693*, 286.

time required for fishing boats to get from Apalachicola to the open Gulf. Named the Bob Sikes Cut in honor of Robert L. F. Sikes, the district's congressman at the time, it is located about three miles east of New Inlet.

Little Saint George Island widens abruptly into an elbow before narrowing into a thin sliver of sand, trees, and grasses at its western end. Known as Cape Saint George, the elbow is the site of a light-house erected in 1852. At the western end of Little Saint George Island, periodic storms caused another division. A few acres known as Sand Island would be separated only to be rejoined later.

Big Saint George or, more simply, Saint George (4,039 acres), contains all of the island east of Little Saint George. It stretches like a thin but highly irregular strand of spaghetti. The novelist Alexander Key described Saint George Island: "For more than seven leagues it parallels the coast, a gleaming white-and-green pine-covered barrier enclosing the bay and the sound, a wall of dunes cast up by the sea in sullen resentment against the spreading red of the river. Occasionally, at the whim of hurricanes it becomes two islands, and sometimes three, but always when the wrath is past the sea hastens to repair these breaches and make it whole again."[2]

The western end of Little Saint George Island is separated from another island, Saint Vincent, by West Pass. During the antebellum period West Pass was the main entrance for ships using the port of Apalachicola. Saint Vincent Island contains 12,358 acres and re-sembles a giant marine plowshare, graceful and forever in motion, parting the waters of the bay. The handsome, winglike island has several freshwater lakes and a variety of trees and plant life. It is separated from the mainland by Saint Vincent Sound, opening on the west to the Gulf through narrow Indian Pass and widening on the east into Apalachicola Bay.

East Pass lies at Saint George's eastern extremity. The waterway separates the landmass from Dog Island, and although deeper than West Pass, it is further from Apalachicola, and was not used ex-tensively until the latter part of the nineteenth century. Dog Island has 1,550 acres and topographically is a smaller version of Saint George.

2. Alexander Key, *Island Light*, 113.

Flanked by Saint Vincent and Dog islands, Saint George Island
dominates the barrier chain that protects the mainland. Its name
appears on eighteenth-century maps as "San Jorge"; like the con-
tiguous land and water formations, it was named by early Spanish
explorers. All of the islands are bounded on the south by the Gulf
of Mexico. Across from Saint George Island on the mainland the
Apalachicola River empties into the bay at a point of deep incursion, creating an inner sheet of water known as East Bay. The town
of Apalachicola lies on the river's western bank. Fresh river water
flowing into East Bay forms a true delta: a complex of swamps,
bayous, creeks, and such streams as the Little St. Marks River, the
St. Marks River, and the East River. To the east, Apalachicola Bay
becomes Saint George's Sound, which extends past Saint George
and Dog islands.

The whole sweep from Indian Pass beyond Dog Island is thirty-
six miles long and from one to fourteen miles wide. Commonly
referred to as the Apalachicola Bay area, it contains some 104,320
acres.[3] From early times, explorers, visitors, and settlers always
noted its two major characteristics: shallow waters and an abundance of marine life, especially oysters. In 1784 the geographer
Thomas Hutchins wrote that the "bay is full of shoals and oyster
banks, and not above two or three feet [of] water at most in any of
the branches of [the Apalachicola]."[4] Saint George's Sound was "so
full of oyster bars, and shoals," according to the surveyor Andrew
Ellicott (writing in 1799), "that it is difficult to navigate it, without
a pilot."[5]

The town that became Apalachicola had its beginning in the
early 1820s. As the seat of government for Franklin County, Apalachicola moved from provincial village to important shipping cen-

3. Among the various technical, scholarly, and general descriptions of the bay
area see Robert J. Livingston, *Resource Atlas of the Apalachicola Estuary*, 8–11,
21–31; Walter Raymond Boynton, "Energy Basis of a Coastal Region: Franklin
County and Apalachicola, Florida," 7–8; and John O. Simonds, *Earthscape, A
Manual of Environmental Planning* (New York, 1978), 48–93.

4. Thomas Hutchins, *An Historical Narrative and Topographical Description
of Louisiana, and West-Florida* (Philadelphia, 1784; facsimile reprint, Gainesville, 1968), 87.

5. Andrew Ellicott, *The Journal of Andrew Ellicott* (Philadelphia, 1803; reprinted, Chicago, 1962), 236.

ter and became Florida's leading port. One authority translated the euphonious word to mean "those people residing on the other side," adding that the Apalachicola Indians spoke the Hitchiti language, were of Muskogean stock, and thus a part of the Lower Creeks.[6] The word has had a number of spellings, and other meanings have been suggested. The Spanish applied the word to both the river and the Indians living along its lower reaches. The Apalachicola was described by the Englishman William Roberts in 1763 as "a noble river, whose mouth formeth a spacious harbor."[7]

About 106 miles long, the river flows south from Florida's northern boundary at the town of Chattahoochee. At that point the Flint River, flowing southwest out of Georgia, joins the Chattahoochee, an even larger river, to form the Apalachicola. The Chattahoochee rises in northeast Georgia and winds southwest until it reaches the Alabama line. Then it drops south so directly that the river itself becomes the natural and official boundary between the two states.[8]

The Flint was navigable seasonally as far as Albany (194 miles from Apalachicola) and the Chattahoochee as far as the important town of Columbus, 262 miles from Apalachicola Bay. Various other rivers, including the Chipola in Florida, feed into the Apalachicola. A strategic place for exporting and importing, Apalachicola was the trading mart for a large agricultural hinterland in Florida, Georgia, and Alabama. The fresh and constant current that brought the Apalachicola River to the saline waters of the bay carried with it the flow of commerce. Soon steamboats doubled the river's economic benefits by creating a two-way exchange.

Before the first steamboats defied the river's current, a great amount of water had flowed into Apalachicola Bay during the

6. John R. Swanton, *Early History of the Creek Indians and Their Neighbors*, 11, 129.

7. William Roberts, *An Account of the First Discovery, and Natural History of Florida*, 13. Roberts had never been to Florida, but he included several excellent maps by Thomas Jeffreys, the king's geographer.

8. See Mark E. Fretwell, *This So Remote Frontier: The Chattahoochee Country of Alabama and Georgia* (Tallahassee, 1980), 1–112; for the Florida background see Charlton W. Tebeau, *A History of Florida* (Coral Gables, 1971), 3–56.

sweep of time that is conveniently called history. Some scholars calculate that aboriginal Indians crossed from Siberia and migrated south to Florida forty thousand years ago. When the Spanish came in the sixteenth century, an estimated twenty-five thousand Indians lived on the peninsula. The Apalachees—farmers, hunters, and fishermen—were the major tribe of Middle Florida, the area from the Apalachicola River to the Suwannee River. The less numerous Apalachicola Indians were concentrated nearer the coast.

The first European to set foot on Saint George Island or on the mainland at Apalachicola remains unknown. Ponce de León, who discovered Florida, returned to Havana in 1513 without having gone that far north. Other Spaniards followed, and in 1519 Alonzo de Piñeda was responsible for mapping the entire Gulf coast.

Perhaps Pánfilo de Narváez was the first European to sight the area. In 1528 he and his men landed in the Tampa Bay area and moved north into the Apalachee country. Encountering fierce hostility from the Indians, the Spaniards built crude boats at present-day St. Marks and, hugging the shoreline, headed west. Narváez and most of the men perished before their odyssey ended in Mexico. Among the survivors was Alvar Núñez Cabeza de Vaca, who chronicled the ordeal. After leaving St. Marks, Cabeza de Vaca wrote, "We sailed seven days among these inlets, in the water waist deep, without signs of anything like the coast. At the end of this time we reached an island near the shore."[9] The place of their brief stop was either Dog Island, Saint Vincent Island (both have been suggested), or Saint George Island.[10]

Hernando de Soto, like Narváez, landed at Tampa Bay and in 1539 marched north to the area controlled by the Apalachees. The Spanish spent the winter of 1539–40 in the vicinity of the future Tallahassee. In December 1539, de Soto sent an expedition west along the Gulf of Mexico. It seems certain that the exploring party at least sighted Saint George Island.[11]

9. Fanny Bandelier, trans., *The Narrative of Alvar Núñez Cabeza de Vaca*, 34.
10. Making the case for Dog Island is Morris Bishop, *The Odyssey of Cabeza de Vaca*, 54. Cleve Hallenbeck, *Álvar Núñez Cabeza de Vaca: The Journey and Route of the First European to Cross the Continent of North America, 1534–1535*, 45, suggests that the site was Saint Vincent Island.
11. Theodore H. Lewis, "The Narrative of the Expedition of Hernando de

The Spanish failed to settle the Gulf coast in the sixteenth century. They did settle on the Atlantic coast, but there they faced the threat of French encroachments. Pedro Menéndez de Avilés repulsed the French in a series of bloody encounters, and St. Augustine was founded in 1565. From that outpost Franciscan friars established missions up the Atlantic coast and across the interior into the Apalachee country. There were over fifty missions by 1680, but none near the mouth of the Apalachicola River.[12]

British and French colonizing efforts in the last half of the seventeenth century threatened Spanish Florida. From Charleston, English traders penetrated to the Apalachicola and beyond to the Mississippi River. In 1704 Governor James Moore of Carolina and his Indian allies swept through the Apalachee country, destroying the missions and killing and enslaving the Apalachee Indians. The French moved down into the Mississippi Valley from their settlements on the St. Lawrence River and the Great Lakes. In 1682 Robert Cavelier Sieur de La Salle reached the mouth of the Mississippi. Claiming the river and its environs for France, he named the region Louisiana in honor of Louis XIV. Fear of the French prompted the Spanish to establish a foothold near Pensacola in 1698 under the leadership of Andrés Arriola.

Saint George Island figured prominently in the life of at least one Frenchman. In the winter of 1766 Pierre Viaud was among those passengers and crew who survived a shipwreck off the barrier island. According to his sensational account of their adventures, the castaways spent three months wandering desperately from island to island before reaching safety. They faced treacherous Indians, bears, tigers, and lions and subsisted on oysters and birds. The book, embellished and exaggerated, sold well in France and Great Britain.[13]

Soto by the Gentlemen of Elvas," 163; F. W. Hodge, ed., *Spanish Explorers in the Southern United States 1528–1543* (New York, 1907); *Final Report of the United States de Soto Expedition*, 161–64. See also J. Leitch Wright, *The Only Land They Knew*, 1–26.

12. Michael V. Gannon, *The Cross in the Sand: The Early Catholic Church in Florida, 1513–1870;* Mark F. Boyd, Hale G. Smith, and John W. Griffin, *Here They Once Stood: The Tragic End of the Apalachee Missions.*

13. Mrs. Griffith, trans., *The Shipwreck and Adventures of Monsieur Pierre*

Caught up in international rivalry and wars of imperialism, Florida was defended by a declining Spain and her Indian allies. The latter were constantly being enticed by the English and French. Time grew short for Spain in 1733 when James Oglethorpe founded Georgia. The decisive French and Indian War (the Seven Years' War) ended in triumph for Great Britain over France and her ally Spain. The English obtained Florida from Spain by the Treaty of Paris of 1763.

During the years of British control, growth came slowly, although a permanent imprint was made. St. Augustine became the administrative capital of British East Florida and Pensacola the capital of British West Florida. The English returned Florida to Spain after the American Revolution: West Florida in 1781, East Florida in 1784. Spain's second period of ownership was short lived. It ended in 1819 when Spain ceded the peninsula to the United States by the Adams-Onís treaty, although the actual transfer of control did not come until 1821.

From 1783 to 1818 the United States made steady encroachments. In one dispute the Americans insisted on their version of where Florida's northern boundary should lie. The United States complained that Florida was a haven for runaway slaves and demanded that Spain control Indian raids across the border. Indians of Creek culture had migrated from Georgia and Alabama into Florida and became known as Seminoles—runaways. In the meantime the United States was unable to remain detached from the Napoleonic wars of Europe. Violations of American neutrality and expansionist ambitions (in Canada and Florida) led to a declaration of war against Great Britain.

During the War of 1812 Spain hoped to keep Florida and relied on the Creeks and Seminoles as allies. Yet she was unable to prevent Great Britain from using the Gulf coast as a military base. In

---

Viaud, a Native of Bordeaux, and Captain of a Ship, 10, 19–21, 42–54, 63–74, 143–45, 251–52; highly skeptical of Viaud's story was Bernard Romans (*A Concise Natural History of East and West Florida*, 200), who wondered how the shipwrecked party could have suffered in a setting of "plenty provided by providence." Viaud's real name was Jean Gaspart Dubois-Fontanelle.

1813 the Creeks attacked the frontier post of Fort Mims in south-west Alabama. Charging British connivance, the United States retaliated. In the Creek War that followed, Andrew Jackson crushed Indian resistance at the Battle of Horseshoe Bend in Alabama. In a humiliating treaty, the Creeks surrendered vast lands in Alabama and southwest Georgia.

Jackson throttled the British threat against Mobile by seizing and subsequently evacuating Pensacola. Next, he moved to his victory at New Orleans on January 8, 1815. The Treaty of Ghent ended the war, but the Florida frontier remained in bitter dispute. Spain could not control Florida, and Jackson made a controversial return in 1818. His invasion during the First Seminole War, actually a continuation of the Creek War, was successful. Despite its questionable legality, the maneuver provided the final pressure with which Secretary of State John Quincy Adams persuaded Spain to relinquish Florida.

When the United States acquired Florida, Saint George Island, the other barrier islands, and many acres in the interior were a part of the Forbes Purchase. In 1776 three Tory businessmen—William Panton, Thomas Forbes, and John Leslie—arrived at St. Augustine, seeking refuge in British East Florida. Previously active in the Indian trade in South Carolina and Georgia, the men established the trading firm of Panton, Leslie and Company. The company prospered due to the business acumen of its owners and their friendship with Alexander McGillivray, an able half-breed influential with the principal Indian nations of the South. Transferring its headquarters to Pensacola, the firm expanded and was permitted to retain its trading privileges after Spain regained Florida in 1783. By 1802 John Forbes, Thomas's brother, and James and John Innerarity, nephews of Panton, were admitted as partners. As the company grew (one branch store was located at Prospect Bluff, twenty miles up river from Apalachicola Bay), it also accumulated debts from the Indians. Business rivals were envious, and one competing firm aided the machinations of the remarkable William Augustus Bowles. A loyalist during the Revolution, Bowles later lived among the Indians and married an Indian woman. He dreamed of establishing an independent nation in Florida with himself as its

head. His forays in the 1790s inflicted damage on the property of
Panton, Leslie and Company but ended in his capture, escape, re-
capture, and ultimate death in 1806.

The company faced the additional threat of economic competition from the United States. After McGillivray's death in 1794 and
that of William Panton in 1801, John Forbes emerged as the leader.
Unable to collect its debts, the company received Spain's permission to accept land as payment. After various negotiations, the first
transaction was made in 1804. By it the Indians ceded many acres
between the Apalachicola on the west, the Wakulla River on the
east, the Gulf on the south (including Saint George Island), and an
undefined line on the north. A few months later Panton, Leslie and
Company was succeeded by John Forbes and Company. Still another treaty in 1811 with the Indians expanded the original grant.
Another large cession in 1818, this time by the Spanish government to cover the company's losses during the War of 1812, was
nullified by the Adams-Onís treaty.

Forbes retired before the treaty, leaving the Innerarity brothers
the task of managing company affairs. In 1819 the firm's property
was sold to Colin Mitchel, who represented his three bothers and
the Carnochan family of Carnochan and Mitchel, a trading firm of
Savannah and Darien, Georgia. When Florida became a U.S. territory, approximately 1.5 million of its acres were claimed by John
Forbes and Company. Whether the land was legitimately in private
ownership or a part of the public domain remained to be settled.[14]

14. William S. Coker and his staff at the University of West Florida have made
a major contribution in gathering the papers of Panton, Leslie and Company. For
related scholarship see William S. Coker and Thomas D. Watson, *Indian Traders
of the Southeastern Spanish Borderlands: Panton, Leslie and Company and John
Forbes and Company, 1783–1847;* John V. Sherlock, "Panton, Leslie and Company"; John Calhoun Upchurch, "Some Aspects of Early Exploration, Settlement,
and Economic Development within the Forbes Purchase," and "Aspects of the Development and Exploration of the Forbes Purchase"; David H. White, "The John
Forbes Company: Heir to the Florida Indian Trade: 1801–1809"; John W.
Caughey, *McGillivray of the Creeks;* J. Leitch Wright, Jr., *William Augustus
Bowles: Director General of the Creek Nation;* James F. Doster, *The Creek Indians
and Their Florida Lands, 1740–1823;* Peter Zahendra, "Spanish West Florida,
1781–1821"; Robert L. Gold, *Borderland Empires in Transition: The Triple-
Nation Transfer of Florida.*

The history of Saint George Island and Apalachicola are insep-
arable. In 1967 Gloria Jahoda wrote the widely read *The Other
Florida*. Among other things, she wondered if "the wide unspoiled
beaches of Saint George Island" might become the economic boon
to revive Apalachicola, affectionately described as "a proud and
seedy relic of an antebellum cotton town."[15] Looking to the future,
her speculations were based on the past. The details of that past are
the subject of this book.

15. Gloria Jahoda, *The Other Florida*, 86, 103.

Outposts on the Gulf

I

Apalachicola: "A Great and Growing Importance"

WITH Florida finally part of the United States, efforts were intensified to develop the long-contested peninsula. The barrier islands of Saint George, Dog, and Saint Vincent protected Apalachicola Bay, and a town site seemed feasible on the mainland somewhere along the Apalachicola River estuary. There a port city could deal in the agricultural products of the hinterland and take advantage of the coastal and international trade as well. The year of the Adams-Onís treaty, 1819, *Niles' Weekly Register* predicted that the location would become "the seat of a large commercial city—look at the map." [1]

Less admiring were those who knew the area at first hand. An early observer complained of "uncommon swarms of flies, gnats and insects," noting that "at Saint George's Sound and Island they are intolerable." [2] A Pensacola editor, writing in 1825, pointed out that where the river entered the bay the adjacent countryside was low and unhealthy. The water was bad, and there was no convenient situation for a town. [3] A Georgia journalist countered that the Apalachicola River "will at some future time, render this bay, a place of extensive business," and the territory's Legislative Council claimed that "in a few years a town must grow up at the mouth of the . . . river, second in size and importance to none in the South-

1. *Niles' Weekly Register* 16 (Mar., 1819): 44.
2. Romans, *Natural History of East and West Florida*, 227.
3. Pensacola *Gazette and West Florida Advertiser*, Aug. 20, 1825.

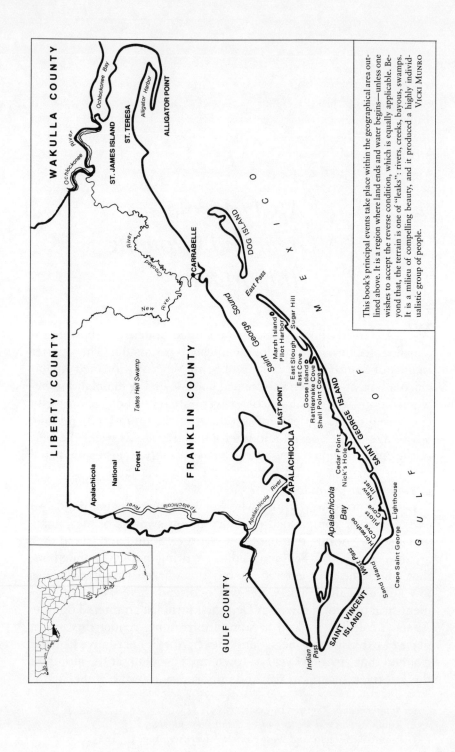

WAKULLA COUNTY

Ochlockonee Bay

Ochlockonee River

Ochlockonee River

ST. JAMES ISLAND

ST. TERESA

Alligator Harbor

ALLIGATOR POINT

CARRABELLE

Crooked River

New River

DOG ISLAND

East Pass

Saint George Sound

LIBERTY COUNTY

Tates Hell Swamp

FRANKLIN COUNTY

Apalachicola National Forest

Apalachicola River

Apalachicola River

EAST POINT

APALACHICOLA

Marsh Island

Pilot Harbor

Sugar Hill

East Slough

East Cove

Goose Island

Rattlesnake Cove

Shell Point Cove

Cedar Point

Nick's Hole

SAINT GEORGE ISLAND

New Inlet

Pilots Cove

Cove

Horseshoe

Lighthouse

Cape Saint George

Sand Island

West Pass

Apalachicola Bay

GULF COUNTY

SAINT VINCENT ISLAND

Indian Pass

M   E   X   I   C   O

G   U   L   F   O   F

This book's principal events take place within the geographical area outlined above. It is a region where land ends and water begins—unless one wishes to accept the reverse condition, which is equally applicable. Beyond that, the terrain is one of "leaks": rivers, creeks, bayous, swamps. It is a milieu of compelling beauty, and it produced a highly individualistic group of people.

VICKI MUNRO

western Country except New Orleans."[4] Several years later a young navy lieutenant, engaged in surveying the coast, had mixed thoughts. Apalachicola was long since a reality, but the town's health was "decidedly bad." That was because Apalachicola was surrounded by "marshes and malaria." He was more impressed with Saint George Island. It and the other sea islands "in the bay are not so objectionable, and would be, in all probability, salubrious enough." The lieutenant admitted that Apalachicola's "peculiar location, and other advantages of a commercial nature" gave it "a great and growing importance."[5]

Applying that view, President James Monroe had set up a customs district in 1821 that stretched from Cape Florida to the Apalachicola River. St. Marks was made the port of entry. By the early 1820s vessels were entering Apalachicola harbor, usually crossing the bar at West Pass, to take on cargoes of cotton. Trade continued to increase, and in 1823 the District of Apalachicola was created with Charles Jenkins as collector. Jenkins's district lay between Cape San Blas and Charlotte Bay, and he established his residence at the mouth of the Apalachicola. As early as 1829, an upriver editor at Bainbridge, Georgia, wrote of the settlement on the bay: "the place is rapidly improving. We think it will be a place of a great city in due time. Many of the eastern vessels now come there, and bring with them, many of the good *notions* of the Eastern people—and for which they can get in a few years, as much good Georgia and Florida sugar, as they wish."[6]

Elsewhere the new Territory of Florida had problems more demanding than the absence of a town on Apalachicola Bay. The Spanish had continued the British administrative system of maintaining governmental centers at St. Augustine and Pensacola. What Florida needed was a permanent, centrally located capital. In 1823 the Legislative Council empowered the governor to appoint two commissioners who were to select an appropriate site. Governor

4. Bainbridge [Georgia] *Southern Spy*, July 28, 1829; Clarence E. Carter, ed., *The Territorial Papers of the United States, Florida Territory* 22: 55–56, 558 (hereinafter cited as *USTP*).

5. The report was made in 1841 by Lieutenant L. M. Powell. See 27th Congress, 1st sess., Senate Document 38, 5–6.

6. Bainbridge *Southern Spy*, Oct. 13, 1829. See also Carter, *USTP* 22: 55–56, 558; *Niles' Weekly Register* 22 (June, 1822): 224.

William P. Duval chose Dr. William H. Simmons of St. Augustine and John Lee Williams of Pensacola. With St. Marks as the agreed place of rendezvous, Simmons and his party set out in the fall of 1823. He reached the small fort and village after an uneventful journey. There the physician waited impatiently for Williams, who took twenty-five days to make the 250-mile trip from Pensacola. The Williams party had embarked in an open boat without a map or chart of the coast. Their route carried them into Apalachicola Bay, where they visited Jenkins, the port collector.[7]

After a storm blew them ashore on Saint George Island, the amateur seamen spent over four days trying to get off and past the island. There were several false starts, delays, and bitter arguments before Williams (who was a lawyer) and his men joined Dr. Simmons. The combined parties moved north and ultimately selected an overgrown Indian village called Tallahassee (which meant "abandoned fields" or "old fields") for the capital. It was officially named in 1824 and incorporated in 1825.[8]

The Territory of Florida began to grow: Pensacola, St. Marks, Marianna, Madison, Quincy, Jacksonville, and Palatka emerged as commercial and plantation centers. Tampa, Sanford, and Ocala, which had been military forts, later became towns. Key West developed into an important naval base and salvage center.

Apalachicola seemed to be fulfilling the prophecies of its advocates. Collector Jenkins departed in late 1825 and was replaced by David L. White in the summer of 1826. Trade had steadily increased—coming downriver were cotton, hides, hogsheads of sugar, lumber, staves, cedar, and live oak timbers. In the winter and spring of 1828 the steamboat *Fanny*, the first of many to come, penetrated to the falls of the Chattahoochee at Columbus, Georgia. By the mid-1820s a settlement had grown up around the collector's office at the mouth of the Apalachicola. It was known informally as Cottonton. Then the name became West Point because of

7. John Lee Williams, "Journal of John Lee Williams, Commissioner to Locate the Seat of Government of the Territory of Florida"; William H. Simmons, "Journal of Dr. W. H. Simmons, Commissioner to Locate the Seat of Government of the Territory of Florida"; and Bertram H. Groene, *Ante-Bellum Tallahassee*, 3–23.

8. Williams, "Journal of John Lee Williams," 40–42; Florida, Territory of, Legislative Council *Acts*, 1823: 111–12; 1825: 68–72, 164–66 (hereinafter cited as *Legislative Council Acts*).

its location. The hamlet was assigned trustees by the Legislative Council in 1828 and following several petitions was incorporated in 1829.[9] The new town was governed by an intendant and a four-man council. Other than accomplishing a geographical clarification, the name West Point was uninspired. The Legislative Council was flooded with additional petitions from the residents, and in 1831 the village was given the historic name of Apalachicola.[10]

From 1822 to 1824 a commission appointed by Congress studied the legality of land grants in Florida, mostly those of the Forbes Purchase. A report favoring the ownership of Carnochan and Mitchel was completed, but Congress took no action. With its title unclear, the company had difficulty selling its lands. Some debts were paid once the firm received permission from the U.S. District Court of West Florida to assign lands to its creditors. All the while squatters were moving in. Soon Congress was petitioned to declare the Forbes Purchase a part of the public domain. Carnochan and Mitchel complained that unless Congress acted they faced unbearable economic hardship. Relief, or what appeared to be relief, came in 1828 when Congress permitted claimants to resort to the courts.

Colin Mitchel and his partners immediately petitioned the U.S. District Court of Middle Florida to validate their claim. Then, after two years of effort, the firm was denied its petition by the court. By late 1830, the status of Saint George Island, Apalachicola, and the entire Forbes Purchase was uncertain.[11]

Even though the final disposition of the Forbes Purchase claim remained uncertain, the creation of counties went forward. Apalachicola was originally a part of Jackson County, created in 1822; then of Washington, established in 1825; finally it became the county seat of Franklin, founded in 1832.[12] The creation of a county court and a court of common pleas aided the townspeople,

9. *Legislative Council Acts,* 1827–28: 22–23; 1829: 49–55. This chapter has benefited from the work of Harry P. Owens, especially his "Apalachicola before 1861." The theory about the name Cottonton was widely held and is based here on a statement by H. L. Grady in Apalachicola *Times,* Apr. 12, 1930.

10. *Legislative Council Acts,* 1831: 7.

11. Upchurch, "Development of the Forbes Purchase," 126–28.

12. *Legislative Council Acts,* 1832: 44–45; Owens, "Apalachicola before 1861," 80.

especially the merchants. Despite petitions to Congress, an admiralty court was not established until 1838.[13] Statutory provisions establishing courts did not, unfortunately, guarantee their effective operation.

In 1834 the citizens complained of the long intervals between sessions of the superior court. J. J. Adams, a local lawyer, pointed out that often prisoners had to wait long periods before being tried. Thus, "if innocent, [they] will have suffered a severity of punishment which would scarcely be awarded to the guilty."[14] In 1837 a Franklin County grand jury, reflecting the pains of growth, emphasized the need for a jail and a courthouse and discussed ways to control professional gamblers.[15]

Unplanned, haphazardly laid out, Apalachicola grew from the riverbank to the west and north and to the shoreline of the bay on the south. Churches, schools, homes, stores that sold dry goods, groceries, and clothing, and hotels, warehouses, and wharves were constructed.[16] Proof that the town had life was that it had death. The Apalachicola cemetery was begun, and the oldest marker would be that of Aretta Schuyler Farmer Jenkins. A native of New Brunswick, New Jersey, she died on November 25, 1832.[17] As demonstrated by a recent scholar, Apalachicola could not become a major port until it was reorganized administratively and physically, until the Creek Indians in the Chattahoochee River valley were moved west to make room for cotton planters and farmers, and until the formidable and bitter rivalry of nearby and newly established St. Joseph was overcome.[18]

When Florida became a territory there were approximately five thousand Indians within its borders, less than six hundred near the Apalachicola River. Because the Indians had surrendered their lands in the Forbes Purchase, only a few lived around Apalachicola Bay. By the Treaty of Moultrie Creek in 1823, the Seminoles exchanged their holdings in northern Florida for acreage in the ter-

13. Owens, "Apalachicola before 1861," 81.
14. See the petition and comments in 23d Congress, 2d sess., H. Rept. 19, 3.
15. Apalachicola *Gazette*, Nov. 29, 1837.
16. Ibid., Apr. 13, 1836.
17. Margaret Key and Ann Haupt in Apalachicola *Times*, Oct. 1, 1973.
18. Owens, "Apalachicola before 1861," 89.

ritory's southern section and monetary compensation. In both the amount and the quality of land the Indians were shortchanged. Small reservations north of the Forbes Purchase and near the Apalachicola River were provided for six leaders.[19]

In the Indian Removal Act of 1830, Congress provided for the transfer of Indians to lands west of the Mississippi River. In Florida the act was implemented by the Treaty of Payne's Landing in 1832 and the Treaty of Fort Gibson in 1833. The Indians resented the terms of the treaties, and, led by Osceola, Caocoochee (Wildcat), and others, they resisted. The resulting Second Seminole War lasted from 1835 to 1842. The Indians were removed, and the few remaining Seminoles disappeared into the Everglades.[20]

Southwestern Georgia and the Chattahoochee River valley helped determine Apalachicola's economic well-being. Although Georgia was an original colony, its map was patched with irregular tracts of land wrested from the Indians after a controversial and complex series of treaties and agreements stretching from 1735 to 1835. By the terms of the land session agreement of 1802, Georgia surrendered her western claims. In turn, the United States agreed at some time to remove the Indians. The attitude of most white Georgians was "the sooner the better." As previously noted, the Creek War of 1813–14 spilled over into Florida and became a part of the War of 1812. After Andrew Jackson defeated the Creeks in 1814 at Horseshoe Bend in Alabama, they signed the Treaty of Fort Jackson. The document provided for the surrender of some twenty million acres of Indian lands in southeastern Alabama and southwestern Georgia.

The Creeks ceded two more areas in Georgia to the United States in 1818; another large region was relinquished in 1825 by the Treaty of Indian Springs. Georgia's Creeks, now concentrated between the upper Flint and Chattahoochee rivers, gave up their last tract by the Treaty of Washington, concluded in 1826. The

19. John K. Mahon, *History of the Second Seminole War 1835–1842* (Gainesville, 1967), 44–50.

20. Besides Mahon, *Second Seminole War*, see M. M. Cohen, *Notices of Florida and the Campaigns*, and John T. Sprague, *The Origin, Progress, and Conclusion of the Florida War*. See also Charles J. Kappler, *Indian Affairs Laws and Treaties* 2: 344–45, 388–91.

Lower Creeks were agreeable, but the Upper Creeks protested the treaty's terms. Even so, Governor George M. Troup, who had arranged the treaty, insisted that land surveys go forward. The Treaty of Washington was expanded by two supplementary agreements, and by late 1827 the Creeks had ceded all their lands in Georgia.[21]

In Alabama the Creeks had lost most of their holdings by the Treaty of Fort Jackson. Their remaining lands on the west side of the Chattahoochee were subjected to ongoing encroachments by the whites. The incursions were legalized by the Treaty of Cusseta in 1832. The sporadic resistance that followed was put down, and by 1837 the Creeks had been removed from Alabama.[22]

Quickly moving onto the fertile lands, white farmers in Alabama planted crops, especially cotton. Apalachicola became their port of shipment. Merchants in the developing river towns relied heavily on goods obtained from Apalachicola. One such settlement was Irwinton (later named Eufaula after the Eufaula Creeks who lived there originally). Eufaula became the principal town in Barbour County, 201 miles by river from Apalachicola.[23]

In 1827 the Georgia legislature recognized the establishment of a "trading town" at or near the Coweta Falls of the Chattahoochee River. The town became Columbus. Incorporated in 1828, Columbus soon burgeoned and established powerful economic ties with Apalachicola. An early historian noted that the two towns had a "direct and indispensable communication."[24]

Two other interior towns of southwestern Georgia, Bainbridge

21. See Angie Debo, *The Road to Disappearance*, 90–96; Grant Foreman, *Indian Removal: The Emigration of the Five Civilized Tribes of Indians*, 315–97. See also Kappler, *Indian Treaties* 2: 107–10, 214–17, 264–68. Highly useful is Charles M. Hudson, *The Southeastern Indians*.

22. For the general picture see Mary E. Young, *Redskins, Ruffleshirts, and Rednecks: Indian Allotments in Alabama and Mississippi, 1830–1860;* Kappler, *Indian Treaties* 2: 341–43.

23. Anne Kendrick Walker, *Backtracking in Barbour County*, 9, 26, 59–61; Fretwell, *This So Remote Frontier*, 234.

24. John H. Martin, comp., *Columbus, Geo., from Its Selection as a "Trading Town" in 1827, to Its Partial Destruction by Wilson's Raid, in 1865*, 39; see also Etta Blanchard Worsley, *Columbus on the Chattahoochee*, 1–11; Georgia, General Assembly, *Acts*, 1827: 183–86; 1828: 153–54 (hereinafter cited as *Laws of Georgia*).

and Albany, were served by the Flint River, and they also developed extensive trade with the port of Apalachicola. Bainbridge was originally the site of an Indian village and later became a trading center. From 1817 till 1824 it was called Fort Hughes. A year after Decatur County was created in 1823, the settlement, renamed Bainbridge, became the seat of government. Located on a bluff on the east side of the Flint, Bainbridge grew into a substantial town.[25]

Northeast of Bainbridge and commanding the head of navigation on the Flint was Albany. It was named for the capital of New York, another river city, which engaged in extensive shipping on the Hudson. Alexander Shotwell, a Quaker from New Jersey, came south in the 1830s and purchased a town site on the west bank of the Flint. He carried out a survey and laid out lots but left without ever developing his property. Nelson Tift, a twenty-five-year-old native of Connecticut, was the real founder of Albany.[26]

In October 1836 Tift and several companions brought a stock of goods up from Apalachicola. Unloading their supplies from the steamer *Mary Emeline,* the men began constructing log cabins. At first a part of Baker County, Albany was named the seat of government when Dougherty County was established in 1853 (state legislator Tift authored the bill of creation). Tift's trading firm shipped its first cotton to Apalachicola in 1837. Under the leadership of the abstemious and religious Tift—he smoked and chewed but declined to drink tea or coffee, let alone liquor—Albany became the leading town in southwestern Georgia.[27]

Chattahoochee was located just below the point where the Chattahoochee and the Flint converged to form the Apalachicola River, making it a significant link between East and West Florida. It was the first town on the river, about 106 river miles north of Apalachicola, and the site of a federal arsenal. The crossroads town was in-

25. Frank S. Jones, *History of Decatur County* [Georgia], 182, 200; *Laws of Georgia,* 1823: 57–60.

26. Mary Ellen Bacon, *Albany on the Flint: Indians to Industry, 1836–1936,* 16, 26, 28, 33.

27. Thronateeska Chapter, Daughters of the American Revolution, comps., *History and Reminiscences of Dougherty County, Georgia,* 1, 6, 14; *Laws of Georgia,* 1853–54, 296–98.

corporated in 1834. Several of the warehouses on its landings were owned by Apalachicola merchants. The larger town of Quincy, nineteen miles to the east, was the county seat and center of life in the rich agricultural county of Gadsden.[28]

A traveler who crossed the river at Chattahoochee and proceeded west for twenty-four miles would arrive at Marianna, the prosperous center of Jackson County. Founded in 1827, it was the creation of Robert Beveridge, a Scotsman who came to the United States in 1822. He and his associates planned their town carefully and won the designation as county seat over a rival community known as Webbville. Marianna was located on the Chipola River, which wound southeast sixty miles before flowing into the Apalachicola fifteen miles above the bay. The clear, pure waters of the Chipola were shallow, and falls prevented steamers from utilizing the river commercially. Yet there was considerable traffic on the Chipola by flatboats hauling cotton and logs to the bay.[29]

Apalachicola developed as the key link in an extensive river system, and by 1844 the town served twenty-six regular landings. Pensacola to the west and St. Marks to the east were shipping rivals (Apalachicola never seriously challenged Mobile or New Orleans), but the new port's greatest threat came from St. Joseph, twenty-eight miles to the northwest and still in Franklin County. West of Apalachicola lay an impressive expanse of water known as St. Andrew Bay. Curving north like a scythe for sixteen miles, Cape San Blas formed a slender protective barrier that helped create an inner body known as St. Joseph Bay. The area had a deep natural harbor, but as late as 1834 trade was limited, and with good reason: there was no link between the bay and the Apalachicola River.

Real estate speculators and commercial visionaries saw immense possibilities in connecting the Apalachicola River with St. Andrew Bay by means of a canal or a railroad or both. Elaborately conceived, the Chipola Canal Company was chartered in 1828, but the project lay in limbo until it was dramatically revived following

28. J. Randall Stanley, *History of Gadsden County*, 9–54; Miles Kenan Womack, Jr., *Gadsden: A Florida County in Word and Picture*, 1–62.

29. J. Randall Stanley, *History of Jackson County*, 7, 9, 45, 48; Janie Smith Rhyne, *Our Yesterdays*, 12, 50, 52.

a decision by the U.S. Supreme Court.[30] After the adverse ruling by the District Court of Middle Florida in 1830, Colin Mitchel and his associates appealed the case to the Supreme Court. The disputed issue was placed on the docket for the January term 1831. Pleading the need to assemble more documentation, the government got the case postponed. Then, using the same grounds, federal lawyers got additional delays in 1832, 1833, and 1834. Finally, the court denied yet another attempt to defer action, and in March 1835 it ruled unanimously for the claimants. The government's case was handled by Richard Keith Call, protégé of Andrew Jackson and a powerful figure in Florida politics. Call was bitter at John Marshall's majority decision (it was the last one that the chief justice handed down). The land of the Forbes Purchase was judged to be private property, and the surveyor general was ordered to survey the tract.[31]

The proprietors reorganized themselves on November 28, 1835, as the Apalachicola Land Company. Initially there were three trustees and six directors, and the stockholders divided their holdings into shares of five hundred acres each.[32] The Supreme Court decision was all that they had worked for, and the owners envisioned large profits from land sales. By then Apalachicola was carelessly dotted with a number of businesses and homes and had a growing population. When the Apalachicola Land Company proposed a new town plan and reorganization, many of the older residents objected. How valid were their land titles? What new taxes would the company impose? A number of worried citizens began to speculate that perhaps the proposed port on St. Andrew Bay, which lay outside the property owned by the Apalachicola Land Company, was not a bad idea.

30. James O. Knauss, "St. Joseph, An Episode of the Economic and Political History of Florida," Part 1; Louise M. Porter, *The Chronological History of the Lives of St. Joseph,* 17–20; *Legislative Council Acts,* 1827–28: 80–86.

31. Colin Mitchel et al. v. the United States, 9 Peters, 711–62. See also *Niles' Weekly Register* 47 (Mar., 1835): 58; Herbert J. Doherty, Jr., *Richard Keith Call, Southern Unionist,* 57–69.

32. Apalachicola Land Co., *Articles of Agreement and Association,* 4. See also Gadsden County Deed Book A, 317–24.

It was further true that Apalachicola's setting had mixed blessings. The bar entrances in the bay were shallow, the channel was winding, and the surrounding countryside was unhealthy. The maze of rivers, creeks, bayous, and swamps that formed the delta made access by land difficult. The Compte de Castelnau, a French naturalist and scientific traveler who spent the winter of 1837–38 in Middle Florida, commented on the environs of Apalachicola. He mentioned the "thick vegetation": while among "the huge trees that crowd together one notices the live oak and the magnolia, which here reach a huge size; they are bound together by wild creepers and vines, and everywhere the high grass and the reeds offer an almost unsurmountable obstacle to the progress of a traveler."[33] Unswayed by esthetic and botanical descriptions, practical men argued that a better site than Apalachicola could be found.

In 1835 the Legislative Council chartered the Lake Wimico and St. Joseph Canal Company. The next year the words "Rail Road" were appended to the official title. It was no accident that three-eighths of the subscribers were from Apalachicola, three-eighths from Columbus (here was an opportunity to own their own port), and the rest from Tallahassee (rich men such as the planter Benjamin Chaires were caught up in the speculative times).[34] Their plan seemed sound: the Jackson River flows into the Apalachicola at a bend called Pinhook, a few miles north of the bay. The plan was to have steamboats bound downriver turn west into the Jackson River. Shortly they would emerge into Lake Wimico (a large bayou), cross it, and connect with a canal that would terminate with a port on St. Joseph Bay. Rather than negotiate the last hazardous miles into Apalachicola, the worst stretch of the trip, steamers could avoid it altogether. Apalachicola would be bypassed and its economy would be strangled.

The canal idea proved unfeasible; it was abandoned and was replaced by one calling for a railroad. Construction was begun, and in September the first steam railroad in Florida, running the eight miles from St. Joseph Bay to Lake Wimico, was opened. Lots in the

33. Compte de Castelnau, "Essay on Middle Florida, 1837–1838," 204.
34. Knauss, "St. Joseph," 181–82; Porter, *Lives of St. Joseph,* 23–27; *Legislative Council Acts,* 1836: 8–10.

proposed town of St. Joseph were advertised early in 1836, and building began by late spring. A town, four feet above sea level, had come into being.[35]

From the first, St. Joseph grew rapidly. Among the immigrants was Dinsmore Westcott, who, in 1833, had established the Apalachicola *Advertiser,* that town's first newspaper. Editor Westcott promoted the interests of St. Joseph with his *Telegraph,* later the *Times.* The Apalachicola Land Company countered by bringing in the combative Cosam Emir Bartlett to edit the *Gazette.* Gabriel Floyd, the port collector, tried manfully to get the customs office moved to St. Joseph. He was tactful enough not to make his efforts public, but he let it be known that with the increase in business, he needed extra help.[36]

St. Joseph had barely been incorporated in 1836 before its citizens demanded that it be made the county seat. The Legislative Council agreed, but the U.S. Senate disallowed the change. As a compromise the new county of Calhoun was created and St. Joseph became the seat of government.[37] The town's rise to prominence was evident by 1838 when it was selected as the site for Florida's constitutional convention. Some Saints, as the citizens came to be called, even suggested moving the territorial capital to St. Joseph.[38]

As economic and social rivals Apalachicola and St. Joseph had spokesmen who dealt in praise and denunciation. Apalachicolans contended that they had the safer bay.[39] St. Joseph's response was more personal. "Apalachicola is sadly thinned by absenteeism and sickness," a St. Joseph paper reported. "We infer that its present

35. It was even predicted that Apalachicola's citizens would move en masse to St. Joseph. See *Niles' Weekly Register* 47 (July, 1835): 337, quoting unnamed Apalachicola newspaper. See also Dorothy Dodd, "Railroad Projects in Territorial Florida," 16–26; Frederick T. Davis, "Pioneer Florida: The First Railroads"; and Frank Albert Unger, "Some Aspects of Land Acquisition and Settlement in Territorial Florida: The St. Joseph Community," 3–18.

36. Mobile *Commercial Advertiser,* Dec. 16, 1835; Knauss, "St. Joseph," 184; Porter, *Lives of St. Joseph,* 30–32; James O. Knauss, *Florida Territorial Journalism,* 29–31, 53–55; Owens, "Apalachicola before 1861," 121.

37. Carter, *USTP* 25: 270–71, 360; Knauss, "St. Joseph," 188; Owens, "Apalachicola before 1861," 124.

38. Porter, *Lives of St. Joseph,* 43–63.

39. Apalachicola *Gazette,* Feb. 19, 1838.

population is made up of old women and children, with now and then a feeble representative of the other sex."[40] Furthermore, in Apalachicola the fleas were "more numerous and larger, than in any other part of the world."[41]

Much of the vilification was real, but some of it was bombast. Citizens in the towns visited each other and maintained friendly relations. St. Joseph acquired the reputation of a free-wheeling place where money could be made and spent. The Saints developed an active social life. Innocent indulgence, "the opportunity of taking an ice cream," was available, but, according to a local editor, one might indulge in the pleasure of "drinking a glass of hock or iced burgundy."[42] By 1840 a jockey club and racecourse drew fans dressed in their finery and anxious to make bets.[43]

A dependable connection between St. Joseph Bay and the Apalachicola River was vital for the new town's survival. When Lake Wimico proved too shallow for steamboats, a new settlement, Iola, was built on the river's west bank. A second railroad, the St. Joseph to Iola, was begun. Before it was completed a much-needed highway was opened from Georgia to Marianna and from there to St. Joseph and Apalachicola. The railroad was completed in November 1839. Yet that same year stockholders in the Apalachicola Land Company were told "there is but little to fear from competition."[44] The report was correct. St. Joseph's swift emergence was matched by its precipitous decline. Upriver tradesmen were unwilling to pay shipping charges twice: on the railroad as well as on the steamboats. They refused to equate railroad fees with the lightering charges required in Apalachicola Bay. St. Joseph never matched Apalachicola in the shipment of cotton. A rapprochement between the towns was proposed in 1840 but failed because the Apalachi-

40. St. Joseph *Times*, Sept. 4, 1840.

41. Ibid., Aug. 1, 1838.

42. Harold W. Bell, *Glimpses of the Panhandle*, 15, quoting St. Joseph *Times*, May 5, 1840.

43. St. Joseph *Times*, June 9, July 28, 1840; see also Dorothy Dodd, "Horse Racing in Middle Florida, 1820–1843"; Unger, "St. Joseph Community," 31–82.

44. Apalachicola Land Co., *Annual Report*, 1839, 5; see also Knauss, "St. Joseph," Part 2, 5–7.

cola Land Company insisted on sharing in a railroad project to connect them.[45]

A series of damaging hurricanes struck St. Joseph in the late 1830s. The final calamity came with a yellow fever epidemic in 1841. St. Joseph was decimated. Many people died, and those who survived moved away. Most of them returned to Apalachicola, which also suffered from storms and contagious diseases but less severely. By the summer of 1841 St. Joseph was practically deserted. It never recovered. Economic overexpansion, storms, and disease combined to destroy a town that had glittered brilliantly for a few years.

With condescending sympathy, the editor of the Apalachicola *Journal* viewed the demise: "Of St. Joseph we would speak as of a deceased foe, who has warred long and magnanimously against us, and at last fell a victim to her own delusive theories. . . . While we chant her funeral requiem, we would throw the broad mantle of charity over her manifold improvidence and indiscretions, and receive her citizens as the father did the prodigal son."[46]

Apalachicola's growth seemed assured. The Apalachicola Land Company held a series of lot sales during the first week of April 1836. Apalachicolans were permitted to purchase their lots before the public sale.[47] The company laid off its property in an orderly fashion, generously giving the town streets and squares and lots for public use (a courthouse, cemetery, churches), and it deepened the channel from anchorage to wharves. Those purchasing lots along Water Street, which fronted the river, were required to build substantial wharves and to erect three-story, fireproof, brick buildings. H. A. Norris, a civil engineer from New York, apparently drew the original plans. The company established its headquarters on the second floor of a building on the corner of Chestnut and

45. Owens, "Apalachicola before 1861," 128; Unger, "St. Joseph Community," 83–99.

46. Quoted in *Niles' Weekly Register* 59 (Feb., 1841): 416. For a fictional account of the rivalry between the towns see Alexander Key, *The Wrath and the Wind*.

47. Apalachicola *Gazette*, Apr. 9, 20, 27, 1836. For later sales see ibid., Feb. 18, 1837; Mar. 19, 1838.

Water streets, and soon the stairs echoed a steady thump as patrons mounted them intent on negotiating some kind of business. Samuel S. Sibley, editor of the Tallahassee *Floridian,* visited the town in the late 1830s and declared that "Apalachicola is a proud specimen of American enterprise."[48]

The company realized $443,800 from early lot sales in Apalachicola. After that, sales began to decline. Financial panic hit the country in 1836 and had a particularly adverse effect on Florida. Adding to the misery was the Second Seminole War, interminable and bitterly contested. Difficulties developed between the Apalachicola Land Company and the townspeople. There were lawsuits over taxes. The company charged high rents and granted only short-term leases. Inevitably, trouble ensued when attempts were made to foreclose on various lapsed mortgages. Despite its initial success, the company soon faced a serious decline in the demand for its lots in Apalachicola.[49]

The story was even worse in the remainder of the Forbes Purchase. A number of surveys were made, but despite expectations no valuable mineral lands were discovered. Most of the lands were ill suited for agriculture. Saint George, Saint Vincent, and Dog islands never fulfilled predictions that they were "some of the finest sea islands for the cultivation of cotton."[50]

The Forbes Purchase was rich in timber. Besides vast stands of pine and swamps crowded with cypress, giant live oaks were abundant on parts of the company's tract. In 1831 a survey revealed a large number of live oaks around Apalachicola. Some were growing on Saint George Island, and Saint Vincent's was particularly wooded with the stately trees that were important in the shipbuilding industry.[51]

48. Tallahassee *Floridian,* Aug. 17, 1839. See also Apalachicola *Gazette,* May 18, 1837; *The Apalachicolan,* Dec. 26, 1840; Apalachicola *Times,* Aug. 12, 1938, quoting New York *Sun,* 1896.

49. See Apalachicola Land Co., *Extract from a Report to the Trustees,* 1–2.

50. James Grant Forbes, *Sketches, Historical and Topographical of the Floridas; More Particularly of East Florida,* vii. For the several surveys see Upchurch, "Development of the Forbes Purchase," 131–38.

51. Apalachicola Land Co., *Annual Report,* 1838, 16–17. For the importance of live oaks see Virginia Steele Wood, *Live Oaking Southern Timber for Tall Ships,* 14–15, 58, 80, 85.

Saint George Island remained unsold and, except for its lighthouse keeper, uninhabited. Soon the company's annual reports were a gloomy litany that applied to Saint George Island and the remainder of its lands: "few purchasers appeared" (1838); "no sales of either land or lots to any important amount have been made" (1842). Even so, the company continued to provide public notices of its sales as late as 1843.[52]

Independent of the company's difficulties, Apalachicola itself had to fight to survive. The port depended on commerce to the exclusion of manufacturing, and Franklin County had few planters or slaves—even small farmers were in short supply. The area was atypical of Middle Florida as Apalachicola became a shipping town, a cotton town that depended on a crop produced many miles away. It was geared to satisfying the needs of people far beyond its confines.

In 1840 Apalachicola had 1,030 persons. The mayor and town council raised money by taxing real estate and businesses. A sales tax was levied, and there were special taxes on professional men as well as billiard tables, ten-pin alleys, and shuffleboard. White males paid a poll tax as did free persons of color and slaves who hired out their labor.[53] By 1850 there were 1,562 people in Apalachicola, and on the eve of the Civil War there were 1,906 residents. If the growth had been unspectacular, Apalachicola was still the sixth largest town in Florida and had a cosmopolitan population. The Irish were the leading immigrant group, most of them dwelling in a boisterous workingmen's section called "Irishtown." Next in number were the English, Germans, and Italians. The Italians and Sicilians were the leading and most active fishermen and oystermen. Decidedly nonprovincial were a group of New Englanders and people from New York and Pennsylvania. They dominated the port's shipping traffic. A number of them were temporary residents who lived in Apalachicola only during the business season, which lasted from late fall to late spring.

52. Apalachicola Land Co., *Annual Report*, 1838, 18; ibid., 1842, 2; see report of Thomas Baltzell, the company's agent, in Apalachicola *Commercial Advertiser*, February 23, 1843, and Gadsden County Deed Book A, 21, 317.

53. Apalachicola *Gazette*, Jan. 19, 1836; *Niles' Weekly Register* 59 (Nov., 1840): 192.

Apalachicola's geographical setting made it both unique and vulnerable. On August 30–31, 1837, a powerful hurricane lashed ashore. Saint George Island absorbed the first tidal surge, and the waters sliced an opening—known as New Inlet or West Gap—through the island. Boats drawing ten feet of water would soon pass through New Inlet.[54] Washing onto the mainland, the storm raged for three days. Apalachicola's thoroughfares were filled with logs. Water Street was covered by ten to fifteen feet of water, and later over ten barrels of fish were picked up from the streets. The steamboats *Henry Crowell* and *Edwin Forrest* were broken up, and in town property damage was put at $200,000. A survivor recorded, "I write from the midst of ruins. A hurricane yesterday swept our town and half destroyed it."[55]

At Saint George Island, New Inlet would remain open for the remainder of the nineteenth century. Vessels often lay in the storm-cleaved pass and received their cargoes from lighters towed across the shallow bay from Apalachicola. A series of storms after 1900, especially the hurricane of 1906, filled the gap.[56] The storm of 1837 provided the additional benefit of deepening the channel by two feet.

For the most part, the storms were highly destructive. Damaging hurricanes, usually called gales, occurred in 1842, 1844, and 1850. A storm in August 1851, the worst in twenty years, caused widespread destruction. Thomas Hutchinson, who owned one of the area's earliest sawmills, watched helplessly as his entire operation washed away. The winds were so violent that the lighthouse on Cape Saint George was blown down.[57] Over eighty miles away at Tallahassee the Capitol building had several tin sheets ripped off its

54. Apalachicola *Gazette*, Sept. 2, 1837. The same storm badly damaged St. Marks but did little harm to St. Joseph.

55. Apalachicola *Times*, August 30, 1940, quoting Lieutenant Colonel W. Reid, *The Law of Storms* (London, 1838). See also Tallahassee *Floridian*, Sept. 9, 16, 1837, quoting Apalachicola *Gazette*.

56. See report of City Manager Newton W. Creekmore in Apalachicola *Times*, Nov. 13, 1953. See also Apalachicola *Times*, July 15, 1976.

57. Benjamin S. Hawley to S. Pleasonton, Sept. 29, Dec. 22, 1841, Hawley file, Record Group 26, National Archives.

roof, and the legislative chambers were flooded.[58] The lighthouse on Cape Saint George was rebuilt and withstood a powerful gale in August 1856 that destroyed the beacon at Cape San Blas. The same gale damaged crops in Franklin and surrounding counties, drove ships ashore, and caused the deaths by drowning of a family of three at Cat Point (directly across the bay from Apalachicola) and a family of six on Saint Vincent's Island.[59] A visitor who admired Apalachicola made the wry admission that the town was "subject to inundations during extraordinary gales from the sea."[60]

Adding their own form of destruction were frequent fires. A fire in 1833 occurred before the waterfront district was built up, but still it destroyed one-third of the town's buildings. An inferno followed the hurricane of 1837, and another preceded the storm of 1842. Fires broke out periodically, some the work of arsonists. A fire company, organized in 1841 and chartered in 1844, battled heavy odds. The year the unit was chartered provided a sardonic note: the customhouse, several stores, and six houses burned. Still another fire in 1857 caused heavy damage. The town marshal required businesses to possess fire buckets and citizens to keep their chimneys repaired. Through all the period of recovery from fires and storms, Apalachicola reeled from the blows, rebuilt, and continued to develop its coastal shipping and trade with the interior.[61] Saint George Island, a long sliver of serene repose, belied the struggles that occupied the mainland residents it protected.

Apalachicola developed a style that was considered open and friendly by some, wild and wicked by others. Dissatisfied with widespread disorder, a group of Apalachicolans petitioned Congress for judicial aid in 1837: "Like other seaport towns in new countries, our population is transient; we are visited by a number

58. Tallahassee *Floridian*, Aug. 30, 1851; Tallahassee *Florida Sentinel*, Aug. 26, 1851.

59. New Orleans *Daily Picayune*, Sept. 13, 1856, quoting Apalachicola *Commercial Advertiser*, Sept. 3, 1856.

60. Bainbridge *Argus*, Apr. 22, 1857.

61. Apalachicola *Commercial Advertiser*, Apr. 13, June 29, Aug. 19, 1844; Bainbridge *Argus*, Apr. 29, 1857; Harry P. Owens, "Sail and Steam Vessels Serving the Apalachicola-Chattahoochee Valley," 195.

of strangers and adventurers from all quarters; our streets are sometimes filled with seamen and boatmen, who soon discover that offenders cannot be brought to justice here, and avail themselves of such opportunities to indulge their vicious propensities." [62] Besides depending on their hard-pressed marshal, the town officials sought other protection. In 1839 they passed an ordinance requiring all white males between the ages of eighteen and fifty to patrol the streets, beginning at nine o'clock each night. The men were divided into five classes (substitutes were permitted) and given wide powers. The patrol could arrest drunken and disorderly whites, including sailors on shore leave. Blacks without written passes could be punished with twenty blows from a rawhide or a switch. The ordinance was practical, especially since there was no courthouse or jail in 1839, and as a judge complained, "there should be Court Houses and Jails—more especially in Pensacola and Appalachicola [sic], which are Sea Port Towns, and where the necessity of Confining Criminals will often arise." [63]

As befitted a trading town, Apalachicola had a number of banks. The Commercial Bank of Apalachicola was established in the 1830s. Others were chartered, although it is unclear how many actually opened. Some of the financial institutions included the Bank of Apalachicola, the Franklin Bank of Florida, the Marine Insurance Bank of Apalachicola, and branch offices of banks in such towns as Tallahassee, Pensacola, and Columbus. A month after Florida seceded from the Union, still another bank was chartered at Apalachicola: the Western Bank of Florida. [64]

Apalachicola was well served by newspapers before and after Westcott took his newspaper to St. Joseph. Bartlett's editorials so aroused his opponents that he sometimes had to use the sword to defend the pen. [65] In 1839–40 his *Gazette* was the only daily pub-

62. 23d Cong., 2d sess., H. Rept. 19, 4.

63. Carter, *USTP* 24: 852; 26: 18–20; Apalachicola *Courier*, May 8, 1839.

64. Apalachicola *Times,* Aug. 5, 1938, quoting New York *Sun*, 1896; Owens, "Apalachicola before 1861," 214–16; Florida General Assembly, *Acts and Resolutions*, 1860–61: 93–99 (hereinafter cited as *Laws of Florida*). For the overall picture see J. E. Dovell, *History of Banking in Florida, 1828–1954*.

65. Bartlett once scattered a lynch mob by holding a match to a barrel of "gunpowder" (it actually contained liquor). See Apalachicola *Times*, Jan. 7, 1966.

lished in territorial Florida. Bartlett moved to Tallahassee in 1840, but other papers followed to Apalachicola: the *Florida Journal*, the *Courier*, the *Apalachicolan*, whose masthead proclaimed "Not The Glory Of Caesar, But The Welfare Of Rome," and the most important, the *Commercial Advertiser*, begun in 1843 (although an earlier paper had borne the same name). Two picturesquely titled publications were the *Star of the West*, which advocated "Principles Not Men," and the *Watchman of the Gulf*. For much of the time after the mid-1830s, Apalachicola had two newspapers, but their editorial policies were commercial, not political.[66]

A local library association had two hundred volumes by 1839 and was chartered in 1840 by the Legislative Council.[67] Novels were serialized and local poets basked in the glory of being published in the town's newspapers. Several merchants sold books, and a portrait painter had enough customers to work full time at his profession. An Agricultural Society and a Historical Society were active by 1839. A debating society organized in 1844 attracted audiences to hear argued such topics as "Are Brute Creatures Endowed with Reason."[68]

In the persons of John Gorrie and Alvan W. Chapman the town had two men, contemporaries and friends, who achieved international distinction. Gorrie, a young physician from South Carolina, became mayor and spokesman for the Apalachicola Land Company. As a doctor he worked tirelessly to combat disease, especially yellow fever. Noting how a drop in room temperature benefited fever patients, he invented an ice-making machine and devised a method to cool a room artificially. He died in 1855 without ever raising sufficient financial backing to market his pioneering work with air conditioning.[69] A native of Massachusetts and a

66. See Tallahassee *Star*, Mar. 13, 1839. See also Knauss, *Territorial Journalism*, 31, 119.

67. Apalachicola *Gazette*, Nov. 6, 1839; *Legislative Council Acts*, 1840: 12–14.

68. Apalachicola *Commercial Advertiser*, June 22, 1844; Owens, "Apalachicola before 1861," 160–61.

69. For Gorrie see V[ivian] M. Sherlock, *The Fever Man: A Biography of Dr. John Gorrie*. See also her "Medical Practices in the Port of Apalachicola, 1830–1850."

physician, Chapman moved to Florida in the 1830s. Settling at Apalachicola, he soon abandoned medicine for botany and became distinguished in the field. He wrote papers, exchanged letters with colleagues, and in 1860 published his monumental *Flora of the Southern United States*. Chapman remained in Apalachicola carrying out his scientific investigations until his death in 1899 (*illustration,* Group 1).[70]

Apalachicola had private schools in the 1840s, and some young people went to academies in other towns. In 1848 Samuel J. Bryan and his "competent Female Assistant" opened the Apalachicola Academy. For its two terms of twenty-two weeks each, attended by boys and girls, classes were conducted in separate rooms. The county commissioners carried decorum even further by enclosing and dividing the playground.[71]

By law, a part of the revenue received from the sales of public lands was set aside to support education. Because Franklin County had no public lands, schools had difficulty securing public funds. Yet more than most Florida counties, Franklin provided education for poor people. No true public school system was developed in Florida at the secondary level, but in 1860 Franklin County had four "common schools" with four teachers and 182 pupils. The schools were supported in part by local taxation.[72] A high percentage of young white boys and girls could read and write.

There was much religious activity in Apalachicola. Christ Church, organized by the Episcopalians in 1836, was chartered by the Legislative Council as Trinity in 1837. The first rector was the Reverend Charles Jones, and the original structure of white pine was shipped in sections from New York and assembled on its arrival.[73]

70. Rowland H. Rerick, *Memoirs of Florida* 2: 160–61; Apalachicola *Times,* Jan. 29, 1976, reprint of Winifred Kimball's article on Chapman that appeared in *The New York Botanical Garden* (Jan., 1921).

71. Apalachicola *Star of the West,* June 22, 1844.

72. Social Statistics, Florida, 1860, Manuscript Census, no pagination. By the late 1840s the county commissioners were empowered to levy a tax to help support the poor schools. See *Laws of Florida 1847–48:* 50–51.

73. Joseph D. Cushman, Jr., *A Goodly Heritage: The Episcopal Church in Florida 1821–1892,* 16, 22; Apalachicola *Times,* Feb. 1, 22, 1936.

Methodists were holding services by 1839 but did not organize until 1844. The Reverend Peter Haskew served both the St. Joseph Station and the Apalachicola Mission in 1839. He would rent a horse in St. Joseph, ride down to Apalachicola on Saturday, preach to the Methodists on Sunday, and return home on Monday. Because the Methodists in Apalachicola had no church building, the Reverend Haskew filled his appointments in hotels and private homes, and sometimes the Episcopalians offered him the use of Trinity. One Sunday in November 1839, the minister wrote, "I have endeavoured to preach twice today to these Apalachicolans. Whether I have done them any good or not I cannot tell. They have done me some good—they have given me twenty-nine dollars and eighteen cents and three-fourths, which will pay all my traveling expenses to and from this place."[74]

The Baptists first established a church in Florida in 1821. A congregation was organized at Apalachicola in 1848, and the members affiliated themselves with the West Florida Baptist Association. From the first, black members were permitted freedom in church matters "in view of the intelligence and piety they manifest."[75]

There was an active Catholic congregation. In 1845 the Reverend Timothy Birmingham was appointed to serve churches at Columbus, Georgia, as well as various missions, including the one at Apalachicola. The Reverend Patrick Coffey took charge of the mission at Apalachicola in 1851 and was instrumental in getting Saint Patrick's built. Completed in 1853, Saint Patrick's served a number of Irish, Italian, and other families. A rectory was constructed later.[76]

Services for slaves were usually conducted separately in white

74. F. W. Hoskins, ed., "A St. Joseph Diary of 1839," 147. See also Apalachicola *Commercial Advertiser*, Apr. 26, 1845.

75. Edward Earl Joiner, *A History of Florida Baptists*, 47.

76. See informational sheet provided at St. Patrick's Church. An appealing legend has the Rev. Juan Juares holding the first mass on the present site when he landed with Narváez in 1528. The original church structure lasted until 1929. See also Thomas J. Burns, "The Catholic Church in West Florida, 1783–1850," and Gannon, *Cross in the Sand*, 161–62, 169.

churches. At Trinity, blacks and whites heard the same sermons, but the slaves occupied special pews in the balcony. By 1858 black Baptists had their own church, which had more members than the white Baptists'. Services were held on Sunday afternoon and evening and were conducted by local white preachers with the assistance of a black minister. Many whites, especially men of the sea and their families, went to the black church, attracted there by the beautiful singing of the congregation.[77] In 1860 there was a black Methodist church. The building could accommodate three hundred persons and was valued at $2,000.[78]

If the need to attend church manifested itself, or if one felt compelled to join the strongly emerging crusade against liquor, that was because antebellum Apalachicola offered numerous temptations. The Apalachicola Temperance Society was holding regular meetings at the Methodist church by the mid-1840s.[79] The arrival of ice shipments was always the signal for increased trade in mixed drinks at the town hotels. One editor commiserated with the teetotalers: "God give them the strength of resolution to resist the temptations they must encounter! Ice, Sugar, Wine, and Madeira!"[80]

Several hotels flourished in the convivial atmosphere of Apalachicola. Some of the earlier establishments were noted for their patrons' disorderliness. Staying overnight at one of them, the Reverend Haskew was outraged because "there was so much cursing and noise that I could not rest well until they got down and quiet." His sober judgment was that such conduct would have a "deleterious effect," and he noted that "this is, in its present garb a cruel place; even the hostler was drunk."[81] As time passed the hotels improved, among them Mansion House, Sans Souci, Southern Coffee House, and City Hotel. Seth P. Lewis's Mechanics & Merchants Exchange featured oysters and billiards; it was rivaled by W. H. Kelton's Phoenix House, which offered board and lodging for seven

77. Apalachicola *Commercial Advertiser*, Mar. 10, 1858, quoting "Traveler" to Bainbridge *Argus*.
78. Social Statistics, Florida, 1860 Manuscript Census, no pagination.
79. Apalachicola *Commercial Advertiser*, May 2, 1846.
80. Ibid., Apr. 11, 1846.
81. Hoskins, "St. Joseph Diary," 141.

dollars a week.[82] Occasionally a hotel would burn, while another might enjoy a vogue only to decline for various reasons. The more elaborately appointed hotels were the scenes of stately dinners, formal balls, and glittering celebrations. At Mansion House a band played in a flower-scented garden; and after late suppers in dining rooms, sporting patrons drifted toward the barroom or into private rooms for faro, poker, and roulette. Whatever the contents of the traveler's purse, Apalachicola could accommodate his desires.[83]

Theatrical performances were considered sinful by some, but they were legal by 1840. That year saw the performance of "Honey Moon" and "Fortune's Frolic" to raise money for the benefit of the Fire Engine Company.[84] Before that, in the late 1830s, a company headed by Emanuel Judah, his wife, and two sons was popular in the town. After the entire Judah family perished at sea in 1840, they were succeeded by W. R. Hart and Company. Hart was gifted comedian. While he excelled at farce, his wife was more versatile. A local critic explained, "She may be termed in Theatrical Parlance the Star of Florida."[85] Citizens of St. Joseph swallowed their pride and not only flocked to see the Harts but were effusive in their compliments.[86]

Boat races were held periodically, but horse races were more popular. The Franklin Course was host yearly to a five-day meet that featured blooded horses from Alabama, Georgia, Tennessee, and the Carolinas. The town became part of a circuit that included St. Joseph, Marianna, Quincy, and Tallahassee. The jockeys wore racing silks, purses of up to nine hundred dollars were offered, and wagers were plentiful.[87]

82. Apalachicola *Commercial Advertiser*, Feb. 12, 1844.

83. Apalachicola *Times*, Aug. 5, 1938, quoting New York *Sun*, 1896.

84. Apalachicola *Florida Journal*, Jan. 25, 1844. See also William G. Dodd, "Theatrical Entertainment in Early Florida."

85. Apalachicola *Commercial Advertiser*, Feb. 12, 1844. See ibid., Nov. 4, 1843, and *The Apalachicolan*, Dec. 26, 1840. For comments on the Judah family see Apalachicola *Gazette*, Mar. 30, Nov. 20, 1839.

86. St. Joseph *Times*, Dec. 23, 1840.

87. Apalachicola *Florida Journal*, Dec. 24, 1840; Apalachicola *Commercial Advertiser*, June 29, 1844. See also Dorothy Dodd, "Horse Racing in Middle Florida, 1830–1843."

Military musters were rollicking events, and over the years Franklin County had a number of volunteer companies. The Franklin Volunteers fought in the Second Seminole War, but despite some saber rattling no unit from Franklin and only a few companies from Florida served in the Mexican War.[88] Among the several companies formed in Franklin County were the Alaqua Guards, City Cavalry, Apalachicola Guards, and City Dragoons. Each unit reached its peak—a bristling display of military tactics and a resplendent splash of dress—during Fourth of July celebrations.

Independence Day was the year's major holiday in Apalachicola and throughout the South. The occasion brought out the county officials, veterans' groups, and delegates from such organizations as Odd Fellows, Typographical Society, Soiree Club, Florida Benevolent Society, City Hospital, and Marine Hospital. On the morning of July 4, 1837, a parade was followed by a reading of the Declaration of Independence and a patriotic speech by the Orator of the Day. At a dinner hosted by Mansion House formal toasts were proposed. Receiving the accolades were national figures such as George Washington, Andrew Jackson, and John Hancock. Local statesmen were not neglected, nor were states, territories, towns, and counties. To "The Fair of Apalachicola, Precious Though Few," was a toast that damaged few female egos.[89]

The Fourth was celebrated as usual in 1844 but with the added attraction of two chartered boat trips to Saint George Island. At West Pass the celebrants went swimming. Later, they cruised around the island to East Pass, crossed over to Dog Island, and enjoyed a picnic before returning home.[90]

The people of the area had great affection for Saint George Island. There was no end of trips and excursions to the narrow land

88. Apalachicola *Gazette*, Apr. 27, 1836; Apalachicola *Commercial Advertiser*, May 23, 1846. See also Frederick T. Davis, "Florida's Part in the War with Mexico." Concerned about their defenseless Gulf coast, Apalachicolans sent a memorial to the president asking that their town be fortified and protected. See Beverly Marchetta, "Florida's Part in the Mexican War," 26–27, 57–58.

89. Apalachicola *Gazette*, Apr. 27, 1836; Apalachicola *Commercial Advertiser*, May 23, 1846.

90. Apalachicola *Advertiser*, June 8, 22, 1844. The announced itinerary was followed. For other celebrations see ibid., June 8, July 12, 1839.

mass. A visitor from Georgia in 1829 described its physical layout —the forests and hammocks, the bays and lagoons—and was amazed by the large dunes.[91] The Frenchman Castelnau was less awed but wrote that the island's "banks are indented, irregular and marshy; it is covered in general with pine woods and scattered cedar and live oaks, on its southern end there are sandy dunes which in certain places are forty-five feet high."[92] Unconcerned with recording their impressions, young people marked the island as a favorite spot and frequently chartered boats to take them over to the lighthouse. More than once the lightkeeper fought high seas and violent winds to rescue inexperienced townspeople who were trying to get ashore.[93]

In the antebellum period Saint George Island was most important for its role in protecting the mainland. Its lighthouse helped Apalachicola function as a port. The town itself, despite superficial trappings, was a place of business. The exchange of goods was its reason for being.

91. Bainbridge *Southern Spy,* Aug. 4, 1829.
92. Castelnau, "Essay on Middle Florida," 209.
93. Apalachicola *Gazette,* Oct. 20, 1838.

2

A Place of Commerce

APALACHICOLA developed four interrelated but distinct commercial activities: receiving goods from upriver farmers and producers, shipping goods to individuals and merchants in the interior, exporting and importing goods in the coastal trade, and exporting and importing goods in the international trade. As an important way station of deposit, sale, and distribution, Apalachicola lived a double life. The town hummed with activity and the port collector had scarcely a free moment during the winter and early spring months (*illustration,* endleaves). In the summer there was a dramatic exodus—commission merchants closed their offices, lawyers locked their doors, temporary residents returned to the North. There was little shipping, and without it Apalachicola slumped into a lassitude that extended to late fall.

"The summer has been upon us for six weeks," one resident wrote in 1844. "We are preparing for a long and lonesome season in our deserted Town." A local physician admitted earlier, "From 4 to 5 months during the year there prevails a most malignant fever . . . and all who are able, abandon the place during the sickly season."[1] The compensation for one editor was that "what we lose in

1. Samuel W. Spencer to Mrs. E. H. Hayward, May 24, 1844. Letter in P. K. Yonge Collection, University of Florida. William D. Price was the candid doctor. See Carter, *USTP* 24: 903.

number is made up by increased sociality, and our time is passed quite pleasantly in reading, visiting, and occasionally a quiet rubber at Whist in the evenings." Even better, the "Aspelaggi Band . . . have frequent meetings, and enliven the citizens with their delightful serenades. Taking it altogether, we get along very well, considering the scarcity of ladies among us."[2]

Activity returned in November and December when steamboats began arriving. Their main cargo was the new cotton crop, and as the bales were unloaded they overflowed the warehouses, spilled out on the wharves, and had to be stored in lines along the street.

Several commission merchants operated cotton presses. Once the sausage-like bales were unloaded, they were dismantled and "pressed" into smaller sizes, which made them more convenient for shipping and storage. Various types of presses—steam, screw, lever, and hydraulic—handled the elongated bales. In 1850 Apalachicola had four cotton presses, employing sixteen, twenty-five, thirty, and forty hands.[3]

Despite financial distress and threats of Indian attack, Apalachicola had "continued to improve in buildings and population," stockholders in the Apalachicola Land Company were told in 1839. "Its ascendency in that neighborhood is gradually and constantly becoming more evident and permanent."[4] Less inclined toward such favorable comments was a recently arrived New Englander. Writing about Apalachicola that same year, he told a friend in Connecticut, "the only articles of natural growth here is *cockadiles*, & *snakes*, & *fleas* (which I might have neglected noticing if I had not some ten or twelve on me at this time) and every other *varment* known as a pess to mankind."[5]

Such detractors were the exception. Proudly describing Apala-

---

2. Apalachicola *Commercial Advertiser*, July 29, 1845; see ibid., Mar. 21, 1846.

3. Statistics for Industry, Florida, 1850 Manuscript Census, 201. A steam press was erected as early as 1841. See Apalachicola Land Co., *Annual Report*, 1841, 5.

4. Apalachicola Land Co., *Annual Report*, 1839.

5. Frank Betts to Robert Raymond, Mar. 13, 1839. Letter in P. K. Yonge Collection, University of Florida.

chicola as "exclusively commercial in its character," the editor of the *Commercial Advertiser* noted the whirligig of 1844–45: "The scene has regularly opened for a winter's campaign, and already you may see the cotton buyer anxiously examining samples. . . . The river's rise—steamboat follows steamboat—each wharf has its pile—every merchant has his business—every clerk his duty— loafers are out of fashion, and it is all business, bustle, bustle— exclusively *masculine* business." [6] Not much had changed by 1858 when a traveler from Georgia declared that Apalachicola had a "very industrious population, among the lower classes. I have seen few if any loafers; have not seen a drunk man since I have come here." If all of that seemed to contradict the relaxed life-style of southerners, it was because "there is a good deal of 'Yankeedom' in this place"; in fact, "all hands are at work, and always at it, is the motto here." [7]

Among the workers were blacks, both slave and free. Blacks were fairly unrestricted, some living apart from their masters in rented houses. They hired themselves out, paid their masters money, but otherwise were uncircumscribed in their conduct. The arrangement prompted occasional protests, and there were chronic complaints that white barkeepers openly sold whiskey to slaves. [8] State laws— one in 1849 that forbade all trading with slaves and another in 1851 that limited the prohibition to agricultural products—were no more enforceable in Apalachicola than in the rest of the state. By 1856 a legislative statute made trading with a free person of color a criminal act unless the guardian had previously consented. [9]

Besides the usual charges that blacks lived in squalid conditions, committed frequent thefts, and competed with them for wages, whites had another cause for dissatisfaction. Many of the slave laborers, local citizens maintained, were owned by nonresidents. Because slave wages were going to masters in Georgia and Alabama, Apalachicolans were urged to hire native whites. By 1845 there

6. Apalachicola *Commercial Advertiser,* Nov. 30, 1844.
7. Ibid., Mar. 10, 1858, quoting "Traveler" to Bainbridge *Argus.*
8. Franklin County grand jury report in Apalachicola *Gazette,* Jan. 29, Dec. 2, 1837.
9. *Laws of Florida* 1848–49: 70; 1850–51: 132; 1856: 27.

was a local tax of five dollars for every slave brought into the city for sale or hire, and in 1850 the legislature required owners to pay a license tax before importing slaves for hire into the state.[10]

Most of Florida's small population of free blacks lived in old Spanish ports such as St. Augustine and Pensacola, where restrictions were fewer. In 1860, of the state's 923 free blacks, 606 lived in towns and cities. Apalachicola had only six persons of color.[11]

In 1827 the Legislative Council prohibited free blacks from entering Florida. Yet in 1828 an act excluded black sailors on foreign or American vessels in Florida's territorial waters from punishment. The territory and later the state were empowered to regulate free blacks, but of the laws passed or amended many were never fully enforced. In Apalachicola most free blacks were transients, sailors who came into town from anchored ships. The men were permitted entry and then lodged in jail until their ship sailed. Few people advocated giving them the freedom of the town. Opposition to their entry grew, and in 1849 the legislature passed a special act requiring free black sailors to remain on ship while their vessel was in port. They were to get no closer to Apalachicola than five miles and were forbidden to communicate with the crews of other ships.[12]

Saint George Island played a brief and unnoticed part in the deepening controversy over slavery in the 1840s. By the fact of its presence, the island had, on occasion, bumped into history. It had been temporary host to men of note or notoriety: Narváez and Cabeza de Vaca (possibly); Viaud; Colonel Edward Nicolls, a British officer on the Gulf coast during the War of 1812; William Bowles, who was shipwrecked there in 1799; Andrew Ellicott; and John Lee Williams. In 1844 a white man named Jonathan Walker left Pensacola with a boat containing seven fugitive slaves. A native

10. Apalachicola *Commercial Advertiser*, Mar. 11, 1844; Feb. 22, 1845; *Laws of Florida* 1850–51: 114.

11. *Eighth Census*, 1860, Population 1: 54

12. *Laws of Florida* 1848–49: 70–71. See also Russell Garvin, "The Free Negro in Florida before the Civil War," 9–10; Julia Floyd Smith, *Slavery and Plantation Growth in Antebellum Florida, 1821–1860*, 110–21; and Jesse J. Jackson, "The Negro and the Law in Florida, 1821–1921."

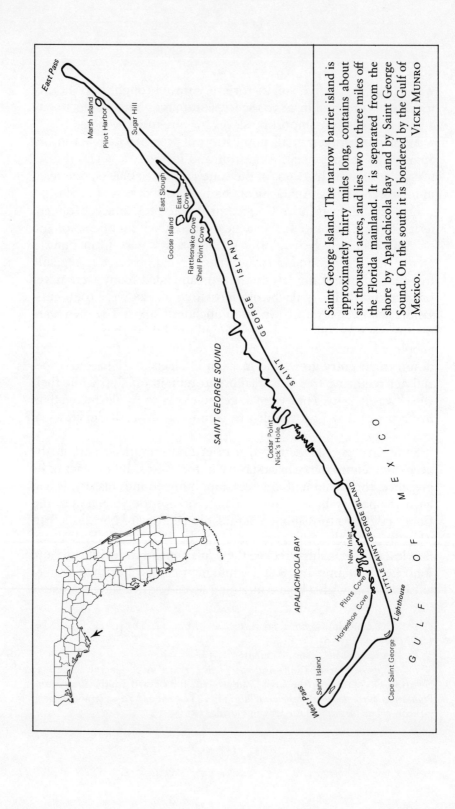

Saint George Island. The narrow barrier island is approximately thirty miles long, contains about six thousand acres, and lies two to three miles off the Florida mainland. It is separated from the shore by Apalachicola Bay and by Saint George Sound. On the south it is bordered by the Gulf of Mexico.

VICKI MUNRO

of Massachusetts who had settled in Florida, Walker was deeply opposed to slavery. He was attempting to carry the slaves to the freedom of British-owned Nassau. Writing about the exploit later, Walker remembered "stopping a few hours at Saint George Island to cook a little, and recruit our water."[13]

Walker and the slaves were captured at sea near Key West. The captive was returned to Pensacola for trial. He was found guilty and branded on his right hand with the letters *SS* (for Slave Stealer). The affair became a national cause célèbre and added to the sectional tensions.

In Apalachicola slavery functioned in relation to commerce, not agriculture. The same was true of practically everything else in town, and the condition of the harbor was an ongoing concern. Before the Civil War, West Pass was used more frequently than East Pass. Ships drawing up to twelve feet could enter West Pass and get within three miles of town before anchoring. Although East Pass permitted ships of greater draft, they had to anchor ten miles short of the wharves. Depending on conditions, the depths of water over the bars might vary several feet. The Apalachicola Land Company dredged the harbor in 1836, and surveys were taken from time to time. Responding to petitions, the federal government appropriated money in the 1830s to remove obstructions from the Apalachicola River and to deepen the channel in the bay and Saint George Sound. The work was sporadic, and silt deposited by the river prevented the bay from becoming a deep-water harbor. The port continued to develop because much of Apalachicola's trade was coastwise and conducted in vessels of shallow draft. Yet by 1842 the port shipped 48,070 bales of cotton to domestic markets, and 38,794 bales were sold abroad.[14]

The cotton trade followed a fairly consistent routine. Farmers and planters in Florida, Georgia, and Alabama shipped their bales to Apalachicola. As a Georgia editor explained, it was a matter of simple economics: "Apalachicola is emphatically a *cotton city*—a

13. Jonathan Walker, *Trial and Imprisonment of Jonathan Walker, at Pensacola, Florida, for Aiding Slaves to Escape from Bondage,* 11.

14. Carter, *USTP* 23: 1034–35; 24: 767–69, 879; 25: 95, 557, 559; 26: 625–26.

commercial emporium, and although within the boundary, and subject to the law of Florida, is a Georgia and Alabama mart, deriving all its nourishment and support from these two Southern states."[15] Bales arriving at Apalachicola were received, handled, and shipped by merchants who imposed various charges and commissions for their services. On occasion the factors were bypassed and the cotton was taken directly to a vessel in the harbor by the steamboat that brought it downriver.

Ships that cleared the bay loaded with upland cotton had arrived earlier laden with goods from New York or other ports both American and foreign. Apalachicola was served by four types of sailing vessels: ships (full square-rigged vessels of three masts, the aristocrats of the high seas), barks, brigs, and schooners. The smallest—schooners with one or two masts—were the most widely used in the coastal trade. Schooners also served in the harbor as lighters and in the Cuban trade. Most active of all were the steamboats, which were utilized in the coastal trade and as packets, lighters, and riverboats.

Typically a New York–based ship unloaded its merchandise at Apalachicola, took on a cargo of cotton, and departed on a second leg to Liverpool or a European port. There the bales were unloaded, and the vessel completed the final leg by carrying foreign goods and passengers back to New York. A number of variations were possible. A ship might return directly to New York or Boston from Apalachicola, the cotton then to be transported across the Atlantic to Europe. The return voyage then became the journey from Europe to Apalachicola with a cargo of manufactured goods or salt in ballast. Often Apalachicola merchants sailed on the ships to northern cities to select goods for their stores.[16]

Saint George helped make possible the development of Apalachicola as a shipping center. The strategically located island soon became important in how the port functioned—a lighthouse was

15. Bainbridge *Argus*, Apr. 4, 1857. See also William N. Thurston, "A Study of Maritime Activity in Florida in the Nineteenth Century," 101–3.

16. Harry M. Owens, "Port of Apalachicola," 5, 8–11; Carter, *USTP* 24: 59–62. See also Robert G. Albion, *The Rise of the Port of New York, 1815–1860*, 105, 95–121, and Harold D. Woodman, *King Cotton and His Retainers: Financing and Marketing the Cotton Crop of the South, 1800–1925*.

erected there. Among the annual rituals of Congress was that of appropriating funds for lighthouses. Money went for the construction of new ones, the repair of old ones, and various matters relating to their maintenance. The annual law coming out of Washington was usually lengthy because it included specific allocations for all the states and territories having lighthouses. Florida's extensive coastline required an increasing number of beacons as the territory became more involved with shipping.

Boston light on Little Brewster Island, America's first lighthouse, was put into service in 1716, but not until 1825 was one erected in Florida.[17] The site was Cape Florida at the southern tip of Key Biscayne. Pressure mounted for more, and Joseph M. White, Florida's territorial delegate to Congress, served Apalachicola's interests in an act passed March 3, 1831. The measure appropriated $11,400 for "building a lighthouse on the west end of Saint George Island, near the entrance of the Appalachicola [sic] bay." An additional $400 was provided for placing buoys in the bay between Saint George Island and the river's mouth.[18]

Acquiring land for the lighthouse posed problems. The island was controlled and owned by the Apalachicola Land Company, but the firm's lands were still in litigation in 1831 and the boundaries were unclear. Because a number of individuals owned portions of the original Forbes Purchase, Louis McLane, secretary of the treasury, made two separate transactions. In January 1833, he paid Peter Mitchell, agent for persons owning three-fourths of the tract, fifty dollars for an unspecified ten acres of land, and in March he paid David V. Ogden two dollars. Ogden acted for those owning one-fourth of the purchase. The only stipulation was that the lighthouse would be located outside of Apalachicola's town limits but within a radius of fifteen miles.[19]

Gabriel I. Floyd, already in charge of the Collector's Office,

17. Robert Carse, *Keepers of the Lights: A History of American Lighthouses*, 11.

18. *U.S. Statutes at Large* 4: 491; Carter, *USTP* 24: 532, 923–24.

19. Lighthouse Deeds and Contracts, June 12, 1839, to November 28, 1847, Fifth Auditor's Office, Bureau of Lighthouses, Record Group 26, National Archives. McLane's first purchase was made at Savannah, Georgia; the place of the second purchase was not recorded.

assumed a new responsibility as superintendent of lights at Apalachicola. He made periodic reports to Stephen Pleasonton, a government official with the imposing title of fifth auditor, whose headquarters were at Washington. Floyd performed the preliminary work—clarifying questions of landownership, procuring buoys, and putting them in place. Even though the western end of Little Saint George commanded the bay's main entrance, Floyd did not want the lighthouse located there. He knew West Pass intimately and pointed out that when the summer and fall gales came the area would overflow.[20] Town merchants and masters of various vessels agreed. They all argued that the proper location was Cape Saint George, the broad elbow of Little Saint George Island. A Mr. Knowlton arrived to make final arrangements, and, after examining Cape Saint George, he estimated that building a landing and hauling materials there would cost $20,000. That amount exceeded by over $8,000 the amount appropriated, so construction went forward at the island's western tip instead.[21]

Work began in the late spring of 1833. A dwelling and the lighthouse, a graceful structure built of bricks and standing sixty-five feet high, were completed by the end of the year. Maintaining a lighthouse was not always easy, as Superintendent Floyd quickly discovered. For one thing, he was never satisfied with the site; for another, a succession of keepers quit out of boredom or were fired. Floyd complained about one Allen Smith in 1835, accusing the keeper of being totally unfit and of relying on others to do his work. Smith, according to Floyd, was often drunk, and the result was that the light kept going out.[22]

There was a need for a beacon at East Pass, and in 1837 Congress made $10,000 available for a "light-house on the most suitable site at or near the east entrance from the Gulf of Mexico into

20. Gabriel I. Floyd to S. Pleasonton, Jan. 12, 1832, Superintendents of Lights at Apalachicola, 1831–32, Record Group 26, National Archives. Floyd's reports covered the period 1831–37. See also Floyd to Pleasonton, Aug. 4, Dec. 5, 1831.

21. Floyd to Pleasonton, May 5, 1833, Floyd file, National Archives.

22. Mrs. Dolores Cassel, a resident of Saint George Island, has collected data on the area lighthouses, and some of her material is used, with gratitude, in this chapter. See also Floyd to Pleasonton, Jan. 22, 1834, Sept. 30, 1835, Floyd file, National Archives.

Appalachicola [sic] bay." An additional $1,000 was provided to mark the channel from East Pass to Apalachicola. The port's trade had become international, and larger vessels engaged in European commerce needed the deeper waters at East Pass. At first the petitioners asked for a lighthouse on the eastern end of Saint George Island, but later the town merchants sought the expert advice of masters of packet vessels. Thirteen of the captains responded formally. They suggested that the western end of Dog Island was a better site, and their counsel was followed. Completed in late 1838, the tower was lighted in February 1839. It was forty-eight feet high, could be seen for thirteen miles, and was more functional than the light at West Pass. Unfortunately, in October 1842, a severe gale washed away lightkeeper Latham Babcock's house, and a portion of the lighthouse fell. The unfortunate Babcock lost not only his house and its furnishings but also a boat and his poultry and hogs. "Imperfect construction" was blamed for the mishap, and the necessary repairs were made.[23]

Hiram Nourse became superintendent of lights in 1842. He continued Floyd's earlier efforts to remove the beacon at West Pass and relocate it on Cape Saint George. It was true that the light had withstood the recent hurricane, but its location remained a basic error. The Apalachicola Chamber of Commerce supported Nourse's arguments and memorialized Congress for a new light. President David G. Raney and other chamber members contended that the West Pass lighthouse was useless. Its beacon was no more than a harbor light and was largely obscured by Cape Saint George. Ships approaching the coast could not see it until long after they made land. Since most vessels used West Pass to take advantage of the easterly trade winds and to avoid the westerly currents, safe navigation required a new lighthouse.[24] Petitions, requests by ship cap-

23. *U.S. Statutes at Large* 5: 185; Gabriel I. Floyd to S. Pleasonton, June 10, 1836, Floyd file, National Archives; Apalachicola *Commercial Advertiser*, Aug. 1, Nov. 4, 1843; Carter, *USTP* 24: 923–25; 25: 70–71; 26: 865–67. A. J. Castleberry and David L. Cipra, *Lighthouses and Lightships of the Northern Gulf of Mexico*, 9. Dog Island had a revolving light to help distinguish it from the beacon at West Pass and later on Cape Saint George.

24. Hiram Nourse to Walter Forward, Secretary of the Treasury, Dec. 9, 1842, Nourse file, National Archives; Carter, *USTP* 26: 584–86.

tains, advice from Nourse, and general pressure finally got the desired action. In 1847 Congress appropriated $8,000 for a light at Cape Saint George.[25] By that time Samuel W. Spencer had succeeded Nourse as superintendent of lights.

Spencer opened negotiations with the Apalachicola Land Company. The island had never been surveyed, but the company employed H. F. Simmons of Franklin County to perform the task. His survey of Cape Saint George was filed in New York City, and the company sold between six and eight acres to Spencer. The superintendent paid $150 for the land, recorded his purchase, and forwarded a report to Washington.[26]

In the meantime Simmons assumed that the land at Cape Saint George would become valuable and purchased several lots in the vicinity. Other people bought land nearby, and later Simmons made an unsuccessful claim that the lighthouse was on his land. Nor was it clear whether Florida, which became a state in 1845, owned the site jointly with the federal government. In the summer of 1847 the Florida legislature formally deeded ownership to the United States, and Governor William D. Moseley signed an engraved document affirming the transfer.[27]

Edward Bowen of Franklin County was selected as contractor, and despite interruptions—illness among his workers and an October gale—got on with the project. Lanterns and lighting apparatus were taken from the old lighthouses at West Pass and at St. Joseph. Work on the keeper's dwelling and the beacon progressed, and the sixty-five-foot structure was lighted on December 20, 1848. Its beam was visible fifteen miles at sea.[28]

Benjamin S. Hawley, who became superintendent in 1849, had a

25. *U.S. Statutes at Large* 9: 177.

26. Samuel W. Spencer to S. Pleasonton, 1849, Hawley file, National Archives. Spencer's letter, written after he was succeeded by Benjamin S. Hawley, clarified the situation.

27. Department of Commerce, Lighthouse Service, Cape Saint George file, National Archives, contains all of the documents pertinent to the transfer: Spanish, federal, state, county, company, and individual.

28. Samuel W. Spencer to S. Pleasonton, Oct. 6, Dec. 20, 1848, Jan. 1, 1849, Spencer file, National Archives. For letters regarding building disagreements see

difficult tenure. Sick and absent much of the time, Hawley had to contend with the effects of a powerful gale in the summer of 1850. He lost his boat, a chimney from his house was blown down, and the lighthouse was badly cracked and undermined. Repairs were made, but Hawley's request for the construction of a breakwater protection was ignored.[29] No barrier could have withstood the force of the hurricane that hit in August 1851. Hawley made a terse report: Cape Saint George and the other district lights were "thrown down."[30]

Rebuilding began in the winter of 1852. The old site at Cape Saint George was retained, but the new structure was moved to a point 400 yards from the shell-strewn beach (the old light had been only 150 yards from the low-water line). The foundation was made deeper and stronger, and the tower's height was increased to seventy-five feet. By the early summer of 1852 the work was completed.[31] The last structure still stands. The lighthouse's beam (kerosene was not replaced by dry cell batteries until well into the twentieth century) functioned efficiently for vessels that used West Pass and New Inlet. As a work of architecture the lighthouse was a sentinel, tapered and solitary, made more impressive by its lonely setting. The people who serviced that light were the island's permanent population, and the tower became a focal point for social occasions and for fishing and hunting expeditions (*illustration, Group 1*).

Entering and leaving the port at Apalachicola was a demanding effort that required skill and experience. Disasters could occur swiftly and unexpectedly. In 1834 the *American,* loaded with cotton and bound for New York, had almost cleared the bar when

Cassel file; see also Apalachicola *Commercial Advertiser,* Oct. 14, 1847; Castleberry and Cipra, *Lighthouses and Lightships,* 8.

29. Cassel file; A. R. Taylor, substituting for Hawley, to S. Pleasonton, Aug. 27, Sept. 10, 1850, Hawley file, National Archives; Benjamin S. Hawley to S. Pleasonton, Sept. 3, 1850, May 24, 1851, ibid.

30. Benjamin S. Hawley to S. Pleasonton, Sept. 29, 1851, ibid.

31. Cassel file; Benjamin S. Hawley to S. Pleasonton, Oct. 20, 1851, Feb. 7, Apr. 30, 1852, Hawley file, National Archives. Two-thirds of the bricks were salvaged from the toppled tower.

a fire broke out in the hold. The ship was run ashore, but the flames could not be extinguished. The *American* burned to the water's edge, and nothing was saved but the baggage.[32] Even an uneventful entry was never routine, and the top seamen were the harbor pilots.

A typical pilot would cruise for two or three weeks off Saint George Island. He and another crew member manned a fast, small schooner and waited for any ship that wanted to come through West Pass or East Pass or New Inlet. The two men maintained their vigil despite the elements. Sometimes they ran out of supplies because sailing ships had no sure schedules and communication with them was difficult. Often several ships would converge at once, and a pilot could bring in several in a day. The pilot would board the vessel, leaving his companion to return in the schooner. Completely familiar with the channel and the effects of wind and tide, the pilot gave sure commands to men who manipulated thousands of feet of canvas. A pilot's fee depended on the ship's draft (the deeper the draft, the higher the fee). Whether the ship was exchanging goods for cotton or, later, for timber and naval stores, it was the harbor pilot who moved the vessel in safety to an exact spot for loading.[33]

The foreign ships that entered the harbor rarely held cargoes of manufactured goods. The port's international trade was mostly in foodstuffs: bananas, coconuts, wines and liquors, olive oil, and especially salt. It was the coastal trade that supplied manufactured goods. From New England and the Middle Atlantic states came hardware, books, clothing, ice, and machinery. Food and whiskey also arrived from American ports, particularly New Orleans. Besides serving the carrying trade, ships ran as regularly scheduled packets. Even so, carriers such as the Mobile Packet Line or the Charleston and Apalachicola Line followed an arrival and departure timetable that varied considerably. They operated primarily during the business season.

Many steamboats engaged in the domestic trade visited Apa-

32. *Niles' Weekly Register* 46 (Aug., 1834): 380.
33. For details of how a harbor pilot operated see Apalachicola *Times,* June 28, 1940.

lachicola, but, more important, they served the Apalachicola-Chattahoochee-Flint river system. Between 1828 and 1861, sixty-four steamboats listed Apalachicola as their home port, and over twice that number were active on the river system at one time or another. Most of the steamboats were built in shipyards along the Mississippi and Ohio rivers (eight were constructed in Apalachicola and twelve others along the Chattahoochee and Flint).[34]

Designed for both freight and passengers, the steamboats were overwhelmingly side-wheelers. Only 14 out of 115 were stern-wheelers because "hog-backing," an engineering difficulty relating to weight distribution, was not overcome until late in the period. Side-wheelers were more powerful, and their maneuverability made docking easier. The river system was dangerous, especially in the summer months, because of rocks and snags. Fires broke out frequently on the steamboats. The shallow draft steamers had no holds, and the deck cargoes were exposed to sparks from the wood and numerous other hazards. Violent explosions occurred, but they were less frequent than fires. In 1835 the *Eloisa* caught fire on her maiden voyage from Apalachicola to Columbus. The passengers jumped overboard and were saved, although the steward, a free Negro, was drowned. Six people were killed in 1840 when the *Leroy*'s flue collapsed between Chattahoochee and Iola (the engineer was drunk, and there was no water in the boilers). Another accident occurred near Chattahoochee in 1842 when the boilers burst on the *Chamois*, killing three persons. The *Robert Fulton* snagged and sank on the Apalachicola in 1843, and the same river claimed the *Fanny Ellsler* in 1844 when her boilers caught fire and the steamboat burned to the waterline. One of the worst years for accidents was 1845: on the Flint the *Viola* struck a rock and was a total loss; on the Apalachicola the *Sirn*'s boilers exploded, causing the deaths of ten people; on the Chattahoochee the *Lowell* hit a snag and sank. Then in 1849 the *Palmetto* caught a snag at Chimney Bluff on the Chattahoochee and was sunk, although its cargo of cotton was saved.[35]

34. Owens, "Port of Apalachicola," 5; Owens, "Sail and Steam Vessels," 198–201.
35. Author's interview with John H. Moore; Owens, "Apalachicola before

With shipping made uncertain by varying river conditions and the competence and vigilance of any particular crew, insurance rates were inevitably high. In fact, the anticipation of instant and ongoing profits led Apalachicola businessmen to establish three insurance companies in the decade before the Civil War.[36]

The Apalachicola was almost always open to traffic as far north as the junction of the Chattahoochee and the Flint. During periods of low water, ships could not ascend the river, and prices dropped sharply in Apalachicola. High water also posed difficulties. Ships caught above the bridge at Eufaula could not descend. Despite navigational problems and complaints about exorbitant charges and unfair freight rates, Apalachicola developed an extensive inland trade. In the 1840s the port began receiving shipments of tobacco from Decatur County producers along the Flint. Cotton remained the most valuable commercial item, but rice, corn, and timber provided diversity to the cargoes and profits for the interior planters and farmers.[37] Yet by 1860 there was evidence of serious trouble.

In 1850 the port received 80 percent of the cotton produced in the hinterland drainage area. By the end of the decade the total had dropped to 43 percent, and there was a comparable decline in the shipment of other products. Some commission merchants in Apalachicola were forced out of business. In view of the South's expanding economy in the 1850s, how could the deterioration be explained? An outsider blamed it on an inert citizenry. Unless the people activated themselves, Apalachicola would "dwindle to nonimportance, and some other gulf port will rise at her expense."[38] The real reasons lay deeper.

River conditions were bad because of low water and inadequate attention to removing obstacles. The harbor at Apalachicola was

1861," 231–33. For the wrecks see Pensacola *Gazette*, Jan. 17, 1835, quoting Apalachicola *Advertiser;* New Orleans *Daily Picayune*, Nov. 5, 1840; Apr. 8, 1843; Tallahassee *Florida Journal*, Nov. 12, 1842; Apalachicola *Commercial Advertiser*, Mar. 1, 8, 22, 1845; Jan. 4, 1849.

36. *Acts of Florida*, 1850–51: 25–31, 31–34; 1860–61: 154–57.

37. W. A. Karin to A. R. Johnston, Mar. 20, 1847, P. K. Yonge Collection, University of Florida; Apalachicola *Commercial Advertiser*, Mar. 2, 1847.

38. Bainbridge *Southern Georgian*, July 23, 1858. See also Owens, "Apalachicola before 1861," 249.

filling up with silt, and there was limited federal funding for dredging. Magnifying the problem was a lack of rainfall that slowed the current. Disinterest by the national government was matched by that of the state. Competition from railroads was already being felt. Lines in Georgia, Alabama, and Florida were laid in the 1850s and significantly diverted traffic from Apalachicola. Textile mills newly opened at Columbus began using the area's cotton, a development sure to reduce shipments to Apalachicola.

The people of Apalachicola and Franklin County had no diversified economy to fall back on. There was so little farming in 1850 that only thirty-seven men in the county were listed in the agricultural census. The total value of all livestock was an embarrassing $10,550, and no farmer reported any acres planted in row crops such as cotton and corn.[39] The unpromising situation had actually worsened by 1860, when a total of only three farmers made census returns. Each planted only one crop: Irish potatoes.[40] Gardens maintained by town residents almost matched the production of the county. One realist posed a question and answered it himself: "Blot out the Flint and Chattahoochee rivers and what would be the condition of this flourishing city? It would soon be deserted, and its streets overgrown with sea-weeds and bushes."[41]

In 1860 Franklin County had no industrial economy at all. No census taker in the United States made a bleaker report than the local enumerator. The official scrawled a cryptic statement across the ledger of his book: "There are no manufactories in the county & nothing made or produced that can properly come under this schedule."[42]

The fishing industry had great potential; but because seafood was perishable, no true export market was established. The natural oyster beds were extensive, but they were exploited only at the local level. By the 1850s some oysters were being shipped in bulk

39. Manuscript Census, 1850, Agriculture, Franklin County, Florida, 70. Although the returns were incomplete, they were fairly accurate.

40. Ibid., 1860, 14.

41. Bainbridge *Argus*, Nov. 25, 1856.

42. Manuscript Census, 1860, Productions of Industry, Franklin County, Florida, 1.

in the shell. Joseph S. Lawrence and John Miller were among the pioneer oyster dealers.[43]

Was Apalachicola a classic story of rise and decline? Its rapid rise was undeniable. In 1837 the port received 32,291 bales of cotton, population increased, and the next year a merchant wrote, "I find there is an important accession of new inhabitants here this season, many of whom are of a character that would be considered a valuable acquisition to any place."[44] Between October 1842 and June 1843 at least 287 vessels dropped anchor in Apalachicola Bay, and the value of cotton shipped was $1,282,365.08.[45] From 1837 to 1850 Apalachicola was the third largest cotton port on the Gulf of Mexico (after New Orleans and Mobile). But by the 1850s, Galveston, Texas, had become the beneficiary of newly opened cotton lands and was number three. There was truth to the statement made by one auditor in 1859: "Of late years it has been common, yea, even fashionable to say, 'Apalachicola is going down.'"[46]

Still, Apalachicola remained an important port, and its problems could have been solved. Between September 1, 1859, and August 1, 1860, Apalachicola received 133,079 bales of cotton valued at $7,139,345, and during the year 148 vessels cleared the customhouse. More bales went to domestic markets than to Europe, although the latter claimed a large number. Long staple or "sea island" cotton was in greater demand in Europe than in the United States, and Apalachicola became an established international supplier. The total value of goods handled through Apalachicola in 1860 exceeded $14 million.[47]

Apalachicola was equally competitive with St. Marks and other ports that dealt primarily in the domestic trade. Departing from Apalachicola in 1852, a satisfied captain wrote, "I am all ready for sea bound to Boston with a six thousand dollar freight in the ship,

43. For a brief summary of the oyster industry see Apalachicola *Times,* Nov. 13, 1953. The subject is treated in detail in chap. 6.

44. Charles Rogers to Caleb Hawkins, Nov. 30, 1938. Letter in P. K. Yonge Collection, University of Florida.

45. Apalachicola *Watchman of the Gulf,* Aug. 12, 1843.

46. Bainbridge *Southern Georgian,* Feb. 25, 1859.

47. For economic data based on earlier records see Apalachicola *Times,* June 16, 1939.

rather better than I could have done in New Orleans."[48] In 1859 an unabashed promoter declared that Apalachicola "has a better cotton market at all seasons of the year, than any other market on the Gulf, and is equal to any other in the United States."[49] Real and personal estate taxes in the county amounted to $1,280,174 in 1860.[50] A number of local leaders—including Thomas G. Ormond, William G. Porter, and David G. Raney—were determined to make improvements (*illustration*, Group 1).

What might have happened invites speculation. Continued attention to expanding and improving a system of roads would have freed the region from its isolation by land. Too often a charter like the one granted to the Apalachicola and Middle Florida Plank Road Company in 1851 was never implemented.[51] A memorial from Apalachicola to Congress in 1860 to improve the harbor came too late. So did state legislation authorizing funds to improve the channel of the Apalachicola River and reclaim overflowed and swamp lands.[52] Railroads were not by definition enemies of a port, and there was talk about Apalachicola as the terminus for a line or lines from Georgia and Alabama.[53]

In 1860, Franklin County had a total population of 1,904. There were 520 slaves.[54] Apalachicola had not achieved the greatness predicted for it, but it was a considerable port and added much to the economy of Florida. Few doubted that with some adjustments the town would grow and prosper. The same could not be said for the ill-fated Apalachicola Land Company.

The actual transfer of lands in the Forbes Purchase had been ac-

48. E. B. Mallet to "Friend Thomas," Mar. 15, 1882. Letter in P. K. Yonge Collection, University of Florida. With few exceptions, St. Marks and Newport, which was nearby, handled the cotton produced in Florida and shipped it to New York. See Thurston, "Maritime Activity in Florida," 120, 125.

49. Bainbridge *Southern Georgian*, Apr. 1, 1859.

50. Manuscript Census, 1860, Social Statistics, Franklin County, Florida.

51. *Acts of Florida*, 1850–51: 72–81.

52. Tallahassee *Floridian and Journal*, Dec. 1, 1860; *Acts of Florida*, 1860–61: 165. The improvements would have been carried out by the trustees of the Internal Improvement Trust Fund created by the state in 1855 to administer its lands.

53. See Bainbridge *Argus*, Apr. 4, 1857.

54. *Eighth Census*, 1860, Population 1: 51–54.

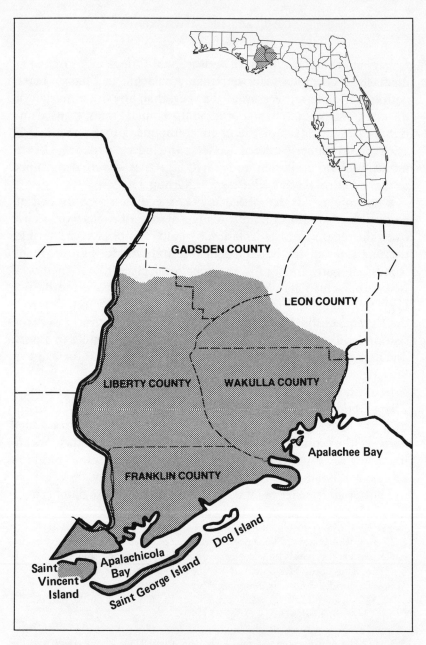

The Forbes Purchase contained about 1.5 million acres and was obtained from Spain by the British trading firm of Panton, Leslie and Company as a settlement for debts. A successor firm, John Forbes and Company, took over in 1804. Once the United States acquired Florida, disputed ownership of the Forbes Purchase set off extended legal battles.   VICKI MUNRO

complished in 1835 when the Apalachicola Land Company was formed. The necessary but endless paperwork was finally completed in 1842 when President John Tyler signed the patent with the seal of the General Land Office. To its pleasure the company found that the amount of land exceeded previous estimates and came to 1,427,290.17 acres.[55] Yet after the success of the early sales in Apalachicola, nothing went right for the stockholders.

Between 1808 and 1856 there were ten surveys of the grant. Some were superficial, others detailed; most were privately commissioned, although the federal government conducted one.[56] In effect the surveyors informed the owners that despite the tract's immensity, much of it was without value. (After a personal inspection, Governor Duval concluded that "nine tenths of [the company's property] is as poor as any lands in Florida.") The purchase had hammock, pine, swamp, and marsh lands, but most of the soil was unsuited for agriculture. Mineral resources were almost completely lacking, although the grant contained vast stands of timber. Land lying east of the Ochlockonee River (far removed from Apalachicola) was considered the most productive part of the Forbes Purchase.[57]

Over the years the original administrative arrangement—trustees and a board of directors—underwent alterations.[58] There were shifts in personnel, number of officers, and voting procedures. When a change occurred, the trust deed to the Forbes Purchase lands was transferred to the new trustees.[59] With rising debts and no income of significance, the company was reduced to paying its obligations in land. As time passed the officials had to give up property to pay county taxes.

In 1853 the Apalachicola Land Company's assets were transferred to trustees Lewis Curtis and Nathaniel Thurston.[60] They

55. The patent was rerecorded in the public records of Franklin, Leon, Gadsden, and Liberty counties. See Franklin County Deed Book U, 559–68. The last citation was recorded October 17, 1921.

56. Upchurch, "Development of the Forbes Purchase," 131–38. See Duval's letter to John Quincy Adams in Carter, USTP 22: 848 [February 13, 1824].

57. Upchurch, "Development of the Forbes Purchase," 138.

58. Leon County Deed Book E, 100–104. See ibid., 104–5.

59. See, for example, ibid., Milton, 164–66.

60. Ibid., K, 537.

were no more successful in restoring the company's solvency than their predecessors had been and emerged as the principals in a debt case in 1855. Judge J. Wayless Baker of the Middle Circuit of Florida Leon Circuit Court, in Chancery, ruled against them and appointed John Beard as receiver. He was to take over the company's functions and advertise the sale of the remaining lands at public auctions. The property was bid for at the courthouses in Tallahassee and Apalachicola.[61]

Another case in the spring of 1857 resulted in the appointment of Charles Ellis as receiver to carry out all of the company's contracts.[62] Ellis remained as receiver until after the Civil War, although most of the lands were sold by 1861. In 1866 he made his final report and yielded his position to George S. Hawkins. Most of the land brought only a few cents on the acre, and in the aftermath of the Civil War, much of it was never paid. One result of all the litigation was a legacy of confused land titles.[63]

Thus did the Apalachicola Land Company go its strange way. At one time its territory was a wilderness kingdom larger than Rhode Island. Yet in the end the company failed for two primary reasons: the owners had poor land, and, as many southerners discovered at the individual level, they were land poor.

By 1860, Saint Vincent and Dog islands had been sold to private individuals. The status of Saint George Island was less certain. Cape Saint George had been surveyed by H. F. Simmons in the late 1840s and all or parts of the rest of Little Saint George Island and Saint George Island by M. L. Williams in the mid-1850s. The source title for the smaller island dates from the appointment of

61. Leon County Chancery Order Book 1: 221–22, 222–23, 224–37. For attempts by the company to promote its land, see brochures published in 1849 advertising a sale to be conducted in New York City. Brochure in P. K. Yonge Collection, University of Florida.

62. Franklin County Deed Book B, 194–95; Liberty County Deed Book B, 1–7.

63. Franklin County Deed Book B, 200–201; see ibid., 194–201, for the final accounting of Ellis; Upchurch, "Development of the Forbes Purchase," 139. For example, in 1859 the Apalachicola Land Company sold 6,736 acres of its lands in Franklin and Liberty counties for $251.86. In 1860 another tract of 5,760 acres in the two counties sold for $86.40. See Liberty County Deed Book A, 25, 143, 174.

Charles Ellis as receiver for the Apalachicola Land Company. Any similar source title for Saint George was lost in 1874 when a fire destroyed many of Franklin County's land records. It was not until the period of Reconstruction that certain individuals (and then only a few) became interested in owning Saint George.

As the antebellum period closed, Apalachicola had declined as a port; but there was hope for the future. The expectations of the Apalachicola Land Company had long since vanished, its lands and assets seized and sold for debts. For the moment Saint George Island played a role well described by an Apalachicolan inclined to metaphor: "[It] seems to be a Providential interposition, stretching as it were its beneficent wings over the quiet little city, thus protecting us from the injuries incurred by gales and storms."[64] Yet the Civil War was at hand, and the island would figure in the conflict.

64. See George W. Saxon writing in Tallahassee *Weekly Floridian*, Aug. 19, 1873. Saxon became a central figure in the attempted development of Saint George Island in the first decades of the twentieth century.

3

Apalachicola Must Be Protected

I HAVE returned from the city of Apalachicola, and you may well be assured that the secession fever is raging there as well as elsewhere in the South," a resident of Quincy wrote in December 1860.[1] Caught up in the sectional crises of the 1850s, Florida followed the lead of South Carolina and moved rapidly toward secession. Under Governor Madison Stark Perry, a native South Carolinian anxious for Florida to leave the Union, a convention gathered at Tallahassee to decide what to do. During the debates McQueen McIntosh, a delegate from Franklin County, introduced a resolution declaring the right of secession and the convention's authority to exercise that right. On January 10, 1861, Florida severed its relationship with the United States. Having fewer slaves than Alabama or Georgia, it nevertheless preceded them in secession and was the third state to leave the Union. Its separate existence ended in February when Florida formally joined the Confederate States of America.[2]

Governor Perry would be succeeded in October 1861 by John

1. William T. Gregory to Columbus [Georgia] *Express,* Dec. 13, 1860, clipping in Love-Scarborough papers, Florida State University Library, Tallahassee.
2. Convention of the People of Florida Convened, Third Day of January 1861, 26–27, 32–35. See also Dorothy Dodd, "The Secessionist Movement in Florida, 1850–1861"; Donald R. Hadd, "The Irony of Secession"; Ralph A. Wooster, "The Florida Secession Convention."

Milton. The enigmatic Milton was fifty-three, a native-born Georgian; in 1860 he had defeated Edward A. Hopkins for governor.
The choice had been clear—Milton, Democrat and secessionist, or
Hopkins, conservative and Constitutional Unionist—and the vote
close. Milton edged Hopkins 6,694 to 5,248, but his victory in
Franklin County was total: 146 to 41. After moving to Florida,
Milton established Sylvania, his plantation near Marianna in Jackson County. Few other Southern governors matched Milton's dedication to the Confederate cause. His interest in Apalachicola was
singular and became the source of difficulties between him and an
array of military and civilian authorities at every level.[3]

Apalachicola, Saint George Island, Saint Vincent Island, and
Dog Island comprised a strategic location and influenced the military plans of Northern and Southern leaders. There were no Federal installations near Apalachicola when the Civil War began
other than the lighthouses at Cape Saint George and Dog Island.
Nothing had come of a legislative request in 1859 for the construction of a Federal fort at Apalachicola, but neither side doubted the
region's importance.[4]

Governor Perry began accepting militia companies for the state's
defense as early as November 1860, and that same month he called
for the reorganization of Florida's state troops. In January 1861,
even before the state seceded, the Quincy Guards seized the Federal arsenal at Chattahoochee, and other forces took over Fort
Marion at St. Augustine and Fort Clinch on Amelia Island. Yet Federal forts at Pensacola and at Key West remained in Union hands
throughout the war. Confederate maneuvers at Pensacola almost
preempted events at Fort Sumter in the harbor at Charleston,
South Carolina. Actual fighting seemed imminent; in January,
Governor Perry appointed William Chase commander of Florida's
troops. Chase took control at Pensacola and positioned his men.[5]

3. Manuscript election returns, Oct. 1, 1860. For Milton see William Lamar
Gammon, "Governor John Milton of Florida, Confederate States of America";
Daisy Parker, "John Milton, Governor of Florida; a Loyal Confederate."
   4. *Laws of Florida* 1859: 99.
   5. Edwin C. Bearss, "Civil War Operations in and around Pensacola." For the
Civil War in Florida see John E. Johns, *Florida during the Civil War,* and William
Watson Davis, *The Civil War and Reconstruction in Florida.*

On February 14, 1861, the legislature passed a law establishing Florida's Civil War militia. It created two regiments of infantry and one of cavalry, both subject to call by the governor for six months.[6] Then on March 6, 1861, the Confederate Congress formally created an army, and General Braxton B. Bragg took command in the Pensacola area. Within three days the Confederate War Department requested additional troops for Pensacola, and Florida was asked to supply five hundred men. To answer the need, the First Florida Infantry Regiment was mustered into Confederate service on April 5, 1861, at the Chattahoochee arsenal. One of the companies serving under newly elected Colonel James Patton Anderson was Captain William E. Cropp's Franklin Volunteers, designated "Company B." Because Union Forces controlled the Gulf approaches to Pensacola, the Franklin Volunteers reached their destination by going upriver to Columbus, where they switched to a train for the journey west to Montgomery, Alabama. There they connected with a southbound train to Pensacola.[7]

As requests for troops from the War Department rose (reaching five thousand by the end of 1861), Confederate authorities began enlisting troops directly rather than receiving them through the governor. Governor Perry, his supporters in the legislature, and the secession convention (which continued in session) were agreeable because they wanted the state forces to be absorbed. Governor-elect Milton strongly disagreed. He wanted to maintain the integrity of the militia and to keep the troops as a state army under the governor's control.

There was overall agreement on the importance of protecting the port of Apalachicola and the river basin stretching into the interior of Alabama and Georgia. Saint George Island and the other barrier islands would serve as the front line of defense. Once the Union blockade was in place, Southerners would make every effort to run it. Yet how much better, they reasoned, to break the blockade by destroying it. To that end the construction of gunboats was begun upriver in Georgia at Saffold (Early County) and at the im-

6. *Laws of Florida* 1861: 16–24.
7. Soldiers of Florida, Civil War 1861–1865, 1: 1; Apalachicola *Times*, Mar. 29, 1930.

portant industrial city of Columbus. Pending completion of the ships, the river system had to be protected. Obstacles were placed in the river and batteries and fortifications were maintained at key spots. As time passed, Confederate officials differed on how to effect their program, although Governor Milton relentlessly insisted that military control of Apalachicola was the key.[8]

Union officials wished to maintain and tighten the blockade. Beyond that, they expected to use Apalachicola as a base for vessels operating in the Gulf and as a point from which to launch excursions up the river. The number, size, and maintenance of their blockading ships, the depth of the passes, the bay, and the river channel, and the number of exits to the open Gulf became constant sources of frustration for the Federals.

Early in the war the United States moved to cut off the Confederacy's routes of trade. In April 1861, President Abraham Lincoln ordered the blockade of all Confederate ports, and implementation followed shortly. The U.S. Navy was divided into several squadrons, and Apalachicola fell under the jurisdiction of the Gulf Squadron. In January 1862, a reorganization caused the creation of the East Gulf Coast Blockade Squadron. From then until the war ended, the squadron was active intercepting inbound and outbound blockade-runners, protecting Union sympathizers and runaway slaves (known as "contrabands"), convoying, destroying salt works, and engaging in amphibious raids. The squadron's jurisdiction stretched from Cape Canaveral on the east coast to St. Andrews Bay on the west. Its ships patrolled the northern Bahamas, the northern coast of Cuba, the eastern part of the Gulf, and the Yucatan Channel.[9]

In June 1861, Flag-Officer William Mervine, commander of the Gulf Squadron, ordered Lieutenant T. Darrah Shaw, commander of the *Montgomery*, to blockade Apalachicola. By June 11, Shaw was

8. Maxine Turner, "Naval Operations on the Apalachicola and Chattahoochee Rivers, 1861–1865," is a detailed study.

9. Stanley L. Itkin, "Operations of the East Gulf Blockade Squadron in the Blockade of Florida, 1862–1865"; Alice Strickland, "Blockade Runners"; Joseph D. Cushman, Jr., "The Blockade and Fall of Apalachicola, 1861–1862," 38–39; Marcus W. Price, "Ships That Tested the Blockade of the Gulf Ports, 1861–1865."

in position off West Pass. The *Montgomery,* a steamer with sixty-six men and five guns, was the first of numerous naval vessels to blockade the port. Shaw had been ordered to publicize his mission, and the *Montgomery* moved carefully through West Pass. The Confederates had removed all the markers and buoys, as well as the lighthouse equipment at Cape Saint George and Dog Island, and placed them for safekeeping at Eufaula, Alabama.

On June 12, a pilot and a three-man delegation from Apalachicola approached the ship under a flag of truce. Once on board they were given an official proclamation to be delivered to town officials and "all commercial reading rooms." There was no mistaking the language: "I, T. Darrah Shaw, commanding the U.S.S. *Montgomery,* now off the port of Apalachicola, do hereby promulgate the enclosed declaration of blockade of the said port." No American vessels could enter or depart, although foreign and neutral ships were given several days to clear the harbor.[10]

Union authorities decided that a single gunboat would be sufficient. Yet within a day of his arrival, Shaw informed his superiors that one vessel could not watch the passes at both ends of Saint George Island.[11] The creeks and smaller rivers and numerous tributaries to the Apalachicola were perfect hiding places. The Confederate blockade-runners could lie safely in anchorage and receive cargo. Later, an escaped Union prisoner of war who struggled through the area described it well: "The country [a few miles above Apalachicola] on both sides of the river, nearly to the gulf, seemed to be but one endless expanse of swamp, with scarcely a human inhabitant, or, indeed, any spot or place where a human could make a permanent home. It was . . . forsaken desolate country."[12] From such isolated spots a blockade-runner could make a silent entry into the bay and dash for the open Gulf.

Besides the east and west passes that Lieutenant Shaw complained about, blockade-runners had other possibilities. One exit was by way of Saint Vincent Sound and Indian Pass, and another

10. *Official Records of the Union and Confederate Navies in the War of the Rebellion,* Ser. 1, 16: 530–31. See ibid., 544 (hereinafter cited as *ORN*).

11. Ibid., 546–47.

12. John A. Wilson, *Adventures of Alf. Wilson: A Thrilling Episode of the Dark Days of the Rebellion,* 194.

lay through Saint George Sound and the eastern end of Dog Island (away from East Pass). It seems probable that New Inlet through Saint George Island was also open, although it would have been too exposed for clandestine activity. Confirmation that additional ships were needed was soon supplied by a letter that came into Federal hands: "A married lady residing at Apalachicola, Florida writes to her uncle in [New York state] that the blockade of that port has thus far been only a farce."[13]

Shaw's reasonable request for aid, preferably in the form of a shallow-draft steamer, was partially answered in early August. Captain Francis B. Ellison arrived with the steamer *R. R. Cuyler*. Larger than the *Montgomery*, the *Cuyler* carried ten guns and was manned by 111 men. Although firepower and personnel were now tripled, problems remained. The Union ships were deep water vessels and could not get close enough inshore to be effective. Expeditions of boats in the bay and sounds and to the mainland were made without the protecting range of the Union blockaders. Because equipment was limited, prizes often had to be burned.[14]

Even as the Gulf Squadron maneuvered off Saint George Island and the other barrier islands, the people of Apalachicola strengthened their defenses. Early appeals to Confederate Secretary of War Leroy Pope Walker for an artillery officer got sympathetic but vague replies. The spring of 1861 found the citizens left to their own devices. A large majority of the men able to bear arms organized themselves into four voluntary companies. By public subscription two cannons, 34-pounders, were purchased from the state. A battery was erected on the waterfront "in the most eligible position to command the several approaches to the town."[15]

Apalachicola's main defense became the Florida Fourth Infantry. A state regiment, the Fourth had ten companies and was mustered into service on July 1, 1861. One of the companies was Captain

13. *ORN* Ser. 1, 16: 613; Turner, "Operations on the Apalachicola," 195.

14. Itkin, "East Gulf Squadron," 28–29; Turner, "Operations on the Apalachicola," 195.

15. *War of the Rebellion: A Compilation of the Official Record of the Union and Confederate Armies in the War of the Rebellion*, Ser. 1, 6: 286 (hereinafter cited as *OR*); Cushman, "Blockade and Fall of Apalachicola," 40. *Laws of Florida* 1861: 202, empowered the governor to defend Apalachicola.

Adam W. Hunter's Beauregard Rifles, a unit from Franklin County. Edward Hopkins, Milton's old political adversary, was elected colonel of the Fourth Florida. Milton detested Hopkins, considered him an inept commander, and believed his election had been rigged.[16] Milton's working relations with Confederate Brigadier General John B. Grayson, commander of Middle and Eastern Florida, were better but not cordial. A graduate of West Point, Grayson had resigned from the U.S. Army a month before his appointment in August and was in the late stages of tuberculosis. As Hopkins set about directing the fortifications of Apalachicola, bitter controversy developed.[17] Milton was helpless to take action until his inauguration in October. His harsh estimate seemed accurate when it became clear that Colonel Hopkins was no hard taskmaster; his soldiers enjoyed relative freedom from drill. The presence of spare time and the absence of discipline resulted in dissipation and the widespread consumption of alcohol.[18]

Simon Peter Richardson, a leading Methodist minister, was a tolerant but somewhat shocked observer. Affiliated with the Gadsden ministerial circuit when the war broke out, the Reverend Richardson was urged by his brethren to become a chaplain. Not particularly anxious to enter the service ("I had no idea of going to war," he recalled; "I had been in the Indian war, and had enough of it"), the preacher jokingly agreed to enlist if he were elected a major. Surprised at his selection for that rank, he went off with the "six months' troops." Assigned to Franklin County—"We guarded Apalachicola and the adjacent islands"—Richardson preached to the soldiers every Sunday morning and night. "The general and all the field officers but myself drank," he wrote. The minister pictured tension-free garrison duty at Apalachicola, and once he persuaded an army band and accompanying singers to serenade him with hymns. He refused to reward them with liquor, but they seemed satisfied with a supper of eggs and oysters.[19]

16. Milton to Jefferson Davis, Oct. 18, 1861, 12–16; Oct. 29, 1861, 36, in John Milton letterbook, 1861–63.

17. Edward Hopkins to Milton, Oct. 22, 1861, 630–31; Oct. 23, 1861, 631–32, ibid.

18. Davis, *Civil War and Reconstruction*, 161–62.

19. Simon Peter Richardson, *The Lights and Shadows of Itinerant Life*, 172–75.

Although not universally popular among the men, Richardson was correct about the pronounced imbibing of ardent spirits. Captain Raburn Scarborough, commander of a company from Quincy, remarked of a fellow captain that "he's a good man morally, but drinks lots of Brandy." Scarborough shunned alcohol himself, declaring to his sister, "While other officers drink and swear &c your unworthy one will remain unmoved so far as drinking & swearing is to be regarded."[20]

For some reason Colonel Hopkins decided that the best way to defend Apalachicola was to convert Saint Vincent Island into a fortress. As requests for artillery got results, a battery was erected on the island along with a makeshift fort and barracks. The compound was called Camp Davis. Saint George Island was not considered. The hurricanes of the 1850s had created a separation at the western end of Little Saint George Island, so that the sometimes familiar Sand Island had appeared. It was largely open terrain and ill suited for any kind of defense. The main channel at West Pass ran closer to Saint Vincent Island than it did to Sand Island, a fact that brought Union vessels into closer range. Besides, Saint Vincent Island was heavily wooded and more compact.

The blockaders maintained their vigil, and the first successful action by the Gulf Squadron came in late summer 1861. The Federals spotted the *Finland* lying at anchor in Apalachicola Bay. On the night of August 26, Lieutenant James Parker led an expedition into the bay. The *Finland*, empty and awaiting a cargo of cotton, was taken without opposition, but adverse wind and tide conditions prevented passage over the bar. The next morning a Confederate steamer, towing a schooner, intruded. Bearing down on the Federal sailors, the steamer's fighting force, a small detachment of local guards, opened fire. The Federals quickly set the *Finland* on fire and escaped, leaving the Confederates to salvage what they could (*illustration*, Group 1).[21]

The loss of the blockade-runner caused alarm in Apalachicola,

20. Raburn M. Scarborough to "My Dear Sister," n.d., 1861, Sept. 16, 1861, Love-Scarborough papers. For criticism of Richardson see ibid., Oct. 18, Nov. 27, 1861.

21. *ORN* Ser. 1, 16: 547, 677; Turner, "Operations on the Apalachicola," 201, quoting Eufaula [Alabama] *Spirit of the South*, Sept. 10, 1861.

but the Federals could not view their success as permanent, especially when a handful of inexperienced militia could send them flying. The expedition emphasized the need for a fast squadron of small ships to make the blockade effective. Shortly after the *Finland* incident, the Confederate commander at Saint Vincent Island requested more arms and ammunition. He believed that the Union forces planned to send shallow-draft steamers into the bay and attack and burn Apalachicola. The officer also wanted two 24-pounders to guard the road from Apalachicola to St. Joseph. After visiting Apalachicola and the island, Milton endorsed the request. A coordinated effort followed. The Confederate army and navy departments secured weapons from the Tredegar Iron Works at Richmond, Virginia, and Navy Lieutenant Augustus McLaughlin was assigned to the Apalachicola area.[22]

Local citizens who had welcomed the arrival of Colonel Hopkins and the Fourth Florida became alarmed when he transferred the battery in Apalachicola to Saint Vincent Island. Although several companies were kept on the mainland at Camp Retrieve, about a mile from the town limits, the people felt vulnerable. They pleaded with Hopkins to bring some of the cannons back, and Milton took up their cause. Once inaugurated, he worked to have Hopkins removed. Seeking other support, the townspeople protested to Confederate Secretary of War Judah P. Benjamin that "the approaches to our town by land, as also from the East Pass, are entirely unguarded, and it would not require a large number of such boats as are now being constructed by the enemy to capture the city before any intelligence of an attack could reach Saint Vincent or assistance be rendered by the forces there."[23]

The command at Apalachicola had once totaled twelve hundred men, but now Saint Vincent Island had four ship-mounted cannons and two long 32-pounders. Apalachicola was reduced to one company of voluntary artillery and two companies of undrilled infantry, all coming to "less than 100 invalids and exempts." Besides the troops transferred to Saint Vincent Island, five other companies had been dispatched to places along Florida's Gulf coast.

22. *ORN* Ser. 1, 16: 838–39; *OR* Ser. 1, 1: 471–72.
23. *OR* Ser. 1, 6: 286–87.

Despite feelings of apprehension, the people informed Benjamin of their determination "to perish beneath the ruins of their city rather than ignobly desert or suffer it to become the prey of the vandal hordes who threaten to assail it."[24]

Once his title as governor became official, Milton took action. His critics theorized that Milton wanted to protect Apalachicola so that the interior, including his plantation Sylvania, would be safe.[25] Whatever his motives, Apalachicolans approved the shallow entrenchments and breastworks that soon stretched three miles around the town's land approaches. Milton's repeated letters to Richmond for arms brought little result because Florida's defense was a matter of low priority to Confederate officials. Milton got Hopkins assigned to Saint Vincent Island and made Colonel Richard F. Floyd the commander at Apalachicola. Conditions had so deteriorated in the town that a group of citizens and officers asked the governor to declare martial law. Milton refused, but as he explained to Floyd, "For good and sufficient reasons, the public good requires a change prompt and decided at Apalachicola."[26] The Confederates on Saint Vincent Island approved when some of the cannons were dismantled and brought back to the mainland. The weapons were of limited range, and the force of 175 to 250 men did not have enough small arms to defend themselves in case of an attack.[27]

The War Department approved the construction of new batteries on the mainland, and Floyd saw to it that the men were drilled. By late October discipline was good, and the forces were raised to 612. An artillery expert was brought in, and there was cooperation between the military and the civilians in strengthening the port's defenses.[28]

Milton remained at odds with Confederate authorities and his detractors in state government. The governor still wanted the state militia to remain independent of Confederate control. When the

24. Ibid., 287.
25. Cushman, "Blockade and Fall of Apalachicola," 40.
26. Milton to R. F. Floyd, November 6, 1861, 50–51, Milton letterbook 1861–63. See also OR Ser. 1, 6: 354–55.
27. OR Ser. 1, 6: 287–88, 319, 325–26.
28. Ibid., 354–56.

consumptive General Grayson died October 21, 1861, Milton suggested Floyd as his replacement. Instead, General John H. Trapier received the appointment. A South Carolinian who had finished third in his class at West Point in 1838, Trapier did not prove to be a success. Even so, he and Milton could at least communicate, and the governor clung tenaciously to his theories about the proper defense of Florida.[29]

Besides defending Apalachicola, the Confederates planned to take the offensive. Lieutenant McLaughlin conferred with engineers at Columbus, and a decision was made to construct a wooden gunboat. A contract was signed with a civilian, David S. Johnson, of Saffold. Few efforts would prove more exasperating and tragic than activating the future *Chattahoochee,* but for the moment, optimism was high.[30]

In the first autumn of the war, there was still an air of unreality. Action was taken to keep speculators in Apalachicola from dealing in salt and pork: the commodities were confiscated by the military. The legislature provided for a special mayor's court to try people who sold liquor to slaves or free persons of color.[31] Still, there was no real hardship. The Apalachicola River was open to passengers and goods. J. J. Nixon, a native of Gadsden County and a member of the Fourth Florida, noted that the soldiers had meat, bread, and coffee. He bought dresses for members of his family and even sent them oranges and oysters by steamboat delivery.[32] Captain Scarborough was unable to purchase tea, soda, or flannel, but he managed to buy shoes, stockings, a knife, a keg of nails, and salt. Most of the men wrote home regularly, and as Scarborough mentioned, the stores were soon depleted of writing paper. When the men were

29. Milton to Braxton B. Bragg, Oct. 21, 1861, 21; Milton to Jefferson Davis, Nov. 19, 1861, 58, Milton letterbook, 1861–63.

30. Turner, "Operations on the Apalachicola," 202–3; Juanita Whiddon, "David Saunders Johnston, The Man and His Times," 140–41.

31. Florida, Senate, *Journal,* 1862, 72–77; F. L. Duncey to R. F. Floyd, Nov. 22, 1861, 166; W. K. Simmons to R. F. Floyd, Jan. 10, 1862, 167, Milton letterbook, 1861–1863; *Laws of Florida* 1861: 207–8.

32. J. J. Nixon to his wife, Sept. 9, Dec. 5, 11, 19, 1861, J. J. Nixon papers, P. K. Yonge Collection, University of Florida.

paid they quickly spent their money, and, according to the captain, by October "There are but two stores that have dry goods here now & the Soldiers have bought until there is nothing left."[33]

Even the military action had a sense of the absurd. An encounter occurred occasionally. In September a detachment of the Perry Artillery boarded the Confederate gunboat *F. S. Bartow* for a reconnaissance mission to East Pass. Leaving from an undisclosed site, the *Bartow* was spotted by the *Cuyler*. The Union ship quickly gave chase, firing twenty-one shots. The *Bartow* barely made the safety of Saint George Sound and the Crooked River that emptied into it. Most of the Confederate soldiers jumped overboard and swam to shore. Commander Ellison's ship returned to its position outside the bar, while the *Bartow*'s crew and the soldiers were rescued by land forces.[34]

Almost in a vein of mock seriousness, the *Montgomery* engaged in a four-hour chase off West Pass. The November episode began when Lieutenant Shaw fired a warning shot across the bow of a suspicious ship. Its only effect was to inspire the unknown vessel to greater speed. Shaw finally broke off pursuit. Without ever making identification, he concluded that "if she was an enemy, I have only to say she was a very fast one."[35]

Before the year ended the realities of the conflict settled in. Ineffective chases convinced the Union forces that they needed vessels of shallow draft—with them they could capture rebel ships before they got to sea. The Gulf Squadron soon assigned new ships to Apalachicola: Commander George F. Emmons's *Marion* (a sidewheel steamer with 101 men, five guns) relieved the *Cuyler*; the *Hatteras,* a sloop with eighty men and fourteen guns, replaced the *Montgomery.* Lieutenant George W. Doty was the commander. The Union fleet now had increased maneuverability and strength.[36]

By late fall the changes were evident. Of five schooners that

33. Raburn M. Scarborough to "My Dear Sister," Oct. 2, 18, 1861, Love-Scarborough papers.

34. Tallahassee *Florida Sentinel*, Sept. 17, 1861; ORN Ser. 1, 16: 669.

35. ORN Ser. 1, 16: 77.

36. ORN Ser. 1, 16: 669, 769; Turner, "Operations on the Apalachicola," 203–4.

cleared Apalachicola only one, the *W. P. Benson,* returned safely, and it was captured on a second voyage. The *W. A. Rain* with its cargo of cotton was taken outbound. The *Onward, Franklin,* and *Phoenix* ran the blockade with cargoes of cotton and turpentine, but all were seized attempting inbound voyages.[37] Taking a ship was a military duty, a patriotic act, and a profitable endeavor. Once captured, a ship and its cargo became prizes of war. The ship was taken to Key West, adjudicated in admiralty courts, and sold. The officers and crew of the ship that took the prize shared in the proceeds.

Furious at the losses, Governor Milton used both his military and civilian powers and ordered Floyd (by now a general) to prevent any more shipments of cotton and turpentine. Floyd complied. Seeking clarification, Milton was advised by both the navy and war departments that ships could not be prevented from departing unless their cargoes were intended for the use of the enemy or there was danger of their being captured by Union blockaders.[38]

Milton, always loyal to the Confederate cause, deferred to higher authority, but he never approved of unregulated blockade-running. He had a sound case because the men engaged in the dangerous game placed profits above the Confederate cause. The goods they brought into port ran heavily to luxury items, not the much needed war materiel. Consumer goods brought high prices. For example, in 1826 the *Savannah* ran the blockade and anchored at an inlet on the Gulf coast with a cargo of dry goods, five hundred bags of coffee, and 130,000 "segars."[39]

By November 1861, increased pressure from the expanded blockading forces caused the Confederates to withdraw from Saint Vincent Island. Much time, energy, and money had gone into its defenses. Yet one soldier described the men's reaction to the evacuation: "This is a source of great joy with many."[40] Milton secured authorization from Secretary of War Benjamin and ordered Hopkins to vacate the island. If the officer failed to obey the order,

37. *ORN* Ser. 1, 16: 855–56.
38. Ibid., 856–57.
39. A. B. Noyes to Milton, Apr. 14, 1862, 338, Milton letterbook, 1861–63.
40. Raburn M. Scarborough to "My dearest sister," Nov. 4, 1861, Love-Scarborough papers.

Milton threatened to have him arrested. The controversial Hopkins withdrew and was reassigned to Fernandina.[41]

Dog Island and Saint George Island fell under Northern control also. Elevated and healthy, Dog Island was used by Union sailors as a place for amusement and target practice. Landings were easy, and after William Baker, the light keeper, was forced to flee, his hogs and poultry were confiscated. Baker's furniture, including a sofa, was taken, and the lighthouse became a kind of recreation center. No personnel were stationed permanently on the island, although the tower made a useful observatory.[42]

Stretching long and narrow for thirty miles or so, Saint George Island could not be effectively defended or occupied. The Confederates placed no major installations there, but the shoals on both sides prevented large Federal ships from coming close. Northern landing parties came ashore from time to time, usually to secure wood. Floyd countered late in 1861. He sent to the island a "detachment of 60 men in ambush to surprise and take any party which may land."[43] The lighthouse on Cape Saint George was better preserved and higher than the beacon on Dog Island, but it was more difficult to reach and its best view was to the Gulf, not the bay. It was mainly curiosity that caused Commander George F. Emmons to climb the tower on December 18, 1861. He observed that the apparatus had been stripped from the beacon, "which is very much in character with secession elsewhere," but the officer enjoyed his vantage point: "I had a good view . . . of the town." Gunfire had been heard in Apalachicola, but everything seemed quiet to Emmons. Looking across the bay to the hazy outlines of Apalachicola, he saw a few fishing smacks and a vessel under construction, but there "was nothing afloat inviting attack."[44]

Military activity picked up in 1862, as the Gulf Squadron was deactivated and replaced by the East Gulf Coast Blockade Squadron. Commander H. S. Stellwagen and the *Mercedita* (a steamer with 135 men and nine guns) and another steamer, Lieutenant

41. Milton to R. F. Floyd, Nov. 6, 1861, 50–51; A. B. Noyes to Milton, Apr. 16, 1862, 61–63, Milton letterbook, 1861–63.

42. H. T. Blocker to Milton, Nov. 20, 1861, 82, ibid.

43. R. F. Floyd to Milton, Jan. 10, 1862, 197, ibid.

44. *ORN* Ser. 1, 17: 7.

A. J. Drake's *Sagamore*, took over the blockade. For the men on duty, monotony and dull routine were their daily fare and a chase or a raiding expedition was a welcome diversion. With the Confederates retired to the mainland, exercise and relaxation on Saint George Island could be enjoyed (Floyd's detachment, "Well and full of hope of catching some of the landing parties," had withdrawn from the island in February).[45] The crews celebrated the arrival of supply ships bringing food, water, and ammunition, not to mention books, pay, sometimes a band, and cherished letters from home.

Despite the blockade, a number of vessels entered and left the Apalachicola area without interdiction. Deserters, Union sympathizers, and blacks who escaped to the blockading ships described the process. Small, unarmed Confederate sloops with crews of ten or so men patrolled the harbor. They reported blockading conditions to larger vessels anchored upriver (several lay in hiding at the confluence of the Jackson River and the Apalachicola six miles to the north). Small steamers remained at Apalachicola to tow a loaded schooner to the chosen Gulf pass, and at the right moment the ship made its run.[46]

No matter how well conceived or daring the run, the advantage lay with the Union forces. The increased number of ships and the expertise that came with experience began to pay off. In February 1862 the *Sagamore* spotted a schooner trying to run the blockade to East Pass. The Southern ship was chased back into the harbor, but the *Sagamore* drew too much water to follow. The next day the Union commander sent an expedition of small boats into Saint George Sound. The schooner had disappeared, but the raiders found a small shipyard where two large and two small schooners were being repaired. The Federals destroyed the vessels and returned safely to the *Sagamore*.[47]

The first months of 1862 brought far-reaching developments in Confederate and Florida military policy, and Apalachicola was directly concerned. Florida's secession convention reconvened late in

45. R. F. Floyd to Milton, Jan. 29, 1862, 168, Milton letterbook, 1861–63.
46. *ORN* Ser. 1, 16: 120–21; Turner, "Operations on the Apalachicola," 208–9.
47. Ibid., 124; Itkin, "East Gulf Squadron," 46.

1861, and in February 1862 it ordered the dissolution of the state troops by March 10. The men would then, or before then, be expected to enlist in regular Confederate units.[48] Milton disapproved strongly and challenged the action but to no avail.

If Floyd's Fourth Florida regiment of state troops was disbanded before March 10, Apalachicola would be left defenseless unless the men immediately enlisted in the Confederate army and remained at their posts (an unlikely possibility if they were not first given furloughs of thirty days) or they were replaced by other troops (improbable since the Confederacy needed Florida's soldiers for its hard-pressed armies in Tennessee and Kentucky).

Conditions in Apalachicola were rapidly deteriorating. The shoreline defenses consisted of twelve light cannon mounted on earthen banks. The artillery pieces were positioned 150 yards from shore and laid in a line of 500 yards stretching southeast to northeast. The troops, perhaps 450 to 650 of them, were armed only with flintlock muskets and shotguns, and one company had no arms at all. Most of the stores were closed. Few goods were available, and prices were exorbitant for those that were—half a bushel of salt cost five dollars. Many of the citizens began to "refugee." The word would take on a long-remembered special meaning for homeless Apalachicolans and other Southerners.[49]

Milton maneuvered frantically. He wrote the governors of Alabama and Georgia asking them to send troops. Apalachicola, he pointed out, was the first line of defense for the interior of their states.[50] He got no response. He urged General Trapier to leave the artillery at Apalachicola and send a courier to carry a letter to General Robert E. Lee at Savannah. Lee was in command of the coastal defenses of South Carolina, Georgia, and Florida. Lee was apologetic but asked for even more Florida soldiers to serve out of state.[51] The governor then appeared at Apalachicola and issued

48. Convention of the People of Florida at a Called Session Begun and Held at the Capitol, in the City of Tallahassee on Tuesday, January 14, 1862, *Journal*, 103, 107.

49. *ORN* Ser. 1, 17: 120–21.

50. Milton to Governor Joseph E. Brown, Feb. 20, 1862, 123; Milton to Governor John G. Shorter, Feb. 20, 1862, 124, Milton letterbook, 1861–63.

51. Milton to James H. Trapier, Feb. 21, 1862, 177–78; Milton to Robert E.

personal appeals to the men to remain at their positions. He took an unequivocal stance: "Apalachicola should be defended to the last extremity." [52]

A few of the troops at Apalachicola agreed to stay past the March 10 deadline, and a scattering agreed to go over directly into the Confederate service. Mayor J. N. G. Hunter and the town aldermen feared evacuation and petitioned Milton to look after "1500 women and children wholly unprotected and without the means of removing to safer parts." [53] On March 1, General Lee called on Trapier for all of Florida's soldiers. Partly persuaded by Milton's arguments, Lee added, "the only Troops to be retained in Florida are such as may be necessary to defend Apalachicola River. . . . You are therefore desired to put that River and Harbor in a satisfactory state of defense." [54]

Lee's instructions came too late. Floyd assured his men that they could successfully repel an enemy attack, but the men insisted on their rights. "Many of the men are poor and must necessarily go Home & make a crop," Captain Scarborough explained to his sister.[55] They were patriots, but they wanted to see their families. The secession convention and its short-lived creation, the executive council, made ineffective and belated efforts to aid Apalachicola. Milton and Floyd, left with no alternative, ordered the removal of the artillery defenses and other ordnance. It was taken fifty-six miles upriver to Ricco's Bluff, and Floyd and his men evacuated the town.[56]

Conditions were bad all over Florida. Northern raiders struck

Lee, Feb. 21, 1862, 178–79; Robert E. Lee to Milton, Feb. 24, 1862, 181, Milton letterbook, 1861–63.

52. Milton to James H. Trapier, Feb. 22, 1862, 242–43, ibid.

53. Undated petition to Milton; see also R. F. Floyd to Milton, Feb. 24, 1862, 182; E. Broward to Troops at Apalachicola, Mar. 3, 1862, 194–200, ibid.

54. Robert E. Lee to Milton, Mar. 3, 1862, 61–63, ibid.

55. Scarborough to "My dear Sister," Jan. 13, 1862. On Nov. 8, 1861, to "My dear Sister," he had warned, "most of [the men] are getting very restless & want to leave here very badly" (both letters in Love-Scarborough papers).

56. Convention of the People of Florida, *Journal*, 14; Florida, Senate, *Journal*, 1862, 56, 61–63; R. F. Floyd to Milton, Mar. 3, 1862, 191; Milton to Robert E. Lee, Mar. 5, 1862, 200–202; Milton to James H. Trapier, Mar. 10, 1862, 213–15. Floyd dismissed the troops officially on Apr. 24, 1862. See R. F. Floyd to Milton, Apr. 30, 1862, 344–45, Milton letterbook, 1861–63.

Cedar Key in January. Early in March, Fernandina and St. Augustine fell to the invaders, and Jacksonville suffered the first of four occupations. At Apalachicola the military departure caused a mass exodus by the citizens. Over half the town's population scattered into the surrounding area and into Georgia and Alabama. One group of families attempted to flee up the Apalachicola but encountered a violent rainstorm. They put ashore by a low bluff and spent a miserable night in the pelting rain, lying in mud and fearful that the rising river would drown them. They were rescued the next day. Apalachicola was left with from five hundred to six hundred people. A few men formed a military force. Known Unionists were confined to town but refused to drill despite threats to hang them.[57]

By late March Commander Stellwagen was hearing conflicting reports. Seeking firsthand knowledge, he ordered Lieutenant Trevett Abbot to go to Apalachicola. With a cutter, a whaleboat, and a fully armed crew, Lieutenant Abbot approached by way of West Pass. On his left, Saint Vincent Island was showing signs of spring —trees on the shoreline presented an appealing mix of green. To Abbot's right Sand Island lay in sharp contrast. The land spit was piled high with an incongruous black mountain of coal. It had become a much-used coaling station for the East Gulf Squadron.

Flying a flag of truce, the Federals landed at a town wharf. According to the official report they were met by four men: Mayor Hancock (probably J. N. G. Hunter), Porter (William G.), Benezet (Samuel), and Father Miller, the Catholic priest. Finding no military forces, Lieutenant Abbot demanded the town's surrender. Otherwise, he threatened, a naval bombardment would follow. Citizens who took a loyalty oath would be safe and their property rights protected. The townsmen admitted Apalachicola's obvious vulnerability and spoke vaguely of evacuated troops somewhere upriver who might or might not return. The citizens were positive that no one would take the oath of allegiance. Perhaps some of the "foreign" residents would—the reference was to recent immigrants who had no stake in the war's outcome.[58]

The expedition returned to the *Mercedita*, and Abbot reported

57. *ORN* Ser. 1, 17: 193–94.
58. Ibid., 194–95.

to Stellwagen. A gig was sent to East Pass summoning Lieutenant Drake's *Sagamore* to a rendezvous. It was decided to launch two attack parties. The first, commanded by Lieutenant Abbot of the *Marion* and Lieutenant George A. Bigelow of the *Sagamore*, consisted of six boats, one armed with a howitzer. Stellwagen followed later with two armed gigs and moved directly on Apalachicola. Crossing West Pass, the first expedition entered the harbor and captured the sloop *Octavia*. Stationing three boats at Apalachicola, the commanders took the others upriver seven miles. There they took the schooner *New Island*, lying at anchor in a small creek. The ship was floated to the river's midstream, and the raiders moved on. The schooner *Rose*, laden with cotton, was captured as were the pilot boats *Cygnet* and *Mary Oliver* and the schooner *Floyd*. The prizes were towed to Apalachicola. The Federals had taken six vessels without opposition.[59]

The coordinated raid of April 3 culminated that afternoon when all eight Union boats converged on Apalachicola. The remaining townspeople were waiting. No authorities met the blue-clad invaders, and since no one offered to surrender the town, Stellwagen proclaimed Apalachicola captured. Then, in the tradition of victors, he addressed the people: "My countrymen, for even you who are engaged in this unholy, unnatural war against our Government are my fellow countrymen, we come not to injure the defenseless, or women and children; I like the people of the South, though I hate secession and rebellion, which have brought such calamities and misery upon all parts of our late happy land."[60]

He was interrupted by remarks such as "We have had no part in it" and "The innocent suffer with the guilty," and, from some of the women, "We are almost starving." According to Stellwagen the women and children "had been told we were ruthless Hessians bent on burning, pillage, and destruction" and were surprised to learn otherwise. He mentioned facetiously that no Confederate sympathizers could be found. In fact, "they now protested that

59. Ibid., 202; Itkin, "East Gulf Squadron," 47. The *Octavia* and *Rose* were sent to Key West for adjudication; the remaining four ships were destroyed because they could not cross the bar.

60. Ibid., Ser. 1, 17: 202–3.

they hated secession and rebellion and had always been loyal to the Union, and state that they had no part in the rebellion."[61]

Stellwagen realized that he lacked sufficient forces to occupy Apalachicola permanently. He knew further that the people depended largely upon the bay for their sustenance. In his speech the commander generously permitted the citizens to keep their fishing boats so that oystering and fishing could go on. He warned that "any direct act or indirect act, such as firing our boats, helping a blockade runner, bringing soldiers to town, or any thing of the sort will be severely punished."[62] Concluding his address, Stellwagen ordered his men back into the boats. A salvo of shrapnel was fired into the air, and, their triumph punctuated, the Federals returned to their ships.

From departure to return the venture had taken less than thirty-six hours. Apalachicola had been captured and abandoned almost simultaneously and was now in limbo—open and largely unoccupied. Apalachicolans had waited for the inevitable. They revived tactics they had practiced before but which they would now bring to the level of art: coping and surviving.

61. Ibid., 203.
62. Ibid., 204–5.

4

"Without Our Lines . . . But Not Within Theirs"

AFTER the Northern forces left, Apalachicola became once more an outpost of the Confederacy. Although not occupied by Southern troops, scattered units of cavalry and guerilla bands would drift in and out for the remainder of the war. Even less was it a Union bastion, although Federal raiding parties appeared periodically looking for cotton, crew members from blockade runners, and Southern soldiers. A nucleus of five hundred to six hundred people steadfastly supported the Confederate cause, although there were exceptions. Dr. Alvan W. Chapman found his botanical excursions curtailed and, like everyone else, longed for the fighting to cease. But he differed from most in that he desired a Union victory. The native New Englander made no secret of his feelings, which ran counter to those of his Southern wife. Holding such intense convictions, the couple made a rational decision in an irrational time. Chapman's wife refugeed to her home in Marianna, while the botanist stayed in Apalachicola. They corresponded, their affection undiminished, and, once the conflict ended, reconciled and resumed married life in Apalachicola.[1]

Life was extremely difficult for the inhabitants. "Great destitu-

---

1. Apalachicola *Times,* Jan. 29, 1976, reprinted an article on Chapman by Winifred Kimball in *The New York Botanical Garden* (Jan., 1921).

tion prevails in that town," a sympathetic physician observed.[2] In such circumstances people were careful and tight-lipped. Vocal pronouncements of loyalty to either flag were rare. In May 1862, Governor Milton appointed a committee of public safety for Franklin, Calhoun, and Washington counties. The twenty-man group was charged with preventing communication with the Federals "on the part of Slaves or Traitors or suspicious persons."[3] The town stood silent, permeated by an air of desperation that hung heavy as citizens went through meaningless motions of activity. A small steamer made a weekly run down the Apalachicola River with a welcome cargo of cornmeal. What saved the people from starvation were the abundant fish and oysters in the bay.

Whatever one's loyalties, it paid to be careful. At the George P. Raney home built in 1838, family members alerted Confederates hiding nearby when the Northerners came into town. Their means was simple but effective: a rain barrel placed on a roof meant the presence of Union raiders. The Porters, one of the area's earliest families, were no more anxious than anyone else to have Yankees or Rebels using their residence for target practice. In a move more imaginative than practical, they hung a Belgian flag outside their home. It is doubtful that either adversary recognized the nation symbolized by the banner.[4]

Undermanned and lacking sufficient arms, Confederate land forces engaged in hit-and-run tactics. "The guerrilla bands here in Florida," a citizen explained, "seemed to have adopted the mode of warfare practiced by the Indians in these swamps not many years ago."[5] With Apalachicola seemingly neutralized, military attention shifted upriver. At Saffold, construction on the *Chattahoo-*

2. William J. Schellings, ed., "On Blockade Duty in Florida Waters," 60. The statement was the diary entry of young Dr. Walter Keeler Scofield, assigned to the blockading ship *Sagamore*.

3. Decree issued May 30, 1862, 357, Milton letterbook 1861–63.

4. Apalachicola *Times*, Nov. 17, 1961. Both the rain barrel and the flag stories have been told many times and have passed into the folklore and legend of Apalachicola.

5. Frank Moore, ed., *The Rebellion Record: A Diary of American Events*, 6: 186.

chee went slowly, but the project seemed worth the effort. Fitted with steam and sail (three-masted, square-rigged), the black gunboat was 130 feet long and would carry 110 to 120 men. Lieutenant Catesby ap R. Jones, fresh from fame gained on the *Virginia* (formerly the *Merrimac*) in its encounter with the *Monitor,* was the commanding officer. He recruited another able man, Lieutenant George W. Gift, a graduate of Annapolis.[6]

Convinced that Union forces would send small, ironclad steamers upriver before the *Chattahoochee* was completed, Confederate officials decided to place obstructions in the Apalachicola. William R. Boggs, an able engineer, investigated and found the Confederate garrisons and batteries at Ricco's Bluff and elsewhere inadequate. He urged the placement of obstructions, but no immediate action followed.[7] Finally, in late 1862 obstructions were placed at the Narrows, a five-mile stretch of river thirty-six miles above Apalachicola, and at Rock Bluff, thirteen miles south of Chattahoochee. Batteries were erected at both places. Heavy chains were stretched across the river. While they were being installed, the unfinished *Chattahoochee* was towed downriver and situated so as to guard the workers from attack. Soon the chains began catching limbs, trees, and debris and became effective deterrents to boats bound upriver or down.[8]

Informants passed details about Confederate activities along to the blockaders. Lieutenant A. F. Crossman, commander of the *Somerset,* was particularly worried. In December 1862, he urged his superiors to occupy Apalachicola, "an important strategic point," and then go upstream to destroy the *Chattahoochee* and attack Columbus. Crossman did not believe the Apalachicolans would defend their town and was confident that the expedition

6. *ORN* Ser. 1, 17: 203–5; Turner, "Operations on the Apalachicola," 213–17.

7. James L. Nichols, *Confederate Engineers,* 10; W. R. Boggs, *Military Reminiscences of General William R. Boggs, C.S.A.,* 29–30; Turner, "Operations on the Apalachicola," 213–19. Work on Ricco's Bluff batteries and two others between there and Chattahoochee was completed by April, 1862. See W. S. Dilworth to Milton, Apr. 17, 1862, 61–63, Milton letterbook, 1861–63.

8. Turner, "Operations on the Apalachicola," 220–25.

would require no more than forty men. His proposal was turned down.[9]

There was little need for alarm. That the blockade was more than sufficient was proved repeatedly. In April the patrolling *Sagamore* sent a detachment ashore on Saint George Island and captured five men and a boy. The prisoners were described as Portuguese-Italians and Irishmen, and while they posed no threat, their apprehension was a tribute to vigilance.[10]

More dramatic evidence of Union superiority came in October 1862. The sloop *G. L. Brockenborough* was spotted in a creek near Apalachicola, and two boats from the *Fort Henry* and *Sagamore* were sent to capture it. Apalachicola's population turned out on the waterfront, much as they had done in happier times to watch boat races on the Fourth of July. According to the Federals, shooting was begun "by a set of miscreants from among a crowd of women and children." Three sailors were wounded, and the raiders returned the fire when they passed the town. The *Brockenborough*, loaded with sixty-four bales of cotton, was taken. Her crew had scuttled the ship, but the Union sailors pumped it out and towed it past the town wharves.[11]

By that time a troop of Confederate cavalry had gathered. They joined several of the town guards behind storehouses and resumed firing. The Northerners replied with rifles and were particularly effective with a 12-pound howitzer. Four additional boats came to their aid, and in the exchange both sides suffered casualties. Finally, the roof was blown from a building, and a fire broke out. When the blaze spread to other buildings the Confederates ceased firing and worked to extinguish the flames. In the meantime the Union boats and their prize entered the bay and made their way to safety. Later that day the fleet was approached by a boat from town under a flag of truce. The occupants asked for naval surgeons to come to Apalachicola and care for Confederate wounded in the just-completed encounter. Three doctors volunteered. Their act of

9. *ORN* Ser. 1, 17: 347–48.
10. Schellings, "On Blockade Duty," 60.
11. *ORN* Ser. 1, 17: 321–22.

mercy lent validity to the notion that the conflict was a war of brothers.[12]

Lack of coordination had plagued the defense of Apalachicola and the river basin from the start. An improvement came in late 1862 when the Middle District of Florida was created and placed under General Howell Cobb.[13] Even so, his command had barely a thousand men. Cobb saw to it that the river obstructions were put in place, but he did so over the objections of Milton. The governor feared that the barriers would destroy Apalachicola as a commercial city and benefit Columbus. Such thinking seemed inappropriate for the time, but Milton explained to President Davis that occupying and defending Apalachicola was better strategy than sinking obstructions. There were five hundred helpless women and children in Apalachicola. Should they be allowed to starve? Should the Confederacy abandon them "to disorder and death"?[14]

Each side was more secure than it imagined. The unfinished *Chattahoochee* could not have descended the river even had it been combat-ready. By the end of 1862 the blockade had four ships in place, but not one was capable of going upriver. Had shallow-draft vessels been available, they still would have confronted the obstructions.

As the year closed, the people of Apalachicola maintained secret contact with Confederate units. Seafood kept them going as they could no longer take advantage of the cattle and hogs that roamed wild on Saint George and Saint Vincent. Fine beef cattle were particularly in evidence on Saint Vincent, and one Union officer reported "Thousands of pigs and one bear on Saint George's Island."[15] Some whites, as well as contrabands, asked to be taken away, and the Union commanders honored their requests. Doctors from the blockading ships visited patients in town, and sick civil-

12. Ibid.

13. Horace Montgomery, *Howell Cobb's Confederate Career*, 78–79; Turner, "Operations on the Apalachicola," 222; Governors John G. Shorter, Joseph E. Brown, and Milton to Jefferson Davis, Nov. 4, 1862, 510–20, Milton letterbook 1861–63.

14. Milton to Jefferson Davis, Nov. 11, 1862, 520–23; Jefferson Davis to Milton, Nov. 7, 1862, 525–27, Milton letterbook 1861–63.

15. Schellings, "On Blockade Duty," 50.

ians were permitted to come aboard the ships for treatment. Everything was quiet except for the occasional gunnery practice that the Federals conducted on their ships and on Sand Island.[16]

The year ended in tragedy. A sudden squall capsized a small Union boat patrolling between East Pass and West Pass. Four of the sailors (all of the men were from the *Somerset*) were drowned. A few days later their bodies were found on a lonely stretch of beach on Saint George Island.[17]

On January 1, 1863, Lieutenant Crossman, still worried about a Rebel attack, renewed his earlier proposal. This time he wanted ten thousand men instead of forty and a flotilla of six or seven iron-plated gunboats to clear the river of enemy vessels and reduce Columbus. The force would be fed, partly at least, with beef from the barrier islands. His proposal was rejected again.[18]

Crossman's superiors were concerned enough to increase the East Gulf Squadron's strength. The squadron, a sort of poor cousin to other commands (it had fewer ships and inadequate attention was paid to repairs), was upped to seven ships. The *Somerset* and *Port Royal* were assigned to Apalachicola and the *J. S. Chambers* to Saint George Sound. Each vessel had a definite area of responsibility. Small, light tenders were assigned to the squadron's larger ships. Each tender had a small crew, was armed with one or two guns, and could go in close to shore. Their arrival strengthened the blockade.[19]

Thomas Orman, a respected pioneer settler, landowner, and merchant, had a high opinion of the blockade's efficiency and a low opinion of the blockade runners. He had remained in Apalachicola and in 1861 purchased Little Saint George Island. Like Milton, Orman objected to unrestricted blockade running. He denounced the captains as greedy profiteers whose presence invited Union attacks and reprisals. The townsman fully expected the Yankees to retaliate by destroying Apalachicola. Besides, Orman claimed that three out of four blockade runners were captured, and the effort

16. Ibid.; Turner, "Operations on the Apalachicola," 226–27.

17. *ORN* Ser. 1, 17: 358.

18. Ibid., 357–58.

19. Turner, "Operations on the Apalachicola," 227; Itkin, "East Gulf Squadron," 67–69.

had "on the whole and aggregate been a gain to the enemy and a loss to our citizens."[20]

By 1863 Confederate forces were suffering crippling defeats. As large areas fell under Union control, shortages became increasingly acute. One critical item was salt. When other Southern sources dwindled, Florida emerged as the primary supplier. All along the coast from Cedar Key to St. Andrew Bay people engaged in the manufacture of salt. The numerous saltworks varied in size, but most of them were small, makeshift operations. The East Gulf Squadron was kept busy raiding and destroying the saltworks. No sooner would they break one up than it would be rebuilt, but in the end the squadron succeeded.[21]

In April, Apalachicola was raided by the Federals. Lieutenant Commander George U. Morris of the *Port Royal* led a small armed force into town. A large supply of cannister, chain, and bar shot for 32-pounders was seized as well as twelve bales of cotton. Prisoners were taken, and they confirmed reports of refugees that work on the *Chattahoochee* was progressing at Saffold and, equally alarming, that another gunboat, the *Muscogee,* was being built at Columbus.[22]

The South's Lieutenant George W. Gift was as offensively minded as the Federals' Crossman. When Catesby Jones was transferred, Gift succeeded him as commander of the *Chattahoochee.* Gift soon developed a plan to take a small party of men into Apalachicola, lure the Federals ashore, capture them, and, dressed in U.S. uniforms, board one of the blockaders. Once the vessel was captured Gift planned to engage the remaining ships in combat. The improbable plan was never implemented because the Federals short-circuited it with a raid of their own.

Lieutenant Morris learned that the schooner *Fashion* was taking on a load of cotton for a run at the blockade through Indian Pass.

20. Thomas Orman to Milton, Oct. 17, 19, 1862, 506–7; for the governor's similar conclusions see Milton to Florida's Senators and Representatives in Richmond, Aug. 18, 1862, 421–23, Milton letterbook, 1861–63.

21. Itkin, "East Gulf Squadron," 163–69; see also Ella Lonn, "The Extent and Importance of Federal Naval Raids on Salt Making in Florida," and *Salt as a Factor in the Confederacy.*

22. *ORN* Ser. 1, 17: 421; Turner, "Operations on the Apalachicola," 231.

He moved quickly by sending three boats and forty-one men up-river. Acting Master Edgar Van Slyck and the expedition left the *Port Royal* on May 23. After some diligent searching and laborious rowing, the men sighted the *Fashion* and captured it. Unopposed they towed the prize back. The *Fashion* proved unseaworthy, but the raid was successful. Several prisoners and fifty bales of Sea Island cotton were taken.[23]

Embarrassed and angry, the Southerners attempted to retaliate. Temporarily in command of the *Chattahoochee*, Lieutenant J. J. Guthrie ordered his ship downstream from its anchorage at Chattahoochee. Somehow, he planned to pass the obstacles and recover the *Fashion*. Unfortunately for Guthrie, the gunboat was unable to cross the bar at Blountstown, twenty-eight miles below Chattahoochee. On the morning of May 26, orders were given to return upstream. The inexperienced crew, in attempting to raise steam, misjudged the amount of water needed, and the boilers in the engine room exploded. The blast killed fourteen men; others, badly scalded, ran wildly about the deck: three men drowned when some of the crew, fearing that the magazine would explode, dived overboard. As the *Chattahoochee* began to sink, Lieutenant Guthrie gave orders to abandon ship.[24]

The dead and wounded were transported to Chattahoochee and Columbus by the steamer *William H. Young.* A Dahlgren and a 32-pounder were salvaged and placed as a battery at Blountstown. The partially sunk *Chattahoochee* was hauled to the right bank of the river, and its most valuable parts were salvaged. Two of the crew made their way to Apalachicola and from there to the *Port Royal,* where they reported the details of the accident to Lieutenant Morris.[25] In a summary statement, another Union naval officer reported to his superior: "The vessel is sunk and shattered past the possibility of recovering and making future use of her."[26]

The loss of the *Chattahoochee* left the Union forces free to ex-

23. J. Thomas Scharf, *History of the Confederate States Navy from Its Organization to the Surrender of Its Last Vessel,* 617–18; ORN Ser. 1, 17: 447–48.

24. ORN Ser. 1, 17: 870; Scharf, *Confederate States Navy,* 618; *Tallahassee Weekly Sentinel,* June 2, 1863; Whiddon, "David Saunders Johnston," 142.

25. ORN Ser 1, 17: 870–71.

26. Ibid., 468.

ploit their position without threat. Before they could do so, an unseasonable but powerful hurricane hit the area. Strong winds began on May 25, grew in intensity, and two days later were of full hurricane force. The storm was nonpartisan. No one could remember an out-of-season gale that was so destructive. Accompanied by driving rain, the winds wrought heavy damage to recently planted crops. Many farm animals were killed, and, worse, between twenty and thirty people lost their lives. Saltworks were blown apart, and an estimated fifty thousand bushels of salt were destroyed. Property damage was extensive.[27]

Many of the Northern sailors had never experienced a hurricane before and were shocked at its fury. The coal bark *Andrew Manderson* was wrecked at Sand Island. Much of the coal supply was washed away at West Pass and East Pass. The schooner *Wanderer* rode out the storm, although her foremast was sprung. Acting Volunteer Lieutenant George E. Welch's *Amanda* was not so lucky. High winds drove the vessel aground on Dog Island, and Welch destroyed it. His reasoning was that otherwise the *Amanda* would fall into enemy hands. The officer did not know it, but there were no Confederate troops in the vicinity. Welch was later courtmartialed and convicted of abandoning his ship without cause. Acting Volunteer Lieutenant David Cate, commanding the *Hendrick Hudson,* which was nearby, made no attempt to assist Welch. Found guilty of neglect of duty, Cate resigned from the service.[28]

The hurricane sank lighters and small craft and damaged several merchant ships. The former blockade-runner, the *G. L. Brockenborough,* now converted into a blockader, was beached to save the crew. It lay ashore in Saint George Sound and finally, despite three weeks of efforts to save her, was abandoned as a total loss. The commander was found innocent of any charge of neglect.[29]

After the storm passed and summer set in, the Union forces became active. By the fall a large saltworks at Alligator Bay, east of Dog Island, had been destroyed. Similar expeditions demolished small saltworks at St. Andrew Bay and at Saint George Sound. In

27. Tallahassee *Florida Sentinel*, June 2, 1863.
28. *ORN* Ser. 1, 17: 451–57; Itkin, "East Gulf Squadron," 159.
29. *ORN* Ser. 1, 17: 503–4, 582.

every instance, the raiders met no resistance. Two forays into Apalachicola, one in July and another in October, netted the Federals a few bales of cotton.[30] As blockade running decreased, the East Gulf Squadron before Apalachicola was reduced to three vessels: the steamers *Somerset* and *Port Royal* and the bark *J. S. Chambers*. With little for their crews to do, the commanders permitted the men to fish, oyster, and enjoy the beaches of Saint George and Dog islands.[31]

The people of Apalachicola ended 1863 deprived of most luxuries and many necessities. Governor Milton remained their champion. He continued to urge Confederate officials to reoccupy the town and to reopen the river. At various levels he was turned down with strong arguments: the Confederacy had only limited manpower, and the men had to be deployed where they were needed most; reoccupying Apalachicola would invite a powerful Union attack; river obstructions were both effective and inexpensive.[32] There was complete agreement between Milton and Confederate authorities on the desirability of building ironclads. Superior numbers of vessels possessed by the Union navy could be countered by unsinkable ironclads. Construction of the *Muscogee* had begun at the Columbus Naval Iron Works in 1862. Milton and all Confederates hoped that upon its long-delayed completion, the *Muscogee* would relieve Apalachicola and break the blockade.[33]

By 1864 the citizens of Apalachicola felt abandoned and even began to question their continued loyalty to the Confederacy. Thomas Orman and John Ruan, a respected merchant of the town, were arrested by Union officers because of their alleged involvement in the killing of two Unionists. They were released once it was established that the loyalists were shot by Confederate soldiers. Later, the two men traveled to Marianna, where they were arrested

30. Lonn, "Raids on Salt Making in Florida," 171, 173; for the Dog Island–Alligator Harbor raid see *ORN* Ser. 1, 17: 467–68, 470–71.

31. Turner, "Operations on the Apalachicola," 237, 242.

32. *OR* Ser. 1, 28, part 2: 450–51; Ser. 1, 53: 299; *ORN* Ser. 1, 17: 872; Milton to P. G. T. Beauregard, Oct. 15, 1863, 697–99; for an opposing view see J. F. Gilmer to P. G. T. Beauregard, Oct. 27, 1863, 6–7, Milton letterbook, 1863–65.

33. Turner, "Operations on the Apalachicola," 239–42.

again, this time by Confederate soldiers. Incredulous and angry, they appealed to Governor Milton. Their arrest on grounds that they were interlopers from Union-held territory upset the governor. Milton wrote the military commanders that Apalachicola "*is not now and never has been* within the enemy lines. It may be without our lines but it is not within theirs." For that matter, "Its unarmed citizens have refused to surrender it when summoned to do so and to this day remain true and loyal." Finally, he wrote, at least two-thirds of the town's population were the families of soldiers serving the Confederacy.[34] Ruan and Orman were released, but neither they nor other Apalachicolans were permitted to travel freely between their town and other parts of Florida.[35]

In such an atmosphere of suspicion, Southerners hoped to regain their confidence and commitment by assuming the offensive. The damaged *Chattahoochee* was being repaired and refitted at Columbus. A torpedo boat was being built there as well, but the major cause for optimism lay with the *Muscogee*. Soon the ironclad would make its menacing appearance. After so many delays the anticipated action was dealt a shattering blow in January. Despite the high waters of winter, the *Muscogee* proved too heavy to be launched. It could not be towed into the Chattahoochee River. The failure provided an irate Columbus editor to demand that the ship be rebuilt. The journalist wrote sarcastically (and colloquially), "What ever could have been expected of such a looking [sic] craft we cannot imagine—unless a second flood is expected—and we are quite sure that nothing but a general inundation can ever lift the thing from its present position."[36]

Apalachicolans had to defer their hopes for deliverance by the *Muscogee*. Yet they and other Floridians celebrated a victory in the winter of 1864. Union forces occupied Jacksonville for the fourth time in February. Then General Truman A. Seymour and a force of some fifty-five hundred men began moving west across Florida.

34. Wilton to Patton Anderson, June 6, 1864, 74–76; Milton to P. G. T. Beauregard, Apr. 13, 1864, 50–51, Milton letterbook, 1863–65.

35. Patton Anderson to Milton, June 8, 1864, 78–80; Milton to Patton Anderson, June 9, 1864, 81–82, ibid.

36. Turner, "Operations on the Apalachicola," 244, quoting Columbus *Daily Enquirer*, Mar. 16, 1864.

The goals were to divide east and west Florida, obtain supplies and deprive the South of cattle and agricultural products, and set up a separate state government for Unionists. With a command of comparable size, General Joseph Finegan took a position at Olustee (or Ocean Pond) near Lake City. The battle occurred on February 20, a clear, sunny day, and resulted in victory for the Southerners. In the largest battle that occurred in Florida during the Civil Way, the Union attempt to penetrate the state's interior was thrown back.[37]

Lieutenant G. W. Gift hoped to respond with a similar but smaller-scale triumph in the waters around Apalachicola. Following the abortive debut of the *Muscogee*, Gift returned to take command of the *Chattahoochee*. His assignment was an empty honor since the ship was not operational. It was just as well the general population did not know what Confederate engineers discovered: the *Chattahoochee* need not have sunk at all. By simply driving a pine plug into the feed pipe, the gunboat could have been kept afloat.[38] With action needed, Lieutenant Gift hit on a bold plan, one similar to his previous but untried maneuver. In May the ships blockading Apalachicola were the *Somerset* at West Pass and the smaller *Adela* at East Pass. Gift planned to launch a surprise attack on the *Adela*. After seizing her, the Confederates would overpower the *Somerset*. The vessels could then be run into Mobile or destroyed, and the blockade would be broken. If the scheme seemed far-fetched, the Southern situation was desperate.

On May 3, Gift, ten officers, and forty-seven crew members went by the steamer *Marianna* to Saffold. There they commandeered seven small vessels: two launches, two yawls, two cutters, and a metallic boat. Increased to one hundred men, the mosquito fleet took provisions for fifteen days and crossed into Florida. At Chattahoochee an additional sixteen army volunteers were added. Continuing down the Apalachicola (their knowledge of tributary sloughs and streams enabled them to bypass the obstructions), the raiders took on thirteen more volunteers at Ricco's Bluff. Reaching Apalachicola they crossed the East Bay arm of Apalachicola Bay to

---

37. There are several accounts of the battle of Olustee, but see Mark F. Boyd, "The Federal Campaign of 1864 in East Florida," *FHQ* 29 (July, 1950): 3–37.
38. ORN Ser. 1, 17: 871–72.

Eastpoint. Further down the mainland of Saint George Sound the men took up a position. The Confederates waited for a dark and rough night before moving across East Pass to attack the *Adela*.

To their regret, the Southerners encountered clear nights. The surface of the sound was smooth and calm. When oars were dipped in the phosphorescent waters, a luminous light was instantly shed, and the resulting brightness could be detected for some distance. Edgy and fearful of discovery, Gift and his men grew restless with waiting. Finally, supplies ran low, and a detail was sent to Apalachicola to get provisions. The men returned with word that Union sympathizers had informed the Federals of the proposed attack. Gift decided to abandon the project, and late on May 12 the Southerners made their way west across the sound. At that moment a storm approached. Gift's boat of seventeen men and another manned by ten men attempted to reach Apalachicola across the open bay. The remaining five boats hugged the shore. Their caution paid off, and they reached Apalachicola safely.

Troubles were quickly compounded for the other two boats. When the smaller vessel swamped, its occupants were rescued by Gift's boat. The lieutenant became ill and transferred command to Thomas Scharf. Realizing the impossibility of reaching Apalachicola, Midshipman Scharf managed to get the craft turned toward Saint George Island. With high waters lashing about them, the crew pulled the men clinging to the boat's sides aboard. As they approached the island, baggage, casks, ammunition, guns—everything—were jettisoned. When the straining boat neared bayside shore, the exhausted men abandoned it and, half swimming, half stumbling, made their way ashore.[39]

Even as the Confederates struggled to escape, Commander William S. Budd of the *Somerset* ordered an attack. Anticipating the attempted retreat, Budd sent Lieutenant Thomas Hunter of the 110th New York Volunteers to the mainland. Hunter's expedition left the *J. S. Chambers* and landed below Apalachicola at daybreak on May 13. Budd himself took two launches to the port. There the Union forces discovered the bulk of Gift's command, some seventy or eighty men, attempting to embark from a wharf.

39. Scharf, *Confederate States Navy*, 620.

The Confederates immediately began running for the swamps. After firing two shells from a howitzer, the Northerners followed in pursuit. The chase continued for two miles before the Federals gave up as the Confederates disappeared into dense undergrowth.[40]

At Saint George Island the other Southerners were alive but not safe. The island, having gone from Confederate to Union control, was now, briefly, a haven for Gift, Scharf, and the other survivors of the ill-fated expedition. The men subsisted on palmetto cabbage and oysters for two days. Townspeople took two boats across to Saint George Island on May 14 and picked up the men. Even then the episode was not over. An alert Union craft spotted them and gave close pursuit. Gift, Scharf, and most of the men were in a single craft; three others were in a second and smaller boat. Gift's men made it safely to Apalachicola, but the second boat was overtaken and captured. Gift did not linger in Apalachicola. He and his crew rowed up the river to a bayou, where they sank their boat and proceeded on foot to the sanctuary of the Confederate lines. The only real attempt to break the Union blockade at Apalachicola had ended in failure.[41]

Milton's fears for the safety of the Apalachicola basin were realized in 1864 but not as he had supposed. Instead of a Yankee incursion up the river from the bay, it came from West Florida. In September the bizarre and feared Hungarian, Brigadier General Alexander Asboth, lead a cavalry raid of seven hundred men east from Pensacola. They rode uncontested across the narrow band of the state. Arriving at Marianna on September 27, the cavalrymen were opposed by a force of fifty young and old men. The so-called Cradle and Grave Company gave a good account of itself, but it was no match for Asboth's superior numbers. The Northerners took the town and returned with prisoners of war, contraband, and livestock.[42]

At the bay, naval officials were sufficiently alarmed by Gift's quixotic raid to strengthen the blockade. They assembled detailed reports of the estuarine system and renewed requests for vessels of

40. *ORN* Ser. 1, 17: 697–99; Itkin, "East Gulf Squadron," 138–39.
41. Ibid.
42. Mark F. Boyd, "The Battle of Marianna."

shallower draft. The commanders also kept up complaints about the poor condition of their ships. As for the Confederates, the work at Columbus went on. The *Chattahoochee* was almost ready. Work continued on the torpedo boat, and, amid rejoicing, the *Muscogee* was actually launched on December 22, 1864. Standing guard off Apalachicola, Lieutenant I. B. Baxter of the newly assigned *Fort Henry* was worried about 1865. He was convinced the Confederates were "making every preparation to make a raid on the blockade at this place."[43]

In 1865 events closed in rapidly. The East Gulf Squadron never faced the Confederate gunboats that they expected. There was some activity on the river, but the blockade was total and most of the saltworks had been destroyed. Early in the year the squadron completed an expedition that was a logistical triumph of limited significance. On January 16, a boat set out from the blockading station at St. Andrew Bay. Acting Master Charles Cadieu of the bark *Midnight,* commanding thirty men in a cutter and a launch, went east by creek as far inland as possible. He rendezvoused with Confederate deserters, who supplied a yoke of oxen and a wagon to haul the cutter overland to the Chipola River. By way of the Chipola they entered the Apalachicola above the obstructions and moved against Ricco's Bluff. The party's primary objective was the steamer *W. H. Young,* which regularly transported supplies from Columbus to the Confederate outpost at the bluff.

The Federals waited a week for the steamer, which never arrived. Fearing discovery, the men attacked the garrison at Ricco's Bluff, capturing nine men and a few weapons. Cadieu's raiders burned a storehouse filled with corn and on January 29 returned with thirty contrabands to the *Midnight*. Acting Ensign W. H. Gruff and eleven men took a different course. Circumventing the obstructions, they descended the river to Fort Gadsden. There they captured several men and arrived at their ship by way of Apalachicola and the bay.[44] If the rewards of the expedition were small, the weak condition of the Confederate units was revealed.

In February and March the blockading force was increased off

43. *ORN* Ser. 1, 17: 784; Turner, "Operations on the Apalachicola," 249–53.
44. *ORN* Ser. 1, 17: 797–800.

Apalachicola, and soon most of its units were sent east to St. Marks to participate in what became the Battle of Natural Bridge. The plan was for a combined force to move by land and water against St. Marks from the lighthouse on the coast of Apalachee Bay. Simultaneously, ships would ascend the St. Marks River while soldiers (a majority of them black troops) marched overland to Newport, seized the bridge, and came upon St. Marks from the rear. They would cut the railroad to Tallahassee and, if desired, take the capital city as well. The plan was sound, but its execution went awry. The ships failed to get upriver, and the troops were forced into battle north of Newport at Natural Bridge. The Confederates were waiting for them, and after some brisk fighting on March 6 the Northern forces withdrew to their ships.[45]

The victory was a small one and outnumbered by many Southern defeats elsewhere. Governor Milton realized that the war could not continue. Having given himself unstintingly to the Southern cause, he could not accept a future under the United States of America. Three days after the victory at Natural Bridge, the governor revealed his new attitude of bitter despair. Governor Brown of Georgia endorsed a last-minute effort to outfit a special ship to run the blockade at Apalachicola. The idea required the removal of the river obstacles, an act that Milton had vigorously championed. Now, on March 9, Florida's governor took a different stance. He wrote General Sam Jones: "I do not believe the blockade could be run at Apalachicola and efforts to do so will increase the force of the enemy on our coast." Replying to Brown, Milton refused to cooperate. To run the blockade at Apalachicola would "induce the destruction of that place and invasion of the state."[46] Because the end was near, Milton saw no need to sacrifice the lives of Floridians in a futile venture.

The depressed governor left his office in Tallahassee for a visit to Sylvania. There on April 1, 1865, he shot himself. Abraham K. Al-

45. Itkin, "East Gulf Squadron," 174–86; William Miller, "The Battle of Natural Bridge"; Edwin C. Bearss, "Federal Expedition against Saint Marks Ends at Natural Bridge."

46. Milton to Sam Jones, Mar. 9, 1865, 182; Milton to Joseph E. Brown, Mar. 9, 1865, 183. See also Gov. Joseph E. Brown to Milton, Feb. 18, 1865, 181; Sam Jones to Milton, Mar. 9, 1865, 182–83, Milton letterbook, 1863–65.

lison, president of the senate, became acting governor and informed President Davis of Milton's death.[47] The cumulative pressures of his responsibilities and his passionate belief in a cause that he realized was lost made John Milton a casualty of the war. Allison had been Apalachicola's first mayor and the first county judge of Franklin County, although he built his political and military career at Quincy in Gadsden County.[48] His tenure as acting governor would be brief.

In bewildering fashion the war ended. On the day after Milton killed himself, Richmond was abandoned; and on April 9, Lee surrendered to General Ulysses S. Grant at Appomattox Courthouse in Virginia. Further south, Columbus was thrown into panic as Union troops threatened the city. The attack did not come, as had been constantly predicted, by way of the Apalachicola and Chattahoochee rivers. Instead, it came from General James H. Wilson and over thirteen thousand fresh, battle-tested cavalrymen. Sweeping down out of northern Alabama, the young general captured the important manufacturing city of Selma, then turned east and took Montgomery. Next he moved against Columbus. Frantic efforts were made to defend the city, but Wilson's overwhelming superiority enabled his forces to storm a bridge and capture it on April 16.[49]

For two days Wilson's men destroyed military installations. The *Muscogee*, two weeks away from completion, was set afire by Wilson's men and left to drift in the river. Its wreckage stopped thirty miles south of Columbus. The Confederates set fire to the *Chattahoochee*, and the doomed vessel came to rest twelve miles below the city. The torpedo boat was used to carry the first troops downriver to Apalachicola. The boat was later lost in a storm while being towed to Key West.[50] Wilson's raiders moved on from

47. A. K. Allison to Jefferson Davis, Apr. 7, 1865, 189, Milton letterbook, 1863–65.

48. Allen Morris, comp., *The Florida Handbook 1981–1982*, 149–50.

49. James Pickett Jones, *Yankee Blitzkrieg: Wilson's Raid through Alabama and Georgia*, 126–44. More specialized is Diffie W. Standard, *Columbus, Georgia, in the Confederacy*. The standard work on Georgia is T. Conn Bryan, *Confederate Georgia*.

50. Turner, "Operations on the Apalachicola," 258–60; *ORN* Ser. 1, 17:

Columbus and took Macon. General Cobb surrendered his forces on April 20, and in early May, Governor Brown formally surrendered Georgia's remaining military forces.[51]

Florida was in the department of General Joseph E. Johnston, commander of the Army of the Tennessee. Johnston signed a convention of surrender terms with General William T. Sherman at Durham Station, North Carolina, on April 26. From his headquarters at Macon, General Wilson ordered Brigadier General Edward M. McCook to Tallahassee to receive Florida's surrender, take charge of government property, and parole prisoners. McCook, his staff officers, and five hundred men of the Second Indiana Cavalry and the Seventh Kentucky Cavalry moved south by way of Albany and Thomasville. They reached Tallahassee on May 10, and the formal surrender ceremonies were held on May 20.[52]

The people at Apalachicola could scarcely believe that the war was over. Three ships of the East Gulf Squadron remained in service off the passes at Saint George Island but were removed when a military post was established at Apalachicola in early June. The hated General Asboth headed a convoy that arrived from Fort Barrancas at Pensacola. The steamers carried the 161st New York Infantry Volunteers; the Eighty-Second U.S. Colored Infantry; Company C, First Florida Cavalry; and fifteen men of the Second Maine Cavalry. Once arrived, General Aboth carried out his assignment, including taking charge of 944 bales of cotton. One of the soldiers of occupation noticed that "All the places of business except one cotton press was closed, the streets were covered with grass, the houses and sidewalks were falling to decay, all the churches were closed, and an oppressive quietness everywhere prevailed."[53] But soon buoys were replaced in the harbor, and the lighthouses at Cape Saint George and Dog Island were put back in operation. Once more the port asserted its historic role as a com-

---

853–54. The wrecks of the *Muscogee* and the *Chattahoochee* were restored in the 1960s and are on display at the Confederate Naval Museum in Columbus.

51. Jones, *Yankee Blitzkrieg*, 160–89.

52. James P. Jones and William Warren Rogers, "The Surrender of Tallahassee."

53. Turner, "Operations on the Apalachicola," 258–60, quoting *Military History of the One Hundred and Sixty-First New York volunteer Infantry*, n.d., 48.

mercial conduit. Asboth marveled at the town's resiliency: "People are returning to Apalachicola from rebeldom as well as from the North, anxious to resume their former vocations."[54]

Asboth relinquished his command to Colonel S. S. Zulavsky of the Eighty-Second U.S. Colored Infantry. The white commander oversaw the port resume its activities as a clearinghouse for cotton and captured machinery of war. Besides taking control of various wharves, lots, and buildings, the military authorities seized certain lands. The confiscated real estate included 1,560 acres on Little Saint George Island, although Federal possession was only temporary.[55]

With its military mission accomplished, the 161st New York Infantry commanded by Major Willis E. Craig left town in late July 1865. The men were assigned to Fort Jefferson on Dry Tortugas. As the soldiers departed, the man who had noted the earlier desolation wrote, "Now the levee was covered with bales of cotton, the wharf was astir with citizens, and handkerchiefs were waving from many of the windows and sidewalks." Yet the heavy summer heat had been unbearable for the New Yorker. Nor could he understand how one would voluntarily elect such a locale as a permanent home. "Farewell, sandy, dry, hot Apalachicola," he recorded, "may we never see thee more!"[56]

Units of the Eighty-Second U.S. Colored Infantry remained at Apalachicola until September 1866. The occupation produced few incidents of racial tension between black troops and white civilians. With the war over, the soldiers tended to relax, although their superior officers attempted to maintain strict military discipline. General orders were issued to stop enlisted men from sleeping and taking their meals outside of camp. Personnel were required to have passes when leaving camp and to surrender all weapons not issued by the government. The surest sign of peacetime attitudes

54. OR Ser. 1, 69, part 1: 567–68.
55. U.S. Army, Records of the Continental Commands, Record Group 393, National Archives.
56. *Military History of the One Hundred and Sixty-first*, 48. For more comment on unhealthy conditions see J. W. Merwin, *Roster and Monograph: 161st Reg't N.Y.S. Volunteer Infantry, Rebellion 1861–65*, 132.

was the large number of warnings to soldiers who left their guard posts and went to town.[57]

Although the area's allure was a mystery to Yankee soldiers, it was powerful and profound for the people born there and for many who came expecting to remain for only a brief period. As the town revived, there was little bitterness. The population, always liberally sprinkled with Northerners, was hopeful about the future but pragmatic. As one citizen would write, "We have no capitalists among us, and this is the great secret of Apalachicola's present obscurity."[58] Yet surely the promise of the antebellum period could be realized. The town was still there as were the river and the bay. Perhaps some enterprising person or persons might discover a profitable use for Saint George Island. For the moment, it lay stretched out in its customary indolence, unchanged by the events of the period 1861−65.

57. Adjutant General, Office of, *Records,* Record Group 94; Quartermaster General, Office of, *Records,* Record Group 92.
58. Tallahassee *Weekly Floridian,* Sept. 23, 1873.

5

Decades of Change

THE questions of who owned Saint George Island and Little Saint George Island between 1865 and 1900 and with what degree of legal title defy conclusive answers. The lighthouse and six acres at Cape Saint George on the smaller island remained the property of the federal government. The capricious hurricanes of summer and fall continued to determine whether the islands were physically joined and whether Sand Island was, however small, an independent landmass. As always, silt entering the bay from the Apalachicola River filled in the waterways, and Saint George Island became a continuous strip of land again.

Deeds in the Franklin County courthouse established Saint George Island and Little Saint George Island as separate entities, at least on paper. They usually had different proprietors, although in the last half of the nineteenth century various individuals owned tracts on both. While the persons who claimed all or parts of the entire island of Saint George can be identified, their roles—sometimes independent, often overlapping—are difficult to trace. Frequently the owners knew how much acreage they held but were uncertain about where it was located.

Dog Island and Saint Vincent Island, Saint George's neighbors, would go through several changes of ownership, although no single individual held property on all three. Benjamin L. Curtis and George K. Walker, two Franklin County businessmen, acquired Dog Island in 1859 from the Apalachicola Land Company.

Curtis owned two-thirds of the island, and after the Civil War acquired full control. From then until the turn of the century, Curtis maintained a major interest, although from time to time he sold tracts on Dog Island to various persons, some of them lumbermen or friends. Despite the numerous sales and leases of small parcels, Dog Island remained largely uninhabited. Like Saint George Island, it was popular with Franklin County residents, who considered it a favorite place to spend leisure time.[1]

In 1858 Robert Floyd purchased the large island of Saint Vincent from the Apalachicola Land Company. Ten years later the island sold at public auction for $3,000. The new owner was George Hatch, a banker and former mayor of Cincinnati. He was the husband of Elizabeth Wefing, a resident of Apalachicola whose husband had been killed during the Civil War. The Hatch family, which included Elizabeth's son George F. Wefing, lived on the island. After Hatch died in 1875, Saint Vincent Island became briefly the property of Francis Avery. A Californian, Avery took the island in settlement of a debt, but after considerable litigation he sold his interest to Mrs. Hatch in 1887.

The next owner was a former comrade of General Robert E. Lee, Confederate General Edward P. Alexander. When he purchased the island from Mrs. Hatch in 1890, Alexander was president of the Georgia Central Railroad. Alexander's estate, known as the South Sea Island Company, sold Saint Vincent Island in 1907. The newest proprietor was Dr. Ray V. Pierce, a wealthy manufacturer of patent medicines from Buffalo, New York. He and his family and guests visited the island during the winter months. Pierce developed Saint Vincent Island as a game preserve, adding sambar deer (native to India) to the already abundant native wildlife. After his death in 1914, the island, except for a brief interim in the 1920s, remained a part of the Pierce estate until 1948.[2]

1. For Curtis's early control, see Franklin County Deed Book A, 72–74, 77–79; F, 419–92. For later divisions see, for example, B, 232–34, when he relinquished in 1881 a one-half interest to Carolyn A. Hall and Julia A. Kelley; and F, 606–7, when he sold a part of the island to the Georgia and Florida Investment Company.

2. For articles on Saint Vincent Island see Gene Smith, "St. Vincent's Island." See also William T. Hornaday, *A Mon-O-Graph on St. Vincent's Game Preserve;*

What the future held for Dog and Saint Vincent islands, as well as what would happen to Saint George Island, was unknown to the people of Apalachicola and Franklin County in 1865. The war had ended; no Union ships stood guard to prevent shipping; soldiers were paroled and allowed to return home. Past difficulties kept intruding even as new ones arose, but the critical problem was how to cope with the present. Curiously, Apalachicola experienced an easy and profitable transition to peacetime conditions. Unfortunately, the prosperity did not last. During this period when progress faded into decline, George Sinclair emerged as the major owner of Saint George Island. Sinclair was caught up in the times, and his maneuvers would demonstrate both the will and the ability to survive.

In the last half of the nineteenth century, Apalachicola and Franklin County remained atypical of other Florida and southern towns and cities. The area was almost devoid of such traditional field crops as cotton and corn. The agricultural economy was as limited as it had been before the war, and the citizens placed their hopes on what had sustained them in the past: maritime commerce, particularly the shipment of cotton. The seafood industry and the surrounding tracts of forests offered unlimited potential for commercial exploitation, but they did not attract interest until the temporary postwar prosperity of cotton shipping faded. The difficulties of a shallow harbor would never be solved. Saint George Island, framed on either side by East Pass and West Pass, would have been developed had the drawn-out and agonizing effort to make Apalachicola a deep-water port succeeded.

It seemed incongruous for an area with a broad river reaching into the interior and the Gulf of Mexico for its front door to remain so isolated. Limited and inadequate roads, dwindling water

---

Eugene L. Nixon, "A Doctor and an Island." Useful newspaper articles include Apalachicola *Times*, Jan. 13, 1906; Feb. 7, 1914; Nov. 23, 1935. For the sale of the Floyd Estate to George Hatch see Franklin County Deed Book D, 242–44 and I, 689–90; for that of Elizabeth J. Hatch to Edward P. Alexander see E, 442–43; for that of the South Sea Island Company to Pierce, see M, 683–86. The last private owners were Henry Loomis and Alfred L. Loomis. In 1968 Saint Vincent Island was acquired by the Federal government and made a part of the National Wildlife Refuge System.

transportation, and a total lack of railroads meant that Apalachicola was cut off from easy communication even with the rest of
Florida. No bridge would span the expanse of Apalachicola Bay
until the John Gorrie Bridge was opened in 1935.

The area's failure to revitalize itself was not the result of destruction from the Civil War or the corruption, alleged and real, of Reconstruction. The difficulties came because the port was not improved. The river system was neither dredged systematically nor
provided a consistent channel depth. Equally harmful, railroad
building caused a dramatic change in the flow of trade. Yet in the
latter part of 1865, Apalachicola seemed to be making a remarkable recovery. The port was one of several Florida towns where the
Freedmen's Bureau returned property to its original ex-Confederate
owners without litigation.[3]

If the ironies of geography made the area isolated, its diverse
population created a tolerant and cosmopolitan society not common to the rest of the South. Racial prejudice was present but far
less virulent than elsewhere in Florida. The political structure was
dominated by the Democratic party, but many of Apalachicola's
most prominent people were Yankee-born and Republican in their
politics. Local elections were based more on personalities and the
issues of the moment than on party affiliation. While the Democrats elected the officials who filled county, state, and national
offices, neither the politicians nor the citizenry wasted much time
denouncing Republicans and the horrors of Reconstruction.

The town and county benefited from their antebellum legacy of
religious tolerance. The area continued to reflect the historic Spanish and French presence along the Gulf coast. More influential was
the dominant and eclectic Protestantism of the English and Scotch-
Irish settlers. Beyond that, numerous Italians and Sicilians had
settled in the area, as well as Greeks. Most of the Germans who
came to Apalachicola were Lutherans, and the town had several
Jewish families of wealth. Nonbelievers and those with unortho-
dox concepts were neither ostracized nor stigmatized.

Never reverting to the freewheeling and flamboyant patterns of
prewar days (a city ordinance reinforced a state law of 1879 that

3. Jerrell H. Shofner, *Nor Is It Over Yet,* 20; *Laws of Florida* 1879: 84.

required the closing of stores on Sunday), Apalachicola retained a certain sophistication. Within limitations, a person's manners and morals were accorded the respect of privacy. Surviving the war reinforced among Apalachicolans the importance of adapting to one's situation and of assuming similar adjustments by others.

Cotton that had been stored during the war, the destruction or crippled condition of existing railroads, and the availability of the river system brought prosperity to Apalachicola. George Bucknam, a successful merchant who had operated the first cotton compress in Apalachicola, resumed business. He and his partner, Samuel J. Whiteside, had remained active until Apalachicola was evacuated in 1862. Whiteside, a native New Yorker who fought for the Confederacy, moved to Columbus, Georgia. In the first years after the war he retained business interests in Apalachicola and Savannah. Bucknam formed a new partnership in Apalachicola with George Stevens.[4]

Bucknam and others made money immediately, and in 1866 more than a hundred thousand bales of cotton were shipped through the port. By the winter of that year a line of steamers, the *Linda* and *Key West,* cleared port every two weeks bound for New York. In 1865–66, at least 135 large vessels entered Apalachicola Bay from all parts of the world.[5] Newcomers such as Henry Brash, a native of Germany, moved in. Arriving in 1865, Brash opened a dry goods store at the corner of Chestnut and Market streets. Expanding into lumber, real estate, and the sponge trade, he would remain in business for the next forty years.[6]

By early 1867, river traffic had increased to four or five steamers making weekly trips to and from Apalachicola. Trade was revived with New Orleans, and in February 1866 a group of Tallahassee and Quincy men organized the Florida Line and purchased the *J. L. Smallwood* in New York. It was to run regularly between St. Marks, Apalachicola, and New Orleans, but in less than a year St. Marks

4. Apalachicola *Times,* Apr. 26, 1902, quoting Columbus *Times.* See also Apalachicola *Times,* Feb. 7, 1914.

5. Apalachicola *Times,* Sept. 12, 1903.

6. Ibid., Dec. 9, 1905, quoting a report made in 1903 by Captain J. B. Cavannaugh. A series of stores in Apalachicola was known as Brash's block. One of his sons took over the business.

was dropped because of its navigational inadequacies and a decline in traffic.

William Mackensie and Company operated a banking business in Apalachicola during the late 1860s, but the difficulties of Reconstruction and economic depression, and competition from east-west railroads north of Florida, forced the area into a severe decline. The most calamitous blow was the completion of the Atlantic and Gulf Railroad to Bainbridge, Georgia. The line gave Bainbridge a direct and continuous link to Savannah and diverted much cotton traffic that would have gone to Apalachicola.[7] In 1867 only one ship cleared the harbor for a foreign port, and an observer wrote in 1869 that Apalachicola, "once a place of considerable trade . . . is now extremely dull."[8]

George Sinclair, who owned several land parcels, including wharf lots in Apalachicola, was among the victims of hard times. He had lived in Apalachicola since the 1840s and was an active businessman. Sinclair had also owned three lots in Pensacola and a tract of land in Chicot County, Arkansas, a part of the state's delta region. Among his Florida holdings was an undivided one-third interest in Saint George Island (about 4,980 acres). Most of his land was on the larger island since much of Little Saint George Island had already been purchased by Thomas Orman in 1861. The property remained in the Orman family.[9] Sinclair probably obtained his land from George S. Hawkins, who had been appointed receiver of the Apalachicola Land Company in 1866.[10]

Late in 1868, Sinclair filed a bankruptcy petition. Charles Kenmore was made assignee, and in December 1869 he received per-

7. Shofner, *Nor Is It Over Yet*, 29, 119, 126, 269; William Warren Rogers, *Thomas County 1865–1900*, 98–127.

8. Daniel Garrison Brinton, *A Guide-Book of Florida and the South, for Tourists, Invalids, and Emigrants*, 110. See also Bainbridge *Southern Sun*, May 25, 1871.

9. Sinclair had also operated a draying service. See Apalachicola *Commercial Advertiser*, Mar. 8, 1845. See also Franklin County Book of Probates, 1867–1903, 3: 144–45, 159–60 (hereinafter cited as FCBP). Orman paid the receiver of the Apalachicola Land Comapny $405.60 for 1,560 acres of Little Saint George. See Franklin County Deed Book A, 110–11.

10. Sinclair bought land in Apalachicola from Hawkins in 1872. See Franklin County Deed Book A, 110–11.

mission to sell the insolvent Sinclair's land in order to satisfy his creditors. Sinclair's acreage on the island was imprecisely described, but in any event Kenmore included the property in the public auction. Even for the times, the bidding was slow. George's half brother William Sinclair (who occasionally signed his first name "Wilhelm") made the highest offer: twenty dollars.[11]

George Sinclair's loss of a barren island, one with no human inhabitants except for a lighthouse keeper, aroused little sympathy or conversation. In the troubled era each person had a matching tale of woe. Future means of wealth—the lumber industry, seafood (especially oysters)—were fine topics for optimistic speeches and editorials touting "potential sources." Yet the urgent demands of the present went unanswered. Greater population would assure increased economic activity; but the town of Carrabelle was not yet founded, and only a few scattered homes lay across the bay at the future site of Eastpoint. Such developments took time, and in 1876 an air of gloom hung over the region. While the rest of the nation celebrated one hundred years of independence, Franklin County languished.

The atmosphere of pessimism moved a visitor to describe Apalachicola as "a city of mouldering ruins," one with "streets grown up in grass." Yet somehow George Sinclair was able to revive his fortunes. Reversing his losses in the winter of 1872, he purchased a one-third undivided interest in Saint George Island. That Sinclair's bid of twenty-five dollars was the highest offered did not seem unusual. His purchase at a public auction came at the expense of Samuel Benezet and Company, which had come into possession of a part of the island. The company, a partnership of twelve men, lost a suit to a rival firm owned by Nathan and Robert G. Baker. Ultimately, Sheriff Robert Knickmeyer included the property among the parcels that fell under his hammer.[12] Then, in August 1872, Sinclair regained his original one-third of Saint George Island by

11. Ibid., 101–4.

12. For the dismal appraisal see Tallahassee *Floridian*, June 6, 1871, quoting Bainbridge *Argus*. See Franklin County Deed Book A, 105–6. *Laws of Florida* 1870: 58–60 show Benezet heading the Gulf Steamship Company and planning to improve Apalachicola's harbor and engage in varied shipping enterprises. The 4,980 acres were described as "all that land East of Range Line, Dividing Range 7 from Range 8 and lying in Franklin County." In 1856 Benezet bought a lot from

paying five hundred dollars to his half brother William and Meta, William's wife.[13] His tract and that owned by Benezet and Company are identically described in the courthouse records and may have been the same.[14]

Sinclair, whose fortunes and reputation had so revived that he was elected county treasurer, died before he had much chance to do anything with the island. Because Sinclair died intestate and without a widow or children, William was appointed administrator of the estate. George's death came the day after Christmas 1874. William, who ran a combination dry goods and grocery store, became administrator on January 6, 1875. By the following November, William himself was dead, and his widow Meta relinquished her rights as administratrix to John G. Ruge.[15] To settle certain debts owed by the estate, probate judge Alvan W. Chapman (the judicial salary helped support the botanist's scientific interests) appointed W. T. Orman as commissioner. Orman conducted the sale at a public auction, and on August 1, 1881, Horace H. Humphries was high bidder at twenty-one dollars. Humphries now owned 4,980 acres "more or less" of Saint George Island.[16]

The transfer inaugurated the Humphrieses' period of control. A numerous clan, the relationship of its various members to Saint George Island was often unclear and confused. Yet their presence was real and important. In the meantime, significant events were taking place in Apalachicola and Franklin County.

During Reconstruction and the years afterward, Apalachicola

the trustees of the Apalachicola Land Company. See Franklin County Deed Book A, 354–57.

13. Franklin County Deed Book A, 108–9. The sale included property in Apalachicola.

14. FCBP, 1877–1903, 3: 160, lists George Sinclair as owning two-thirds of Saint George; but when the land was sold in 1881, it was described as 4,980 acres, not 9,960 acres.

15. Ibid., 144–45, 156–58; ibid., 1833–84, 1: 218–29; Franklin County Record of Wills, 1846–94: 209–10. Sinclair was an effective treasurer, although he died owing the county thirty dollars, which was taken from his estate. See Franklin County Commissioners' Record Book, Feb. 2, 1876, 43–44; June 13, 1877, 89.

16. Franklin County Deed Book B, 67–69. Some records, apparently incorrect, show the purchaser as Henry N. Humphries, brother of Horace. See also Franklin County Record of Wills 1846–94, 192, 211.

and Franklin County had no agricultural base to fall back on. In 1870 only fourteen people in the county reported their farming operations to the census taker. No farm was valued at more than seven hundred dollars, and none was larger than 550 acres. The major crops were oats, rice, sweet potatoes, sugarcane, and garden vegetables. The estimated value of all farm products (not one cotton plant grew in the entire county) was only $4,795. Livestock statistics were equally unimpressive, and the census placed the worth of all animals at $4,210.[17] Carpentry, including shipbuilding, was the county's only listed industrial activity, with one exception that was a harbinger of future economic growth. Partners in the firm of Snow, Richards, and Harris listed their ownership of a lumber mill. It had a curved saw and a steam engine and employed fifteen hands.[18] The expanding lumber industry improved the languishing economy and helped revive Apalachicola as a port.

Interrupted by the Civil War, earlier efforts to capitalize on the seemingly inexhaustible forests were revived. Charles M. Harrison opened a sawmill in the late 1860s. Other mill owners, including Snow, Richards, and Harris, followed Harrison's pioneering work, but fires, insufficient capital, and mismanagement thwarted their efforts. In the early 1870s A. B. Tripler founded the Pennsylvania Tie Company. The company cut railroad crossties from cypress logs easily obtained from the swamps surrounding the Apalachicola River. The Pennsylvania Tie Company was sold in 1882 and renamed the Cypress Lumber Company. The firm's headquarters was in Maine, and locally the key figure was A. S. Mohr. The company remained an important part of the county's economy into the twentieth century.[19]

James N. Coombs was the most important man in the lumber industry. From the late 1870s till after 1900 he made a fortune and became one of Apalachicola's wealthiest and most influential men. Coombs's rise was accomplished despite his being a native of

17. Manuscript Census, 1870, Agriculture, Franklin County, 1–2.

18. Ibid., Products of Industry, Franklin County, 7. For the larger picture see Richard W. Massey, Jr., "A History of the Lumber Industry in Alabama and West Florida, 1880–1914."

19. Apalachicola *Times*, Nov. 8, 1957. The issue contains a history of the area by a contemporary, County Judge R. G. Baker. See ibid., July 28, 1900; Mar. 23, 1912.

Maine, a veteran of the Union army, and a Republican. Coombs migrated to Pensacola in 1871, returned briefly to Philadelphia, and came South again in 1876, this time to Apalachicola. By the early 1880s, he operated a store, which he expanded to include a sawmill. His associate was Caleb Emlen, another early lumberman and a native of Chester, Pennsylvania. Next, Coombs established a partnership with Seth N. Kimball of Mobile.

Coombs purchased still another lumbering operation in recently founded Carrabelle. His new partner was Charles H. Parlin. Like Coombs, Parlin was originally from Maine, served in the Union army, and was a Republican. He came South, married Cornelia Elizabeth Grady of Apalachicola, and became owner of the Long Lumber Pine and Cypress Company. Moving his family twenty-two miles east to Carrabelle, Parlin managed his and Coombs's newly acquired Franklin County Lumber Company. Back in Apalachicola, Coombs sold out to Kimball in 1888 and set up his own firm, Coombs and Company. Shortly afterward, he acquired single control of the Franklin County Lumber Company.[20]

Coombs had a sure financial touch and entered several business ventures including banking. That he ignored Saint George Island demonstrated the island's lack of appeal as an economic investment. Coombs faithfully attended Republican party conventions and contributed money to what, at the state level, was a lost cause. Too busy with his lumber mills and other interests to seek elective office, he turned down his party's nomination for governor in 1900. By 1908 he was even mentioned as a possibility for vice president. Coombs was more content to enjoy his family and his profits (Coombs's lumber company was incorporated in Delaware at $100,000 in 1901). His role as a carpetbagger and Republican leader earned him no local embarrassment. The citizens attributed it all to geographical happenstance and political eccentricity. The respected Coombs lived in Apalachicola's most elegant house, built to order by George H. Marshall, the town's leading contractor.[21]

20. Ibid., Aug. 23, 1902; May 2, 1908; Mar. 7, 1931; Mar. 19, 1943. The Franklin County Lumber Company was first established in 1888. See Franklin County Deed Book D, 517–18. For Emlen's sale of his mill interests to Coombs, see Franklin County Deed Book B, 511–14.
21. Apalachicola *Times*, July 24, Aug. 4, 1900; Feb. 2, Sept. 30, 1905.

There were numerous smaller lumber companies and sawmills. Charles M. Harrison's early mill was taken over by Henry Brash, who later sold it to the Cypress Lumber Company.[22] When Seth Kimball took over in Apalachicola from Coombs in 1888, he formed the Kimball Lumber Company. It was capitalized at $100,000 and operated as a partnership of four men. In the early 1880s, C. L. Storrs and R. F. Fowler operated a sawmill in Carrabelle, and by 1890 the new town was the center of an expanding naval stores industry. The landscape around Carrabelle and west toward Apalachicola was dotted by many turpentine stills, property values rose, and shipping was brisk (*illustrations*, Group 1).[23]

The demand for timber products was worldwide: hewn logs were exported to Europe and to South America; railroad ties found ready markets in Mexico; various forms of sawed pine lumber and shingles were sent north; businesses in New Orleans were the major purchasers of cypress.[24] Soon the capacity of the local mills was greater than the area's shipping facilities. At first there were not enough barges. The problem was temporarily solved in the 1870s when the mill owners employed the slow and inefficient process of rafting lumber and floating it out to ships in the bay. The timber industry's profit margin was tied to the efficiency with which lumber could be transported to market. The need for better shipping facilities led to the drive to make Apalachicola a deep-water port.[25]

From 1878 to 1888 lumber was shipped through West Pass. Located eight miles from Apalachicola, the pass would admit ships drawing no more than ten or eleven feet of water. The passage between Saint George Island and Saint Vincent Island, as well as the

22. Ibid., Mar. 23, 1912.

23. See Kimball Lumber Co., Apalachicola, Ledger Book 1888–89. See also Apalachicola *Times*, July 24, Aug. 4, 1900; Feb. 2, 1901.

24. Thurston, "Maritime Activity in Florida," 212; U.S. Congress, House of Representatives, *Annual Report of the Chief of Engineers, United States Army, 1883–84*, 980–83 (hereinafter cited as *ARCE*).

25. Recollections of John J. Berry in Apalachicola *Times*, Dec. 9, 1922. For logging on the Apalachicola see Apalachicola *Times*, Oct. 14, 1938. In 1872 the state legislature memorialized Congress for funds to improve the harbor. See *Acts of Florida*, Extraordinary Session, 1872: 98.

From the 1830s until his death in 1899, Alvan W. Chapman lived and worked in Apalachicola. A native of New England, he gained international fame as a botanist, and in 1860 he published his classic study, *Flora of the Southern United States*.   APALACHICOLA HISTORICAL SOCIETY

Three lighthouses were constructed on Saint George Island. The last one, seventy-five feet high, was completed in 1852 and still stands on Cape Saint George.   BAWA SATINDER SINGH

David G. Raney was a businessman and civic leader in Apalachicola. He is shown wearing the uniform of an officer in the Confederate marines. This is one of the few extant pictures of the regalia.   APALACHICOLA HISTORICAL SOCIETY

The East Gulf Blockading Squadron engaged in numerous amphibious raids against Confederate saltworks and captured war supplies and foodstuffs. Besides blockading the coast, the squadron captured Confederate ships lying at anchor. The action here takes place on the Ochlockonee River, the eastern boundary of Franklin County.

Frank Leslie's Weekly

By the 1880s the timber industry had become Franklin County's primary means of income. Here a three-masted schooner at Carrabelle harbor takes on lumber from the Cypress Lumber Company of Apalachicola.

HERBERT BROWN COLLECTION / FLORIDA PHOTOGRAPHIC ARCHIVES

A lumber mill worker oversees the rafting of lumber along the Apalachicola River. The photograph was taken around 1900. APALACHICOLA *Times*

Three musicians—talented amateurs all—of Eastpoint in 1912. Herbert Brown has the violin, Tobar Williams the mandolin, and Lonner (Bubber) Segres the guitar.
HERBERT BROWN COLLECTION / FLORIDA PHOTOGRAPHIC ARCHIVES

Herbert Brown and his students at the Eastpoint school—the ages and the level of instruction varied as he moved from group to group in his one-room schoolhouse. The photograph was taken in 1906.
HERBERT BROWN COLLECTION / FLORIDA PHOTOGRAPHIC ARCHIVES

Oyster "tongers" working in Apalachicola Bay about 1900. "Cullers" work at culling boards to separate salable oysters from smaller oysters and extraneous material.

FLORIDA PHOTOGRAPHIC ARCHIVES

Peering through the glass at the bottom of his wooden bucket, a "hooker" prepares to use his pole to bring up sponges. The oarsman makes any required maneuvers. Never a major source of income, the sponge industry was active from 1870 until the first decade of the twentieth century. Sheepswool, grass, and yellow sponges were found in waters adjacent to Carrabelle and Apalachicola.

channel to it, badly needed deepening. As early as 1868 a number of leading citizens had formed the Apalachicola Channel Company. Their public aims to deepen the channel upriver from Apalachicola and out to deep waters in the bay proved beyond their private means.[26] In 1870 a congressional appropriation was made to survey the harbor. The U.S. Army Corps of Engineers reported the results in 1872. The Corps of Engineers recommended deepening the passes and affording a deeper and wider channel entrance from the bay into the mouth of the Apalachicola River and up to the city wharves. A reexamination was made in 1878, and beginning in 1882 money was provided for the project. By 1890 about $100,000 had been spent. Separate funds in smaller amounts were expended on clearing the river of snags and overhanging trees. Even so, the amount of money was far from adequate, and nothing was done to deepen West Pass.[27]

After 1888 the volume of commerce shifted to East Pass, Upper Anchorage, and Dog Island Cover. There the water was deeper and larger ships could enter. Both Apalachicola and Carrabelle used the passes. The drawback was that the lumber had to be lightered from Apalachicola across the bay and along Saint George Sound, a distance of over twenty miles. The channel was treacherous, and lightering and insurance costs were high.

With shipping by water an uncertain means of transportation, business leaders in Apalachicola (men such as James N. Coombs, H. L. Grady, the brothers John R. and George H. Ruge, and W. T. Orman) realized the importance of securing a railroad. As the terminus for a line, Apalachicola would become the base for the shipment of seafood and lumber to northern and western markets. A group of townsmen secured a charter in 1885 for the Apalachicola and Alabama Railroad Company. With a generous grant of land from the state, the incorporators planned to build northward through Calhoun County and cross the newly completed Pensa-

26. *Acts of Florida* 1868: 146–49. A similar company, chartered in 1863, proposed to sell its stock after the war ended. See ibid., 1863, 12–16.

27. *ARCE* 1872: 1–25; 612–23; 1879: 123–24; 1883–84: 980–83; 1889: 176–77, 1372–75; 1891: 1694–96. For efforts after 1910 to obtain congressional funds see U.S. Congress, House, *Document No. 834,* 63d Cong., 2d sess., 1–8.

cola and Atlantic Railroad somewhere in Jackson County. The line would then be extended to the Alabama boundary and make connections there. Problems with financing delayed construction, although a time extension was obtained in 1887. The company was given two years to begin work and three years beyond that before land grant benefits would be canceled. Unfortunately, backers of the Apalachicola and Alabama Railroad could not secure the needed economic support, and the line was never built.[28]

Failing to secure a railroad, but keeping their hopes alive, Apalachicolans renewed their efforts to obtain a deep-water channel to West Pass. As president of the Apalachicola Board of Trade, John E. Grady worked closely with officials in Columbus, Georgia, and other river towns. Appeals laden with convincing facts were forwarded to the capital at Tallahassee. In turn the state legislature memorialized Congress for funds to deepen, dredge, and maintain Apalachicola Bay and its tributary waters. Pressure was put on local congressmen and members of the congressional Committee on Rivers and Harbors. Investigations were made by the U.S. Army Corps of Engineers. Reporting the results of a survey in 1896, the Corps of Engineers supported the proposals for deepening West Pass. A congressional appropriation of $20,000 in 1900 helped but was not enough. That same year the Apalachicola and Columbus Deep Water Association was formed, but its lobbying activities failed to persuade the Committee on Rivers and Harbors to release significant funds.[29]

Some Apalachicolans even supported a scheme to separate from Florida and make the area west of Apalachicola a part of Alabama. They were certain that Alabama would develop a deep-water port at Apalachicola. The plan, which had been offered periodically, went the way of previous (and future) proposals of annexation. There was much talk but no action. Even though no real progress was made, the agitation was important. It led to an expanded movement for an intracoastal waterway and for improving naviga-

28. *Acts of Florida* 1885: 85–90; 1887, 1st sess.: 224–26.
29. For typical legislative memorials see ibid., 1887: 291–92 and 1889, Extra Session: 324. See also report of Maj. F. A. Mahan in U.S. Congress, House, *Document No. 129*, 54th Cong., 2d sess., 4.

tion on the river system. In 1900 a satisfactory harbor entrance from the Gulf still did not exist. It could be fashioned at West Pass, East Pass, New Inlet, or, some suggested, by making an artificial cut across Saint George Island. Apalachicola was far behind Pensacola in the amount of lumber shipped, but the industry was the mainstay of the county's economy. In the decades after 1870 most people took for granted the familiar sight of lumber being slowly towed along the dangerous route to East Pass.[30]

As the 1870s closed, Apalachicola was a sleepy, down-at-the-heels village. Agriculture had, if anything, declined since the beginning of the decade.[31] The county's population in 1880 was 1,791, an increase of more than 500 since 1870 but still below the 1,904 figure of 1860.[32] Apalachicola had no sewers, and open ditches were used for water runoff. The streets were sandy stretches. There were no street lights, although lamps were placed throughout town on posts sunk into the ground. Each night the tender went from post to post with a ladder and "alligator" matches to light them. The next morning he retraced his steps and put them out. There were few wagons or buggies. Hauling was accomplished by drays with five-inch tires—John Carrigan, a good-humored Irishman, and his two-wheeled cotton cart seemed to be everywhere. When a funeral occurred, a dray was commandeered for a hearse, and the deceased was usually buried in one of Phil Preston's homemade coffins.

The cost of living was low, but, even so, money was scarce before the rise of the lumber industry. Phillip Schoelles was just eighteen when he came to Apalachicola in 1850. He survived the war and became the town's leading butcher. Purchases were made daily at his meat market. Schoelles had no wrapping paper, and once a sale

30. Apalachicola *Times*, Feb. 2, 9, 1900; Mar. 9, 1901; ibid., Mar. 23, 1912, quoting Pensacola *Journal;* Occie Clubbs, "Pensacola in Retrospect: 1870–1890," *FHQ* 37 (Jan.-Apr., 1959): 377–96. Between 1872 and 1900, Apalachicola received $202,600 in harbor and river appropriations. See *ARCE* 1900: 2092–98.

31. Manuscript Census, 1880, Agriculture, Franklin County, 1–3.

32. *Twelfth Census* 1900, I, Population: 13. A useful compilation of Apalachicola's population covering June 1, 1884–May 31, 1885, was made by City Marshal Patrick J. Lovett. It was transcribed by Rosa Gibbons Lovett in 1968 and may be consulted at the Special Collections Room, University of West Florida.

was made, he ran a cedar stick (extracted from a supply he kept on hand) into the meat and handed it to the customer. A. F. Myer ran a saloon that featured cool lager beer. He also dispensed rye whiskey that was guaranteed to produce four fights to the pint or no charge. A. J. Murat's grocery dealt in a variety of fish, especially mullet and mullet roe. John Cook owned a combination saloon and grocery. Other merchants included George F. Wefing, R. H. Porter, and H. L. Grady.

There was one dentist who, like the town's three doctors, also operated a drugstore. The lawyers had so few customers that Robert Knickmeyer, one of the fraternity, quit for lack of business. Before an armory and opera house were built, the forty-room Curtis House served many purposes. The hotel hosted local and traveling theatrical productions, and until the new courthouse was completed in 1892 it doubled as the meeting place for the circuit court.[33]

Newspapers flourished in Apalachicola before the Civil War, but after the conflict the declining population and deteriorating economic situation caused journalists to shun the town. The *Reporter* ceased publication in 1868, and a journal called the *Times* was unable to survive the depression of the 1870s. Henry Walker Johnston began editing the *Tribune* in 1881. In 1884 he moved to Houston, Texas, where he worked on his brother's newspaper, the *Post*. In Apalachicola the *Tribune* was succeeded by W. B. Sheppard's *Herald*. Longing for Florida, Johnston returned in 1886, bought out Sheppard, and established the *Times*. Under Johnston's editorship, the Apalachicola *Times* became an institution. Until he died in 1922 and was succeeded by his son, Herbert K. ("Duke"), Johnston was a tireless promoter of the region, including Saint George Island.[34]

Blacks, who suffered more than whites from the economic depression, made the most of their situation nevertheless. Several black churches were established during and after Reconstruction.

33. Recollections of Henry W. Johnston in Apalachicola *Times*, Apr. 27, 1912; June 11, 1921; recollections of Berry, ibid., June 25, 1921; Sept. 16, 1922. See articles ibid., Aug. 23, 1902; Nov. 12, 1921; July 25, 1936; Mar. 19, 1943.

34. Apalachicola *Times*, Aug. 23, 1902; June 11, 1921; Mar. 19, 1943; May 19, 1944; Oct. 22, 1948.

The black community, no less than the white, enjoyed excursions, picnics, and baseball. The town's two-man police force was integrated. By the late 1880s, blacks ran the two leading hotels: the Spartan Jenkins and the Fuller. The Spartan Jenkins catered only to whites. Mary Aldine Fuller, a native of Marianna, ran the Fuller with her husband. After he died in 1891, she operated it by herself until 1905. She provided accommodations for the occasional blacks who rented rooms, but her clientele were mainly whites. When she died the African Methodist Episcopal Church was the scene of an outpouring of grief and respect by whites and blacks in the community.[35]

Blacks as well as whites enjoyed the pleasures of Saint George Island, but their visits went unreported in the newspapers. Although segregation was institutionalized, both races frequently passed across the barriers in their personal relationships. Such interaction was evident when entertainment was the goal. When they held a dance, whites hired black musicians. The extra income was welcome, and the blacks became local celebrities.

Square dancing was the favorite kind of such activity. Festivities began at eight in the evening and theoretically ended at midnight. The sponsors employed a black youth to go around town with a list of those invited. On locating a prospect, the courier presented him or her with a pencil. Scratching a line through one's name signified acceptance.

Whether the dance was held in a hotel or in a private home, the musical instruments remained the same: the tambourine, triangle, accordion, and fiddle. The evening's success depended on the caller, and none could match Theodore Jones. His opening cry of "all balance, swing your partners," was as familiar as their preacher's voice to many people in Franklin and surrounding counties. Jones accompanied himself with his tambourine. He was backed up by Sam Hill, who also sang and was renowned for his rendition of "Don't Dare Me Down, My Darling." William Henry Hall, an employee of Coombs and Emlen during the day, was the unrivaled king of Apalachicola's night life. His artistry with the bow was much admired, especially his command of "The Bed Fell Down"

35. Ibid., Nov. 11, 1905; June 24, 1916.

and "Old Aunt Sookey." Later, he settled down, and one person regretted that "Henry Hall has long since given up his fiddle and joined the church."[36] Dressed for the occasion, at the Christmas and New Year's dances the men wore derbies, swallowtail coats, and long, striped cravats. In a time when money was so scarce that mullet was sometimes used for legal tender, square dances were inexpensive entertainment. In general the people of the town and country worked hard, but on occasion they gave time to the pursuit of pleasure (*illustration*, Group 1).[37]

The Carrabelle River empties into Saint George Sound about twenty-two miles east of Apalachicola. It is formed by the confluence of New River and Crooked River some four miles from its mouth. Directly across Saint George Sound, six miles away, lies Dog Island. The area to the north—almost impenetrable with its swamps and forests and the habitat of bear, deer, panther, and other wild animals—came by the 1880s to be called Tate's Hell. According to local folklore, one Cebe Tate, a resident of the interior community of Sumatra, wandered into the wilderness in 1875 searching for straying cattle. He became lost, wandered around feverishly for days, and was bitten by a water moccasin but survived. The forty-five-year-old Tate stumbled out of the swamps to the safety of the beach along Saint George Sound. His hair had turned completely white. Encountering someone, Cebe declared, "My name is Tate, and I've just come through hell." Whether the story is true or not, the wilderness was the domain of wild animals as well as wild turkeys and many game birds.[38]

At the mouth of the Carrabelle, both saltwater and freshwater fishing were excellent. Before the Civil War, hunters and fishermen

36. Ibid., Sept. 27, Aug. 23, 1902; Mar. 23, 1912. Such data came from *Times* editor Johnston, Apalachicola's unofficial historian. See also Berry's recollections ibid., Sept. 30, 1922; and those of Judge Baker ibid., Nov. 8, 1957.

37. Recollections of Berry ibid., Sept. 30, 1922. John L Brown ibid., Feb. 6, 1948, recalled that Theodore Jones was paid $1.50 for calling and Sam Hill $2 for his varied talents.

38. Author's interview with Leo Hance, Jan. 5, 1983. Hance, a longtime resident of Carrabelle, has written extensively about the area. See his article in Apalachicola *Times*, Oct. 24, 1952. See also Audrey Dunham, "Tales of Tate's Hell"; and Jahoda, *The Other Florida*, 106–8.

used the river's east bank as a convenient headquarters for their outings. By 1855 a few settlers had moved in as permanent residents. Among them was the family of McCagor Pickett, and the area along the beach was known as Pickett's Harbor.[39] There the natural harbor was deeper than Apalachicola's, and East Pass was a better entry than West Pass. As mentioned, in the last decades of the nineteenth century, East Pass became the major entrance for ships engaged in the area's lumber trade.[40]

It was inevitable that a town would be established where the Carrabelle entered Saint George Sound. A devastating hurricane in 1873 that destroyed homes, stores, and warehouses in Apalachicola also toppled the lighthouse on Dog Island, but the disaster did not deter the expanding lumber industry. A new lighthouse, located just as effectively but in a safer spot, was built on the mainland about a quarter of a mile off the sound. For some confusing reason the beacon was known and continues to be known as the Crooked River lighthouse. Its construction was authorized in 1889, but it was not completed and put into operation until 1895.[41] Long before that, Oliver Hudson Kelley was responsible for the early growth and naming of Carrabelle.

Kelley was born in Boston, Massachusetts, in 1826, but later moved to Minnesota and helped found a small farming community. Still later he worked as a clerk in the U.S. Department of Agriculture, and in 1867 he was instrumental in founding the Patrons of Husbandry. Better known as the Grange, the farmers' organization had a ritual based on that of the Masons and it admitted women. It became influential through its economic and social activities, and it became a political force in the Midwest but not in the South. There the Democratic party, triumphant over the Republicans, brooked no divisive issues or groups that might threaten a return to Radical Reconstruction. The Grange reached its peak in the 1870s and attracted thousands of farmers to membership.[42]

39. Leo Hance writing in Apalachicola *Times*, Nov. 2, 1935.
40. U.S. Congress, House, *Document No. 622*, 63d Cong., 2d sess., 2–3.
41. Apalachicola *Times*, Jan. 25, 1979. For an account of the storm, see Tallahassee *Weekly Floridian*, Oct. 7, 14, 1873; New Orleans *Times-Picayune*, Sept. 25, 1873.
42. Oliver H. Kelley, *Origin and Progress of the Order of the Patrons of Hus-*

Although the Grange was established in Florida in 1873, none of its officers were from Franklin County, and apparently no subordinate Grange was founded there.[43] Yet Kelley came to Florida in the late 1870s and became interested in land speculation and development along the state's Gulf coast. The visionary Kelley saw the stirrings of the timber industry in Franklin County, realized the possibilities of a seafood industry, and noted the potential of the harbor at Carrabelle. All that was lacking was a town, and Kelley set about to supply one. In 1877 he bought 1,920 acres of land from Benjamin L. Curtis. Already the owner of Dog island, Curtis had bought extensive property and opened a large sawmill in the area.[44]

Kelley moved with his wife and four daughters to the community and urged others to invest in the future. He built and lived in a hotel called Island House. It was managed and operated by Carolyn Arrabelle Hall, Kelley's niece and a national officer in the Grange. He credited her with giving him the idea of including women in the order. Known as Carrie, she became famous locally for her business sense, charm, good looks, and Boston brown bread. In her honor, Kelley named the new community Rio Carrabelle. One contemporary recalled visiting Island House in 1879, an occasion that enabled him to enlarge Carrie's knowledge of southern cooking. He taught her how to prepare what he euphemistically called Kentucky turkey: white pork meat browned in butter.[45]

As lumber mills were established, people moved in and Carra-

bandry . . ., 422; Edward Winslow Martin, *History of the Grange Movement* . . ., 407.

43. Saunders B. Garwood, "Florida State Grange," 166, notes that the first state master was Benjamin F. Wardlaw of Madison; he was succeeded by William H. Wilson of Lake City in 1879, when the Grange received its state charter. See *Laws of Florida* 1879: 151–52.

44. For land purchases by Curtis in 1875, see Franklin County Mortgage Deed Book A, 44. For Kelley's first purchase from Curtis see Franklin County Deed Book A, 399–401. Kelley continued to buy property in the Carrabelle area.

45. Kelley, *Order of the Patrons*, 14–15; Editor Johnson in Apalachicola *Times*, June 11, 1921, credits Kelley with naming the village; Berry in Apalachicola *Times*, Dec. 9, 1922, states that Carrie was Kelley's niece, and in Franklin County Deed Book U, 421–23, two of Kelley's daughters mention Carrie as their cousin.

belle grew. John Van Dyke established a general merchandising store in the early 1880s. A post office was opened in 1878 and in 1887 an official town map was issued. That same year Captain Andy Wing and the *Gazelle* (later the *Crescent City*) opened mail and ferry service between Apalachicola and the new town. The ferry would continue to serve the two locales until 1929.[46]

Kelley and others turned their efforts to obtaining a railroad. Rail connections with Tallahassee would give the lumber industry an east-west route across Florida and an outlet at Jacksonville. There were plans to connect at Tallahassee with a proposed line of thirty-eight miles to Thomasville, Georgia. Carrabelle's timber products would then be accessible to Savannah and northern markets. Beyond that, the Gulf terminus would open New Orleans, Cuba, and South American ports to south Georgia and middle Florida.[47]

Various investors, including Kelley, subscribed to stock in the Carrabelle and Thomasville Railroad Company. Chartered in 1881, the company proposed to build a line from Dog Island harbor to the Georgia boundary by way of Tallahassee.[48] Financial difficulties followed, but in 1883 the Florida legislature chartered the Thomasville, Tallahassee, and Gulf Railroad. Most of the directors were northerners, although local interests were represented by investors from Thomasville and Tallahassee. The line was to extend from Carrabelle to Thomasville.[49]

In August 1883 the first spade of earth for the line was ceremoniously turned in Tallahassee. Not much more was done. There were the usual delays, and twice, in 1885 and 1887, the state legislature amended the original charter and granted time extensions to

46. Apalachicola *Times*, Oct. 24, 1952; May 12, 1977; author's interview with Leo Hance. The name of the post office was changed from Rio Carrabelle to Carrabelle in 1881; see Alford G. Bradburby and E. Story Hallock, *A Chronicle of Florida Post Offices*, 14. See also George Norton Wakefield, *A Florida Sandpiper*, 1–57.

47. For an optimistic statement of the prosperity that railroads would bring, see Tallahassee *Floridian*, Mar. 13, 1883.

48. *Laws of Florida* 1881: 161–64.

49. Ibid., 1884: 114–15. See also Thomasville [Georgia] *Times*, Feb. 10, 1883.

the owners. By 1888, when some twelve miles of track had been laid, the company was absorbed by a new group of investors. In 1889 the line was given a new name and yet another one in 1891: the Carrabelle, Tallahassee, and Georgia Railroad Company. Under that title the road was completed to Tallahassee in October 1893.[50] The severe economic depression of the mid-1890s spoiled plans to extend the line to Thomasville. Unable to erase several consecutive years of deficit financing, the company was sold in 1902 to the Georgia, Florida, and Alabama Railway Company.[51]

In 1890 the small village's population reached 482. Later, Kelley and his family moved to Washington, D.C., where he continued to maintain his interests in Carrabelle until he died in 1913. With both rail and water connections for shipping, Carrabelle became a center for lumber and for the emerging seafood industry. Efforts were made to deepen the channel at the mouth of the river and to improve the harbor. After Hampton Covington established a large naval stores export company, turpentine stills became fixtures no less ubiquitous than the sea gulls that swooped across Saint George Sound. Rio was dropped from the name and, as a tangible mark of progress, Carrabelle was incorporated in 1893. A newspaper, the *Advertiser*, was established shortly after 1900, and Carrabelle entered the twentieth century with a population of 923.[52]

The most direct route from Apalachicola across East Bay, where

50. Thomasville *Times*, Aug. 11, 1883; and ibid., July 23, 1887, quoting Tallahassee *Floridian*, and Mar. 17, 1888, quoting Tallahassee *Tallahassean;* Tallahassee *Weekly Floridian*, Mar. 19, Apr. 16, June 4, 1892; *Laws of Florida* 1885: 78; Extra Session, 1889: 8–9; 1891: 208–9. The company's third name was the Augusta, Tallahassee, and Gulf Railroad Company.

51. Dudley Sady Johnson, "The Railroads of Florida, 1865–1900," 225–26; Rogers, *Thomas County, 1865–1900*, 123–24. The company continued to receive benefits and time extensions from the legislature until 1901.

52. *Twelfth Census* 1900, Population, I, 92; *Laws of Florida* 1893: 285–86. One journal, *Topics*, never got beyond the planning stage, but the *Advertiser* began a brief existence in 1906. See Apalachicola *Times*, May 26, 1906; Jan. 19, 1907. For a legislative memorial to Congress requesting harbor improvement, see *Laws of Florida* 1895: 377. Leo Hance's account of turpentining in the Carrabelle area appears in Apalachicola *Times*, May 4, 1978. Despite Kelley's claim of local businesses worth $2,373,600, only $20,000 was spent in harbor improvement in the 1890s. See ARCE 1900: 2088–91. See also Wakefield, *A Florida Sandpiper*, 115–56.

the myriad creeks and rivers that twisted through the delta of the Apalachicola River emptied, led to Eastpoint. Through the years the site retained a geographical description as its name. There were scattered settlers in the area before the Civil War, and Eastpoint was the connector for Apalachicolans bound by land for Tallahassee and other parts of Middle Florida. The southern shoreline extremity of Eastpoint, often called Cat Point, looked across four miles of water to the center of Saint George Island. In general, Eastpoint marked the end of Apalachicola Bay and the beginning of Saint George Sound.

Eastpoint was established as the result of a combined economic and religious effort that began in the Great Plains. In the mid-1890s a group of families in Nebraska decided to come south. Most of the male adults had been active in the Farmers' Alliance, a social and economic organization that evolved into the People's party. Commonly known as the Populists, the number of embattled agrarians declined after the national election of 1896. Earlier, the Farmers' Alliance had staged successful ventures in cooperative buying and selling. The group of Nebraskans that eventually founded Eastpoint included David H. Brown. Born, raised, and married in Virginia, Brown took his wife, Rebecca Wood, and his three-month-old son, Herbert G., to Nebraska in 1884.

Determined to leave Nebraska, the band of reverse migrants sent Brown to the South to find a suitable location. He visited Georgia and came as far south as Apalachicola. At the port town, he met several people, among them Samuel E. Rice, Sr., a man prominent in the seafood industry and a large landowner. After Brown returned and made his report, the families pooled their resources. They had sufficient funds to charter two freight cars and to purchase an old plantation of a thousand acres located twelve miles east of Columbus, Georgia. It had the advantage of being situated on the Central of Georgia Railroad line. By that time they had formed an organization and adopted a name, the Christian Commonwealth. The collectivistic group was dedicated to forming a colony where the work and the rewards would be shared by all.[53]

53. Author's interview with Herbert Brown and Rebecca Brown, Dec. 28, 1982. The son and daughter of David H. Brown and his wife, Rebecca Wood Brown, they lived in Eastpoint with their sister, Elizabeth Brown. At the time of

Loading their possessions and household goods on the freight cars, the families rattled by train across the country to Georgia. They gave the name Commonwealth to their new settlement in Muscogee County. Shortly after their arrival in 1896, the settlers established a post office, a public school, and a depot. The seventy-five members of the farm community did not all belong to a single religious denomination. The Browns were devout Quakers, and most of the settlers were members of a church.

The experiment at Commonwealth progressed satisfactorily, but the Browns and a few others felt alienated. Their Georgia neighbors were friendly but suspicious. In the meantime Brown visited his home in Virginia, a journey that took him downriver to Apalachicola. Once again he was impressed by the area. Land was available there, and a good living could be wrested from both the earth and the sea. The atmosphere of unease plus the descriptions of Franklin County furnished by Brown were enough to persuade five families and two single men to leave.[54] Brown and the others set to work and completed two house barges in the spring of 1898. They purchased an old barge that was smaller than the thirty-foot boats they constructed themselves. Once more, and for the second time in two years, thirty-one Commonwealth members prepared for a major move. On April 4, a strange flotilla started down the Chattahoochee River. The larger boats were lashed end to end and the older barge was tied alongside. In addition to their human cargo, the barges contained household and farm equipment, horses, chickens, ducks, and a pair of turkeys. If the sojourners were not experienced shipbuilders, at least their barges floated. If they were novice sailors, at least they made it, although leaving as they did at a time when heavy rains made the Chattahoochee River swift and dangerous was hardly advisable. There were no serious mishaps, and the migrants enjoyed the April weather. The foliage along the

---

the interview Herbert was 99, Rebecca 87. Elizabeth, 89, although ill, contributed to the conversation. Brown's recollections, entitled "Long, Long, Ago," are in manuscript in the author's possession. Herbert Brown died Aug. 1, 1984, and his sister, Elizabeth, died Oct. 24, 1984. For the Georgia experiment see Muscogee County Charter Record, Book 1, 227–29; Muscogee County Deed Book KK, 455–57; LL, 554–56.

54. Rebecca Wood Brown to "Dear Sister," Feb. 23, 1898 (in possession of the Brown estate).

riverbanks became increasingly spectacular as they descended. The barges entered the Apalachicola River for the last leg of the journey, and on April 5, after a trip of eleven days, the boats reached the bay.[55]

At Apalachicola they entered into negotiations with Rice, who helped them cross the bay to Eastpoint. There they landed at a place called Godley's Bluff. Later, the practical colonists would disassemble the barges and use the wood in building their homes. Some property was purchased, but larger tracts were bought the next year when an unusual man named Harry C. Vrooman arrived. Vrooman was a late settler at Commonwealth, Georgia, but he decided to follow Brown and the others. Before that the Harvard graduate had been a lecturer and the pastor of a Congregational church at St. Louis, Missouri. He was one of six brothers, all active in social reform. One was an author and founder and president of Ruskin Hall, a workingman's college at Oxford University in England. Another was busy organizing a colony similar to that at Eastpoint on Martha's Vineyard off the coast of Massachusetts (*illustration*, Group 1).[56]

The newcomers did not continue to function under the Christian Commonwealth name. Vrooman bought land from Rice in 1899 and, aided by Brown, set up a cooperative colony. The idea was to establish a group to be called the Co-Workers' Fraternity and to have a separate but related industrial colony. A worker held membership in both: the fraternity was to be concerned with spiritual, philosophical, and religious study, while the colony's emphasis would be on production. By 1900 settlers could obtain land in plots of ten acres. The colony charged a membership fee of one hundred dollars. Later a person was permitted to substitute a year's work in lieu of that payment. Although the workers owned their own land, all profits were shared. The colony expected to engage in farming, the seafood industry, the lumber business, and manufacturing.[57]

When a post office was opened in 1898, the *Crescent City* began

55. Brown, "Long, Long, Ago," 1–4; author's interview with Herbert G. Brown and Rebecca Brown.

56. Apalachicola *Times*, July 28, Aug. 4, 18, 25, Sept. 1, 1900. See V. H. H. Green, *A History of Oxford University*, 194.

57. Apalachicola *Times*, July 28, Aug. 4, 18, 25, Sept. 1, 1900.

stopping daily on its run to Carrabelle with mail, passengers, and supplies. Soon a school was started and a church established. Yet not many settlers moved in. Eastpoint lacked the strategic location and advantages of Apalachicola and Carrabelle. In 1902 an attempt was made to give the village a more practical appeal. Vrooman and Brown joined with Rice and his son, S. Ewing, to charter the Southern Co-Operative Association. Capitalized at $25,000, the new organization stressed and expanded the business side of the venture.[58] But Eastpoint still grew slowly.

Vrooman continued to preach and to discharge the secular duty of promoting the colony. Brown and the farmers were handicapped in the fishing trade by their lack of experience. Nor were the agricultural opportunities along the Gulf coast similar to those of Muscogee County, Georgia, to say nothing of Nebraska. Despite the drawbacks, the resourceful Brown succeeded as a truck farmer. He raised for sale in Apalachicola onions, strawberries, turnip greens, and sweet potatoes; he also planted satsuma oranges and established muscadine grape arbors. But his most profitable crop was sugarcane, which he and his family converted to syrup and sold under the brand name of Bay Croft.[59]

Eastpoint remained more a community than a town, a stopping place for many, an unrealistic but admirable, almost heroic, experiment for the few permanent residents. By 1913 fishing and lumbering had become important. Vrooman went about the piecemeal disposal of land, and the indomitable Brown became a familiar sight on the streets of Apalachicola, vending his fresh vegetables and delicious cane syrup.[60]

As has been seen, after the Civil War, Saint George Island fell into a pattern of shifting, desultory, and confusing ownership. In the meantime, Apalachicola prospered briefly from shipping, then lapsed into decline, only to be revived by the lumber industry. Carrabelle and Eastpoint came into being. A few years after Brown and Vrooman began their cooperative efforts at Eastpoint, William

58. Franklin County Incorporation Book A, 3–10. Bradburby and Hallock, *Florida Post Offices*, 24; Franklin County Deed Book K, 697, 699–701; L, 283.
59. Author's interview with Herbert G. Brown and Rebecca Brown.
60. Apalachicola *Times*, Apr. 26, 1913.

Lee Popham, promoter extraordinary, tried a similar venture on Saint George Island. During the period encompassed by this chapter, the seafood industry became important, and it should be examined before we discuss Saint George Island and the tenure of the Humphrieses and succeeding owners and part owners.

6

Livelihood from the Sea

BECAUSE the waters surrounding Apalachicola—fresh, salt, and brackish—sheltered a variety of marine life, the port was strategically located to become a center of commercial seafood activity. Within the area were oysters, shrimp, red snapper, blue crabs, mullet, skipjack, pompano, spotted weakfish (sea trout), bluefish, catfish, flounder, kingfish, and nonfood fish species such as menhaden.[1] The area extending from Indian Pass through Saint Vincent Sound, across Apalachicola Bay, and through Saint George Sound to Dog Island was rich in natural oyster beds. Warm, brownish, and filled with nutrients, fresh water from the Apalachicola River emptied into the bay guarded by Dog Island, Saint Vincent Island, and the crooked finger of Saint George Island. Oysters flourished in such a sanctuary. It was also a nursery where young shrimp matured before they swam out to sea.

The deeper waters of the Gulf of Mexico were filled with marketable fish, and the area around West Pass teemed with king tarpon, a favorite of sportfishermen. The reefs off Saint George and Dog islands, it was discovered, had a large supply of sponges. The Apalachicola River and the numerous small rivers and streams contained an abundance of freshwater fish: bass, trout, bream, and many others.

What was to become a major means of livelihood for Franklin

1. Apalachicola *Times*, Apr. 4, 1941; Livingston, *Resource Atlas*, 44–53.

County evolved slowly. In the years after Reconstruction, people from Georgia, Alabama, and noncoastal parts of Florida visited the Gulf coast. Their journeys were usually made in late summer and early fall, and their main purpose was to obtain fish. Wagons of all descriptions creaked slowly down and across crude roads that became increasingly sandy nearer the coast. The people often came in family groups, camped out for several days, and combined a vacation with their quest for fish. They enjoyed fresh fish and oysters while salting down the excess catch. Salted fish by the barrel were taken home to be eaten in the winter months. Local residents sold fish to the visitors, especially mullet, and it was reported that "on the coast line of Wakulla and Franklin counties the revenue derived form this industry is considerable."[2]

Before the late 1880s, responsibility for regulating Florida's fishing industry lay with each county. The need for a statewide agency was answered in 1889 with the creation of the Florida Fish Commission.[3] But it never had the funds to regulate the industry, failed to accomplish much, and was abolished in 1905. A new law shifted responsibility back to the counties, where fish and game wardens oversaw local ordinances.[4]

In places such as Apalachicola, where the seafood industry was expanding, the system proved inadequate. Between 1913 and 1915, three important laws were passed by the state legislature. They were enacted during the administration of Park Trammell, 1913–17, a Progressive governor and later longtime U.S. senator. In 1913 the Shell Fish Commission was created and placed in the Department of Agriculture. That same year a Department of Game and Fish was established to direct freshwater fisheries. In 1915 all saltwater fishing regulations were consolidated into a single act,

2. Long, *Florida Portrayed*, 59. See Tallahassee *Weekly Floridian*, Sept. 23, 1873, for a "guano" fish factory (probably utilizing menhaden) at Cat Point across the bay from Apalachicola.

3. *Laws of Florida*, Extra Session, 1889: 71–72; see also Derald Pacetti, Jr., "Shrimping at Fernandina, Florida, before 1920: Industry Development, Fisheries Regulation, Wartime Maturation," 66–73. The U.S. Fish Commission was not created until 1872, as the result of pressure from the American Fish Culture Association.

4. *Laws of Florida* 1905: 116–18. The wardens were appointed by the county commissioners upon the receipt of a petition bearing seventy-five names.

and responsibility for enforcement was placed under a Shell Fish Commissioner.[5] T. R. Hodges—imperious, controversial, and destined to figure prominently in events at Apalachicola and on Saint George Island—was the first commissioner.

Oysters became the first important seafood industry in the Apalachicola area. Capable of changing their sex from male to female, oysters release either sperm or eggs. The sperm is carried away in the currents and forms a dense white stream, which quickly disperses in the water. The eggs are dispelled and fertilization takes place in the sea. Within a few hours after fertilization the eggs develop into tiny larvae, which are called spat. Still microscopic in size, the little oysters are extremely active, swimming about by means of tiny whiskerlike hairs or cilia. Swarming by the thousands in surface waters, they are carried away from the home oyster bed by tides and currents. After two weeks the small oyster, which has grown a shell, sinks to the bottom. It crawls about by means of a powerful foot until it finds some clean, hard surface, known as cultch (or culch). Quickly expelling a jet of cementlike substance from a special gland, the young oyster rolls over and presses its left shell into the adhesive material. Unless transplanted or dislodged, the oyster has no power of movement. In a moment it is planted for life.[6]

After the attachment is completed, the spat continues to develop. The oysters measure one-fourth inch within two weeks. They become marketable, depending on conditions, in two to five years. Conditions in Apalachicola Bay were excellent. In northern waters, oysters hibernate during cold weather and do not feed until the water warms again. In the bay and sounds adjacent to Apalachicola, the water temperature fluctuates with the seasons but never gets cold enough to cause the oysters to hibernate.

Oysters feed on microscopic plants and organic matter in the

5. Pacetti, "Shrimping at Fernandina," 80–94; *Laws of Florida* 1913, 1: 426–52; 460–67; 1915: 163–71.

6. Robert M. Ingle and William K. Whitfield, Jr., *Oyster Culure in Florida*, 2; Apalachicola *Times*, Feb. 26, 1938, quoting *Fish and Oyster Reporter* (Jan., 1938); Donald K. Tressler, *Marine Products of Commerce: Their Acquisition, Handling, Biological Aspects, and the Science and Technology of Their Preparation and Preservation*, 514–28.

water above the bottoms on which they live. Food is obtained by filtering, and an oyster can strain as much as twenty-six quarts of water an hour through its gills. The oysters that survive the developmental process (some 90 percent of the eggs fall on grass or mud and die) have natural enemies: several varieties of crabs, snails, starfish, leeches, and boring sponges. Besides the danger from predators, the fragile oyster bed can be destroyed by disease, fresh water, excessive salinity, cold, heat, shifting, and sudden changes in water levels. In the twentieth century, pollution has become a serious menace.[7]

It was the oyster as food, not its appearance or life cycle, that caught the interest of humans. People have fancied them from early times. The Chinese and Japanese attempted oyster cultivation thirty centuries ago. Natural beds could not meet the demands of the ancient Greeks and Romans, and in the year 95 B.C., oysters were transplanted from Britain to beds at the Roman resort city of Baia. English settlers in North America found them on the Atlantic coast as far north as Maine. By 1840 Connecticut leased underwater grounds for the cultivation of oysters. The state's natural growing areas were almost depleted, but each spring thousands of bushels of oysters were brought in from the rich beds of Chesapeake Bay for planting and marketing the following autumn.

By the 1860s, Americans were practicing the French method of oyster cultivation: the placement of clean surfaces such as oyster shells, tiles, or brush on the bottom near beds of adult spawning oysters. When the larval oysters were ready to set, they attached themselves to the clean cultch, assuring large-scale cultivation. During the same period New Jersey oystermen developed another method. They transplanted young oysters from natural beds to grounds bathed with water of a higher salt content, where they grew more rapidly and reached market size sooner.[8]

The aboriginal Indians who lived along Apalachicola Bay ate

7. Ingle and Whitfield, *Oyster Culture*, 2; William K. Brooks, *The Oyster*, 17–45; C. M. Yonge, *Oysters*, 52–77; Fred Eugene Nichy, "The Effect of Predators on the Mortality of Oysters in a High Salinity Area in Florida," 41, 54; Apalachicola *Times*, Nov. 2, 1978; Livingston, *Resource Atlas*, 38–39.

8. Apalachicola *Times*, Jan. 2, 1938, quoting Dr. Lewis Radcliffe, director of the Oyster Institute of North America, Washington, D.C.

oysters in large quantities and left numerous shell mounds as testimony to their appetites. The numerous explorers and travelers in the region invariably commented on the profusion and delicacy of the bay's oysters. Commercially sold on the local market at Apalachicola as early as 1836, oysters were not harvested in quantity until the 1850s. Packed in barrels, they were shipped to neighboring states and sometimes to northern markets. Experiments with canning oysters failed because the packers did not understand the practical application of sterilization by heat to destroy the bacteria of fermentation.[9] During the Civil War the oyster beds lay undisturbed and by the 1870s were in prime condition. After the conflict, Sidney Lanier commented that the area's "fish, and particularly its oysters, are celebrated for their excellent flavor."[10]

Intensive efforts to exploit the beds began in the late 1870s. Before that, in 1870, John C. Messina and Company (he added the title because he employed one man), Yent and Alexander (with one employee), John Miller, and Joseph Segras earned their livelihoods as dealers in "oysters and fish."[11] In 1881 a state law encouraged individuals to plant oysters in Florida's public waters. By applying to the county commissioners and adding specifications of planting and harvesting, an individual could be awarded exclusive oystering rights in designated waters.[12]

Various beds in the bay area had different amounts of salinity in the waters around them, and each bar enjoyed fame for its characteristic mark and flavor. Harvesting in the nineteenth century was accomplished by tonging, hogging, and, with limitations, dredging.

Tongs were long, double-handled rakes with double vise-grip prongs. From his small skiff the oysterman could reach nine or more feet into the water, scrape shells from the beds, and bring the oysters to the surface. Tonging was (and is) laborious, primitive, and inefficient. It also was and remains an art. The skilled tonger combined stamina, coordination, and dexterity and operated at a

9. John G. Ruge, "The Canning Industry in the South," 15.

10. Sidney Lanier, *Florida: Its Scenery, Climate, and History,* 149.

11. For a contemporary survey see Lieut. Franklin Swift, "Report of a Survey of the Oyster Regions of St. Vincent Sound, Apalachicola Bay, and St. George Sound, Florida," 187–217.

12. *Laws of Florida* 1881: 92–94.

sustained level of production. Like the cotton-picking field hand to the north of him, the oysterman depended for his income on the volume of his harvest. The typical oysterman went out in his boat early in the morning. Besides the tongs, other essentials were a culling iron, culling board, and a drag anchor. As the oysters were brought up they were deposited on the culling board, which extended across the boat. Once the troughlike board was full, the tonger ceased gathering and, taking the iron, used swift strokes to break off extraneous material and small oysters. In turn, the culled matter was returned to the water. Skillful and rapid culling was almost as vital an operation as tonging. Warehouse (or oysterhouse) dealers who purchased the tonger's oysters measured them in large tin buckets or in barrels (*illustrations*, Group 1).[13]

Hogging took place at low tide when the oyster beds were exposed. Then it was possible to walk out and pick them up by hand. The technique was simple but limited. Dredges were used, particularly once canning became popular. The process was much more productive than tonging, but it harmed the beds. When a wire basket or dredge was dragged across the bars, it knocked many oysters into surrounding mud where they died and did physical injury to the beds. Dredges were not used to gather oysters that were shipped raw or in the shell. As early as 1885 a state law prohibited the use of dredges or dragnets in natural oyster beds. In the twentieth century, additional legislation made the use of dredges entirely illegal.[14]

John G. Ruge (already mentioned for his role in property transfers on Saint George Island) was an important figure in the local shellfish industry. Born in Apalachicola in 1854, he was the son of Herman Ruge, who migrated from Hanover, Germany, in the early 1840s. Herman established a machine shop and hardware store in Apalachicola. John and his brother, George H., worked for their father, and after the Civil War the firm of Herman Ruge and Sons became the Ruge Brothers Canning Company. It was organized in

13. Author's interview with Robert L. Howell, clerk of the Circuit Court of Franklin County, December 30, 1982. The author is indebted to many people in Franklin county, who, over the years, have explained oystering techniques to him.

14. *Laws of Florida* 1885: 58–59.

1885, and John emerged as the dominant partner. Taking advantage of new techniques in canning—pasteurization—the Ruges became Florida's first successful commercial packers.[15] John Ruge was among the first Floridians to advocate planting oyster shells near the natural beds. The local *Times* agreed and praised Ruge. The spat would have places to settle upon during the spawning season, and the newspaper was convinced that "the oystermen and dealers who do this thing will be casting bread upon the water to be returned to them a thousand fold."[16]

Stephen Ewing Rice, the man who sold the property at Eastpoint to Brown and Vrooman, and Joseph Messina were two other pioneers who helped establish the sale of shellfish as a permanent commercial venture. Born in Huntsville, Alabama, in 1838, Rice moved to Texas and commanded an infantry unit during the Civil War. He came to Apalachicola in 1882, and, aided by his two sons, Steven E., Jr., and Rob Roy, founded a large and successful oyster-packing company. Locally born Joseph Messina gained control of the Bay City Packing Company in 1896. He expanded from oysters and marketed a variety of profitable seafood products under the trademark "Pearl Brand."[17]

By the twentieth century the oyster industry was a significant part of the county's economy. Steven E. Rice, Jr., headed his own Apalachicola Packing Company, and there were many small dealers. In 1915 some four hundred men manned 117 oyster boats, 250 shuckers worked in various oysterhouses, and a number of other workers were employed in two canneries.[18] Profits were good, but there was strong opposition to Shell Commissioner Hodges,

15. Ruge, "Canning Industry in the South," 15; Apalachicola *Times*, Aug. 1, 1931.

16. Apalachicola *Times*, Apr. 2, 1902. Visitors to Apalachicola who held detached views urged the planting of oyster shells. See the opinion of W. I. Gibbs, a South Carolinian, ibid., May 30, 1903.

17. Ibid., Dec. 20, 1913; Nov. 7, 1936. Rice, a strong character, was captured during the war but escaped from a prisoner of war train near Atlanta, Georgia. When his son, Steven, Jr., married the socially prominent Carolyn Burke Floyd in 1900, it was the social event of the year. See brochure on the Bay City Packing Company in the Special Collections Room, University of West Florida.

18. Apalachicola *Times*, Dec. 18, 24, 1915; Jan. 22, 1916.

who enforced a state law requiring a license tax and a privilege tax of two cents a barrel.[19]

A storm in 1903 damaged some of the beds, but they were replanted. An absence of cold weather and fresh water from the rivers caused demand to outdistance supply in 1906. Then in 1907 the famed Dr. Harvey Wiley of the U.S. Department of Agriculture declared that oysters were safe only if shipped in their shells. His request for a federal law prohibiting bulk shipment sent chills through the oystermen of Franklin and nearby counties but was never acted upon. Despite such occasional setbacks, by 1914 the fishing and oystering industries ranked second in Franklin only to lumbering, and the county emerged as the state's leading producer of oysters.[20]

Harvesting and marketing sponges became a short-lived, limited, but colorful industry. The gathering of the marine animals dates to several centuries before the Christian era (Homer mentioned the efforts of early Greek divers). Down to the 1840s, sponges came entirely from the Mediterranean Sea. In that decade the French began importing them from the Bahamas. Sponge beds were found in the waters of the Florida Keys, and in 1849 the first shipment from Key West to New York City was made. The industry was centered in the Keys until around 1870, when extensive beds were located in the Gulf of Mexico north and south of Cedar Key. In the late 1880s and early 1890s, Greek spongers operating out of Tarpon Springs emerged as leaders of the trade.[21]

A living sponge, one of the oldest branches of animal life, grows attached to the bottom and bears no resemblance to the market product. It reproduces asexually and has a solid, slimy, fleshy body varying from grayish yellow to brown and black. Traversed by numerous chambers and canals, the sponge varies in appearance and

19. Ibid., Nov. 20, 1915.

20. Ibid., Nov. 21, 1903; Nov. 10, 1906; Mar. 9, 1907; see also June 20, 1914, quoting Pensacola *Journal;* John J. Brice, "The Fish and Fisheries of the Coastal Waters of Florida," 263–342.

21. Carolina Johnson Comnenos, "Florida's Sponge Industry: A Cultural and Economic History"; George T. Frantzis, *The Story of the Sponges of Tarpon Springs: Strangers at Ithaca,* 38–65.

consistency but looks like beef liver. After the soft, fleshy matter is removed, the skeleton is dried and becomes the familiar sponge. Several varieties—sheepswool (the most valuable), yellow, grass, and wire—were found off the coast of Florida.[22]

The first sponges in Florida were plucked by men wading or diving into shallow areas. A more sophisticated process was developed when sponge beds were found in deeper waters. From the mid-1870s to the early decades of the twentieth century, Apalachicola was a part of the industry. By 1879 the port's fleet had sixteen vessels. When more beds were discovered in the reefs off Dog Island, local seafood men outfitted additional ships. Larger vessels from Apalachicola—among them the sloops *My Stars, Cootie,* and *NonSuch* and the schooners *Ruge, Lillie B.,* and *Golden Age*—put out to sea for four weeks or more. The sponge boat carried several dinghies or small rowboats about twelve feet long; it served as the mother ship where the sponges were cleaned, strung in long lines to be dried in the sun, and then stored below. Around the turn of the century, a dozen sponge boats still operated out of Apalachicola and Carrabelle.[23]

Sponges were taken by a method known as "hooking." Two men, the oarsman (sculler) and the hooker, used the dinghy to search the area. The hooker (or diver) sat in the bow and scanned the murky waters through a glass-bottomed wooden bucket. By thrusting the bucket a few inches beneath the water's surface, a telescope effect was achieved. When the sponges were spotted on the bottom, the oarsman was signaled. He then maneuvered the boat into position for the hooker, who used his pole—a sharp-pronged tool about one and a half inches thick and fifteen to forty feet long—to bring up the sponges. Most of the hooking was done

22. John M. Gonatos, *The Story of the Sponge,* 6; Tressler, *Marine Products of Commerce,* 671–83.

23. Other sponging vessels were the *Liberty, Clara, Hero, Jessie Mae, Mascot,* and *Henrietta Sharit.* For an account of the local industry see Joseph Messina in Apalachicola *Times,* July 26, 1946. John E. Grady, collector of customs, reported in 1886 that spongers were operating three miles from land. See U.S. Fish Commission, *Bulletin* 6 (1886): 140. For Apalachicola's early sponge trade see Tallahassee *Weekly Floridian,* Sept. 23, 1873; and Comnenos, "Florida's Sponge Industry," 19.

in four fathoms (twenty-four feet) of water. The pole was like a rake and had two to five tines or teeth set at right angles to the shaft. Once the larger vessels had a full cargo, they returned to port.[24]

Some boats took their catch to St. Marks, Tarpon Springs, and Key West. Those going to Apalachicola docked at City Wharf, unloaded the sheepswool, grass, and yellow sponges, and sold them. The three principal buyers were M. Brash, Sr., John G. Ruge, and Joseph Messina. After inspecting the catch, the buyers made sealed bids. The successful bidder later shipped the sponges to firms in San Francisco, St. Louis, Baltimore, and New York.[25]

A crew shared the profits. Sometimes the money was good, as in 1901 when the crew of the *Mascot* earned shares of thirty-two dollars and the catch of the *Lillie B.* reportedly brought seven hundred dollars. In December the *Golden Age* docked at Apalachicola with 275 bunches of sponges. The water was constantly muddy in 1902, and the sponge ships returned from the reefs empty or with greatly reduced catches.[26]

Laws were passed to regulate the size of sponges taken in the Gulf, but profits were uncertain and the known beds became depleted. Boat owners in Apalachicola began withdrawing from the business. At its peak in 1901 the industry at Apalachicola brought in $20,000 annually, but by 1903 the market had declined drastically.[27]

A revival came in 1905 when the development of diving gear allowed sponging in deeper waters. New beds were discovered, and, with the sponging range extended, they could be exploited. Some Franklin County businessmen resumed the trade, but they were soon eclipsed by Greek divers and ships from Tarpon Springs.[28] Operating expenses rose and some, for example, in 1911, Mitchell

24. Gonatos, *Story of the Sponge*, 7–8; see especially Vasil Petrof, "A Study of the Florida Natural Sponge Industry with Special Emphasis on Its Marketing Problems," 21–80.

25. Joseph Messina in Apalachicola *Times*, July 26, 1946.

26. Apalachicola *Times*, July 27, Dec. 7, 1901; June 28, Aug. 2, 23, 1902.

27. *Laws of Florida* 1901: 141–42. Sponges had to be at least four inches in diameter before they could be harvested. See also Apalachicola *Times*, Mar. 30, 1901; May 30, 1903; and Comnenos, "Florida's Sponge Industry," 44–51.

28. Apalachicola *Times*, June 10, July 7, 1905.

Peters of Apalachicola, who had made heavy investments, abandoned their efforts. Yet when important beds were found off Dog Island in 1911, nine or more crews of Greek spongers began operations there. Predictions that a Greek community and a permanent market would be established at Carrabelle did not materialize, and the sponges were taken to the exchange at Tarpon Springs for sale.[29]

The divers, clumsy in their heavy equipment and resembling the astronauts of later decades, engaged in a dangerous occupation. Their early paraphernalia made movement awkward and difficult, and they were wholly dependent upon a flow of air pumped to them from the surface. In 1912 a Greek diver died off Carrabelle when his air tube was accidentally severed.[30]

The uncertainties of supply plus operational expenses caused the sponge industry to decline. People in Franklin County turned more and more to oyster production and later to shrimp. Yet for a number of years sponging was a remunerative activity.

The waters around Apalachicola were known to contain large quantities of shrimp, but little effort was made to develop the industry in the nineteenth century. Historically, shrimp were a by-product of seining operations. The industry evolved at several locations, but the first significant shrimping was begun by a Sicilian immigrant, Sollecito Salvatore, around 1900. Salvatore's operations were at Fernandina on Florida's northeast coast. The resourceful immigrant Anglicized his name to Mike Salvador and by 1902 was using the first power-driven boat with a haul seine. The innovation allowed him to work in deeper water and increase his catch. Before World War I other developments, such as the otter trawl, permitted the industry to expand.[31]

Curious in appearance, like dwarfed refugees from a prehistoric age, shrimp go through complex larval stages. They hatch their eggs offshore in a twenty-four-hour period. The tiny shrimp then

29. Ibid., January 21, Dec. 2, 23, 1911; Feb. 3, Mar. 3, 1912.

30. Ibid., Mar. 23, 1912. See also Comnenos, "Florida's Sponge Industry," 68–83.

31. Edwin A. Joyce, Jr., and Bonnie Eldred, *The Florida Shrimping Industry,* 14; Pacetti, "Shrimping at Fernandina," 2, 34–43; Tressler, *Marine Products of Commerce,* 548–60; Apalachicola *Times,* May 14, 1938.

move slowly toward shore and take up a bottom-dwelling existence in the grass flats of shallow waters. This nursery period is one of rapid growth. As they develop, the shrimp move from the inshore waters to the deeper reaches of the bay. When they attain a growth of approximately four inches, they migrate again, making their way to offshore waters where they complete maturation and spawn.[32]

After 1900 a reliable market was established. In 1919 the state legislature passed a law regulating shrimping operations—the statute referred to the crustaceans as "Salt Water Crawfish." By the 1920s shrimpers shifted their operations from Fernandina to St. Augustine. Later, they skipped across to the area from Apalachicola to Pensacola, across the Gulf coast of Alabama, Mississippi, Louisiana, and Texas, then back to the Tortugas, and over to Campeche, Mexico.[33]

Pink (the largest and most important), white, and brown shrimp became commercially important in Florida, and all three varieties were found near Apalachicola. Fresh shrimp sold on the local market, but as late as 1897 one writer observed that in Apalachicola, as in many coastal towns, "the fishermen throw them back into the water when found in nets."[34] The situation changed quickly after 1900 as some oystermen shifted to shrimping and others engaged in both operations. By 1902 there were efforts to establish a canning factory.[35] For years shrimpers used boats constructed for shallow-water work and seldom ventured to distant grounds. If shrimping proved bad, the owners either tied their boats up or engaged in catching blue crabs for the local crabmeat market.[36] The latter "sometime" operation also became a full-scale industry in the twentieth century.

32. Joyce and Eldred, *Florida Shrimping Industry*, 9–10.

33. *Laws of Florida* 1919, 1: 276–77; Joyce and Eldred, *Florida Shrimping Industry*, 14–15, 21–22.

34. John N. Cobb, "Possibilities for an Increased Development of Florida Fishery Resources," *Bulletin of the United States Fish Commission* 17 (1897): 351. See also ibid., 349–51. Author's interview with Anthony Taranto, May 11, 1983. Like his father, Taranto is engaged in the seafood industry.

35. Apalachicola *Times*, Oct. 4, 1902.

36. Robley M. Miles, "Analysis of the 'Trash Fish' of Shrimp Trawlers Operating in Apalachicola Bay and the Adjacent Gulf of Mexico," 7. For the catching

By 1915 the Bay City Packing Company was shipping canned shrimp to Boston and other markets. Captain Frank Comforter and his crew on the *Grady,* as well as other boats, found that the company paid well. The Bay City Packing Company and other firms also dealt in fresh shrimp. Yet shrimp remained enough of a novelty that the *Times* printed an editorial in 1916 explaining to locals how to fry them.[37] When it was discovered that pink and brown shrimp were nocturnal, night shrimping began and grew far beyond daytime operations for the white variety. Soon the industry became as important to the local economy as oystering.

The catch and sale of sturgeon never became a regular business, but each spring when the large fish appeared in the bay area to spawn, men such as Captain Charles Anderson got busy. In one twenty-four-hour period in 1900, Anderson and his crew caught seventy sturgeon. The fish was in demand for eating and even more so for its eggs, which were popular as caviar. Shortly after Anderson's catch, at least 120 sturgeon were landed near the western end of Saint George Island and exhibited at the wharf in Apalachicola.[38]

The presence of water influenced more than just the economy of Franklin County. Water formed the world for many people and shaped many facets of their lives. The county's southern boundary was a constantly changing shoreline marked by usually tranquil waves of blue-green that washed in with edges of white. The Apalachicola River, sometimes pearl-colored and sometimes the hue of café au lait, formed the western demarcation. When the river's fresh water emptied into the bay, it turned brackish and then salty by the time it was impounded by the restraining arm of Saint George Island. At the eastern extremity was the Ochlockonee River. Narrow and brown where it rose in southwestern Georgia but wide and clear when it reached Franklin County, the Ochlockonee was a broad expanse of slate-blue lined by magnolias, tupelos, black gums, and other marsh trees. In the interior to the

---

and processing of crabs see Apalachicola *Times,* June 24, 1938; Apr. 21, 1939; see also Livingston, *Resource Atlas,* 40–43.

37. Apalachicola *Times,* December 18, 24, 1915; Jan. 22, Mar. 11, 1916.
38. Ibid., Sept. 22, Oct. 6, 1900.

north, accessed through a labyrinth of swamps, waterways, and large tracts of forests, lay Liberty County.

Except in times of storm and flood, the waters were a blessing. Apalachicola's shipping and trade in the antebellum era were made possible by water. Invigorated by abundant moisture and a hot climate, trees and plants grew in amazing variety and profusion. Timber products brought profits for mill owners and paychecks for workers. Readily available seafood was so abundant that it filled local needs and underwrote commercial activities.

To prosper from the sea required hard work and luck, and few became wealthy. To make a modest living from the sea also required hard work and luck, and that was the lot of many people of Franklin County. But their way of life could not be measured by material comforts and bank deposits. They took pleasure from many things that cost nothing. In the spring the county turned into a patchwork of green, and the air was permeated with the perfume of tupelo trees. Formations of Canadian geese arrived at Saint George Island in the fall, when the foliage of the cypress trees turned to burnt orange and other hardwoods smeared the woods with vivid colors.

If the people took their unspoiled environment for granted, they also took advantage of what it offered: hunting for birds and animals, leisurely fishing, and outings to Saint George and other nearby islands. Baiting a hook and dropping it in the water was a relaxing way to pass the time, and the Apalachicola *Times* noted in November 1906, "Pole fishing continues abundant." [39]

39. Ibid., Nov. 10, 1936.

7

Island Owners

BENEFITING from Apalachicola's improving economy and impressed by the success of newly founded Carrabelle, the people of Franklin County entered the 1880s with optimism. In 1881 Saint George Island became the property of the Humphries family. The senior members of the family were Henry and Mary Elizabeth. They had four sons: Horace H., Henry N., Felix J., and Lemuel K. The elder Humphrieses (even before Horace H. bought Sinclair's holdings on the island) owned an undivided one-fourth of Saint George Island (sixteen hundred acres). They acquired the property because of their interest in the estate of J. W. Humphries, a kinsman. In 1882, Henry and Mary Elizabeth gave the sixteen hundred acres to their children. They stipulated that if either parent ever needed and was refused support or assistance by any or all of their sons, the property would revert to the parents.[1]

In 1888, six years later, a part of Saint George Island changed owners. At that time taxes amounting to $77 were paid on the one-third that was the estate of J. W. Humphries and $154 on Horace H. Humphries's share.[2] On December 7, 1888, Emmalee I. Rice and Mary F. Smith bought two-ninths of the island from Mary A. Fuller and W. M. Humphries. The actual number of acres was not

1. Franklin County Deed Book B, 269–71. No reversion was ever made.
2. Franklin County Commissioners' Minutes, Book 2, 123.

mentioned but apparently was part of Little Saint George Island. A search of the county records fails to reveal when or how Fuller and Humphries (not one of the brothers) obtained their title.[3]

The events of 1888 were clear compared to the chaotic developments of 1889. When the elder Henry Humphries died intestate in November 1886, his son Henry N. was appointed administrator. Added later as administrators were William H. Neel (whose relationship with the island would not end there) and John M. Fowler. Mary Elizabeth and her sons could not agree on an equitable division, and, after permitting Samuel E. Rice and Patrick Lovett to arbitrate their differences, the Humphries family put the estate up at public auction in 1889.[4]

While the Humphries family were deciding what to do with the estate, Emmalee I. Rice and Mary Smith relocated the site of their holdings on Saint George Island. In September 1889, they paid the four Humphries brothers one dollar for the sixteen hundred acres they had inherited from their parents.[5] On the same day the two women and their husbands—Samuel E. Rice, who had helped arbitrate the dispute between Mary Elizabeth and her sons, and C. H. Smith—sold their interest in the island to the four Humphrieses for one dollar. That two-ninths interest had mysteriously grown to five thousand acres.[6] No reason for what was, in effect, an exchange of sixteen hundred acres for five thousand acres was ever offered.

Saint George Island's economic attraction was lessened by its inaccessibility. Yet the timber on it, particularly the slash pines, had some value for cutting and even more as a source of naval stores, especially turpentine. The absence of permanent residents made the island an excellent cattle range. Horace H. Humphries decided to make his property yield what profits it could. In October 1889, he made an arrangement with the previously mentioned William H. Neel of Apalachicola. Neel agreed to put one hundred head of

---

3. For the sale see Franklin County Deed Book E, 350–51. The price was one hundred dollars.

4. Franklin County Record of Wills, 1846–94: 288, 324–28.

5. Franklin County Deed Book E, 350–51

6. Ibid., Book R, 334–40.

"fair average stock cattle" on the island at his own expense. Half of the cattle would become the property of Humphries, and one undivided half of the island would be deeded over to Neel.[7] By any measure, Neel had struck a bargain in swapping fifty head of cattle for half an island. The attractions of timber, turpentine, and cattle now were added to Saint George Island's potential as an integral part of the expanding seafood industry. The site of countless fishing, hunting, camping, and swimming excursions—all of them brief outings—Saint George Island had the additional possibility of becoming a place for permanent vacation cottages, perhaps a town (*illustration,* Group 2).

The early 1890s were prosperous, and the Humphries family, as major owners of the island, expected that their investment would somehow pay off. The Rices and Smiths had retained at least part of their holdings—in 1890, they paid fourteen dollars in taxes on fractional sections.[8] Early in 1891 they sold sixteen hundred acres to John A. Murray for one thousand dollars. It turned out to be a bad investment for Murray because the next year he sold the land to Mary E. Humphries for five hundred dollars.[9]

In August 1893, Horace H. and Henry N.—acting for themselves, their two brothers, Mary Elizabeth, and Mary P. Humphries (wife of Lemuel K.)—regained William H. Neel's share in the island. Neel and his wife, Sophronia, sold them two thousand acres as well as the stock of cattle and hogs that ranged Saint George Island. The price was twenty-five hundred dollars, and Neel was also to get 80 percent of all money received from the sale of livestock.[10] Unable to pay cash, the Humphries family executed a mortgage to Neel covering seven thousand acres on Saint George Island.[11]

In the United States, the first half of the "Gay Nineties" turned quickly from what seemed a promising upturn into a crippling economic depression. The entire nation was stunned. Franklin County,

7. Ibid., Book E, 68–69. None of the other Humphries was mentioned as being a party to the arrangement.
8. Franklin County Commissioners' Minutes, Book 2, 247.
9. Franklin County Deed Book E, 739–42; R, 340–42.
10. Ibid., Book R, 242–45.
11. Franklin County Mortgage Book A, 417–21.

like most of the South, had a marginal economy at best, and fore-closures and bankruptcies became common occurrences. Nature appeared to be a part of the conspiracy as the embryonic oyster industry suffered from hurricanes and freezes. Beyond all of that, there was overharvesting of the oyster bars.[12]

Financially embarrassed like their neighbors, the Humphries family struggled to pay off their note to Neel. But when it became due at the end of fifteen months, they still owed $1,331.61. The result was that Neel brought suit, and the island and the livestock were put up for sale. Robert G. Baker served as commissioner, fol-lowed the required legal procedures, and on February 12, 1896, sold Saint George Island. Among the crowd of bidders gathered in front of the courthouse, no one matched Daniel O. Neel's offer of five hundred dollars.[13]

The suit growing out of the mortgage executed in 1893 and still unpaid in 1896 named all of the Humphries family. In truth, Hor-ace H., who was a bachelor, had liquidated his holdings in 1894. First, he sold to Mary E. Humphries his undivided interest of 4,980 acres (as described in Commissioner Orman's deed of 1881); next, he sold her his undivided one-fourth interest in 1,600 acres of the island and certain blocks in Apalachicola (acquired jointly with his brothers from their parents in 1882). Horace included in the transaction a dappled, cream-colored horse, a yoke of oxen, an ox wagon, and all his undivided interest in the cattle and hogs on Saint George Island.[14]

By 1896 it appeared that the Humphries family no longer had any claims to the island, although this would not prove to be so, and that it was the property of Daniel O. and Alma E. Neel. The day before Christmas 1900, the Neels sold Saint George Island, an estimated seven thousand acres, to Paul S. King and F. R. King.

12. See Lieutenant Franklin Swift, "Report of a Survey of the Oyster Regions of St. Vincent Sound, Apalachicola Bay, and St. George Sound, Florida," in *Annual Report of the U.S. Fish Commission for 1896*, Part 22: 213.

13. Circuit Court file, William H. Neel v. H. N. Humphries et al. See also Franklin County Deed Book H, 440–42.

14. Franklin County Deed Book G, 745–47. Mary E. later paid fifteen dollars at a sheriff's sale for lots of Horace H. that were put up for debt in Apalachicola. See Franklin County Deed Book I, 65–67.

The Kings, who lived in Colbert County, Alabama, were outsiders but not newcomers. They had bought and sold land in Franklin County as early as the 1880s.[15] The purchase price of Saint George Island was $507.25. Neel included all of the livestock, which meant some goats as well as the cattle and hogs. The Kings also assumed the balance of an 1896 mortgage of $992.25 from Neel to George F. Wefing of Apalachicola.[16]

Other than the principals involved in the sale, no one in Franklin County was the least bit concerned. The citizens continued to use Saint George Island as if the island were in the public domain (*illustrations*, Group 2). In 1901 Captain Andy Wing carried excursionists twice weekly to the island on board the *Crescent City*, a steamer owned by the Cypress Lumber Company. Each May or June one of his work crews repaired and made fit a wharf on the bay side.[17]

Giant sea turtles were frequent visitors to Saint George Island. Female turtles emerged on the beach, crawled awkwardly across the sand, and, leaving an unmistakable trail, disappeared into the dunes. There they hollowed out cavities, laid their eggs, and carefully covered the nests with sand. Then in their ponderous gait the turtles returned to the sea. Searching for turtle eggs became a favorite pastime for human visitors to Saint George Island. One group found a thousand eggs at a single outing to Nick's Hole, a bayside inlet justly famous for its rattlesnakes.[18]

Fishing for flounder was a favorite activity on Saint George Island and also from the mainland shore. The brown, pancake-shaped flounder was a prized fish because it was delicious to eat and a challenge to catch. The nighttime activity carried over from the nineteenth century into the twentieth with more sophisticated and expensive equipment but with the same basic strategy. As one zealot described the art, the flounder was "most frequently cap-

15. In 1883 the Kings bought land and in 1888 sold land in Franklin County. See Franklin County Deed Book B, 300; D, 537–38.

16. Ibid., Book K, 148–51.

17. Apalachicola *Times*, Apr. 13, June 22, 1901; July 12, 1902.

18. Ibid., July 23, 1902. Capt. Joe Sangree claimed that some rattlesnakes at Nick's Hole had skins large enough to make an overcoat. See ibid., Feb. 4, 1903.

tured with nothing more than a nail-pointed stick, a lantern and an optimistic disregard for sting-rays."[19]

Coming close to shore with the rising tide, flounders sank themselves into the sand, often with only their eyes (both on the same side of their head) protruding, and waited to pounce on smaller fish. If the bottom were smooth it was best to catch them as the tide began to fall. On a rough bottom packed with oyster shells, like much of the shoal waters around Saint George Island, it was best to wade beyond the shells and wait in the smooth gullies as the tide came in. Flounders could be taken from a boat, but the preferred means was for several people to wade forward slowly, making out the forms on the bottom by the light of everything from fat lightwood sticks to, later, gasoline lanterns. After the flounder was speared, it had to be picked up. Its human captor reached under the fish and placed it in a boat or sack. Stingrays (or stingarees) closely resembled flounders, and it was in the final process of landing the fish that the danger lay: stepping on a ray and being spurred in the foot, ankle, or calf. Still, the possibility of a wound from the poisonous spine in the tail of a disturbed stingray deterred few if any from the sport of flounder fishing. Saint George Island was an ideal setting, and more than one romance in Franklin County began during flounder fishing parties on moonlit nights.[20]

At the turn of the century, it was not uncommon for a group of men and women to take tents and spend several days on Saint George Island fishing, swimming, and exploring. By 1902, Captain Andy's men had laid a boardwalk all the way across the island.[21] There were no objections from the Kings and none from the swarm of—technically speaking—trespassers.

Saint George Island was full of wildlife—rabbits, squirrels, raccoons, opossums, deer, alligators, snakes—and was the permanent home of a wide variety of land and sea birds. From time to time the island was leased for cattle and there were goats and wild hogs. In

19. Ibid.
20. Ibid. Author's interview (Oct. 8, 1981) with Audrey Roux, a citizen of Apalachicola who was brought up in the 1930s and 1940s.
21. Apalachicola *Times*, May 24, 31, 1902.

the fall, hunters shot quail, doves, ducks, and geese. On one occasion in the 1890s, Frank Cross took a schooner to Saint George Island and managed to catch several hundred cranes. It was said that his fellow Apalachicolans used the better part of a week eating crane in every form: broiled, stewed, and baked. Although Cross had been able to sell the cranes, his venture proved to be a one-time operation owing to the future lack of supply and pronounced lack of demand.[22]

Edward G. Porter, a son of Richard Gibbs Porter and Mary Tibbitt Salter, helped make Little Saint George Island popular (*illustration,* Group 2). Porter began as the lighthouse keeper at Cape San Blas and later was transferred to Little Saint George Island. The lighthouse and the island had a strong attraction for Porter and his family, and in 1894 he purchased 1,515.85 acres on Little Saint George Island.[23] He soon built a cottage and a storm house and even hired Miss Ola Rhodes to teach a school. It was attended by eleven students, of whom six were members of his own family. The other five belonged to the family of Walter Roberts, the assistant keeper.[24]

The Porters lived in a one-story frame house with a porch all the way around. There was a connecting kitchen. The Robertses' home was two-storied, with a brick lower floor and frame upper floor. Porter always had a garden—tomatoes, watermelons, corn— and as a lover of livestock he maintained 150 to 200 hogs and 200 to 250 head of cattle. He and the assistant keeper supplemented their salaries by butchering meat and carrying it across the bay for sale in Apalachicola. Porter's young daughter Pearl shared his enthusiasm for life on the island. She had fond memories of helping her father and of helping herself to wild grapes (also known as muscadines and "bullaces") and all kinds of berries—black, dew, huckle, and blue—as well as the fruit from sabal (or cabbage)

22. Ibid., Mar. 23, 1912. The crane story remained vivid in the mind of Editor Johnston of the *Times.*.

23. Franklin County Deed Book G, 566–68. Porter paid $500 to Sarah Orman, Annie V. Orman (both silent), and J. F. C. Griggs and Sarah O. Griggs, his wife.

24. Author's interview with Pearl Porter Marshall, Sept. 1, 1981. At that time "Miss Pearl" was 81.

palms. The life of tedium that was thought to be the lot of a light-house keeper was not what the Porters of Little Saint George Island experienced. Pearl remembered the excitement of storms. When a hurricane moved in the family quickly responded. They loaded up in a double-team wagon pulled by a horse and a mule and took refuge in the storm house a mile and a half from the lighthouse.[25]

Porter had visions of building several vacation cottages on Little Saint George Island. His death in 1913 cut short such plans, but he had earlier constructed a cottage two and a half miles east of the lighthouse. A dock was built close by on the bay, and from spring to fall the small house was in constant demand by renters.[26] Porter's cottage was the first commercial use of the island.

At the turn of the century, Little Saint George Island was separated from Saint George Island by a hurricane. In 1902 a change came in the ownership of the larger island. In July, R. R. King and Imogene, his wife, sold Saint George Island to Paul King. Gaining exclusive ownership, Paul paid them two thousand dollars for their part in the island and their share of livestock.[27] A few months later King's wife and three sons arrived from Leighton, Alabama, and the family announced that Apalachicola would be their permanent home.[28]

Apalachicola and Franklin County experienced the bitter economic problems of Reconstruction and the 1870s, but the timber and seafood industries brought a taste of prosperity in the 1880s. Then the area and the nation were numbed by the financial misery of the 1890s. In the preceding thirty-five years, Saint George Island had gone through a succession of owners, but most residents of Apalachicola who bothered to speculate about the island wondered why anyone would want it. Some saw humor, or at least irony, in the fact that twentieth-century Saint George Island would once more have a king—even if the title were only the surname of an uncrowned sovereign.

25. Ibid.
26. Ibid. See also Apalachicola *Times,* May 30, 1908; Aug. 13, 20, 1910.
27. Franklin County Deed Book L, 262–65.
28. Apalachicola *Times,* Nov. 8, 1902.

8

The George W. Saxon Era

As THE nineteenth century unfolded into the twentieth, there was an unusual and highly welcome stirring of economic activity in Apalachicola and Franklin County. The timber and turpentine industries, the mainstays of the county's economy, expanded. The northerner-owned Cypress Lumber Company and the several mills of James N. Coombs continued to operate profitably. The Loxley Lumber Company, the Carrabelle Land and Lumber Company, and other mills were established. Billions of feet of longleaf yellow pine, as well as ash, cypress, poplar, cottonwood, sweet gum, and tupelo gum, were available.

The timber industry meant a large increase in traffic on the Apalachicola River. The commerce of the river system went from $2,000,000 in 1898 to $13,324,000 in 1903, a jump of nearly 700 percent in five years. Remarkably, the upsurge came despite continued but unsuccessful efforts to secure more federal money for dredging and deepening West Pass and the bars. The barks, schooners, and brigs that cleared port gave Apalachicola something of its old international atmosphere. Beginning in 1902, Captain W. G. Barrow brought the steamer *Tarpon* down from Philadelphia and inaugurated weekly trips between Apalachicola, Pensacola, and Mobile, a major link with the Gulf cities for local citizens.

Possibilities for economic growth accelerated with the coming of the railroad. In 1903 Charles B. Duff and his partners chartered the Apalachicola Northern Railroad. Capitalized at $500,000 and given five thousand acres of state land for every mile of track laid, the construction of the line had a time limit of four years. Behind the opening lay the disappointments of the 1880s and the years of propagandizing, public meetings, editorials, and appeals to investors. Unlike similar ventures, this project was completed on time. A tumultuous celebration was staged when the first engine steamed into Apalachicola on April 30, 1907. Sarah Braenard Cullen, a resident of Franklin County since the 1830s, was particularly excited. The retired schoolteacher and native of Connecticut had never seen a train before.

Extending from River Junction in Gadsden County, the seventy miles of track brought a promise of prosperity. At River Junction the railroad linked up with east-west Florida lines and, further north, at Climax, Georgia, with the Atlantic Coast Line. A branch was constructed from Apalachicola to St. Andrew Bay, and in 1909–10 the new town of Port St. Joe was built at the site of historic St. Joseph. In a repetition of past events, Port St. Joe became a busy center for naval stores and lumber. By 1909 Apalachicola had a ferry connection with the Georgia, Florida, and Alabama Railroad at Carrabelle. From there trains could be taken to Tallahassee and Bainbridge (*illustration*, Group 2).

At every hand there was evidence of progress and growth. In 1900 Port St. Joe had three resident physicians, each with his own drugstore. There were two blacksmiths, and E. M. White ran a thriving livery stable. More modern transportation could be obtained by making a small down payment to J. P. Lovett for a Waverly bicycle. There were numerous stores. Visitors stayed at the Central Hotel or at the more prestigious three-story Franklin. Opened in 1907 by James F. Buck, the Franklin featured steam heat and adjoining baths. The owner, a timber and turpentine businessman, entrusted the management to his son, L. G. Buck. The hotel was successful and in the 1920s was renamed the Gibson. Less affluent strangers were accommodated by Mrs. W. W. Jeter, who operated a boardinghouse at Live Oak and Palmetto streets and charged her patrons $3.50 a week.

Any town with three barbers, Apalachicolans informed strangers, had a future. Salvador Lucido was especially popular. The experienced "tonsorial artist" promised his customers clean towels, sharp razors, and polite attention.[1]

Apalachicola had two banks, and a municipal waterworks was opened in 1905. In 1906 the Florida Corporation of Apalachicola was formed to sell lots in town. Its initial success brought about the formation the next year of the Florida Coast Realty Company. Established by local businessmen, the company bought land west of Apalachicola for commercial and residential development.

There was plenty to do, depending on one's preferences. The popularity of whist equaled that of bridge in later decades (*illustration*, Group 2). The card game became so popular that whist clubs were organized. One avid party of players hosted nine tables at the Fuller Hotel. The Masons, Knights of Pythias, Women's Christian Temperance Union, and a Bachelors' Club were prominent; the last gave dances at Fuller's Hotel with Webb's Orchestra supplying the music.

The Philaco Club (its name was taken from letters appearing in the word "Apalachicola") began as a woman's reading club in May 1896. There was a hunt club, and the whites had a City Cornet Band. Not to be outdone, the town's blacks formed a popular brass band, and the Colored Odd Fellows was strongly entrenched by 1900. Unlike many other southern newspapers, the *Times* ran a weekly column containing news about the black community.

No event stirred civic pride more dramatically than the coming of electricity. On August 22, 1900, the Electric Light Company's switches were thrown, and lights with 2,000 candlepower came on. An observer noted that they "burned brilliantly and with scarcely a flicker."[2]

The expansion of the shellfish industry, particularly the oyster

1. See *North & South* (June, 1909). The Louisville, Kentucky, magazine devoted its entire issue to Apalachicola. See also Apalachicola *Times*, May 19, July 14, 1900; Oct. 27, Dec. 1, 1906; Jan. 5, Apr. 27, 1907; Jan. 18, 1913; Oct. 10, 1914; July 29, 1916; July 14, 1967. For harbor improvements appeal see *Laws of Florida* 1905: 450–51. For details of the Apalachicola Northern see Franklin County Deed Book L, 90–95, 96–99; and *Laws of Florida* 1905: 275; Porter, *Lives of St. Joseph*, 125–31.

2. Apalachicola *Times*, Aug. 25, 1900. See ibid., Nov. 17, 1900; Jan. 5, Feb. 23, Apr. 13, 1901; Mar. 22, 1940.

business, had significance for the present and the future. The industry, limited before to a few dealers such as John G. Ruge, Antone Messina, and C. H. Lind, expanded. The county commissioners received numerous applications to form packinghouses. Ruge's successful business was soon rivaled by Joseph Messina's Bay City Packing Company and the Gulf Trading Company. The commissioners found themselves issuing permits to small entrepreneurial ventures owned and operated by local residents.[3]

As more dealers emerged, the oystermen responded. In August 1902, thirty-one of them formed the Oystermen's Protective Association. By September most of the bay area oystermen had joined, and in December the association was chartered. The group was, in effect, a labor union—one organized, its leaders said, not to oppose the dealers but to achieve uniform rates and fair prices. The association had some impact, but it had difficulty maintaining its organization.[4]

The upswing in the shellfish industry was all the more remarkable because it was accomplished in the face of adversity. Franklin County, along with the nation, was just beginning to pull out of the depression of the late 1890s. A setback occurred in 1898 when a destructive hurricane swept along the Gulf coast, followed in the winter of 1899 by temperatures that dropped to 10 degrees above zero—the worst freeze since 1835. Yet the situation improved by spring when a first school graduation seemed to portend hopeful times ahead.

May seemed warmer than usual, especially to the students of Miss Steppie Rice, who ignored the weather and gloried in their role as the first "public school" graduates. They had their class motto, "Not Finished but Just Begun," emblazoned on a banner strung across the school stage. Farley Warren refused to accept his diploma publicly because he did not want to be seen with so many girls, but everyone enjoyed the dance that was held at the armory afterward.[5]

---

3. Ibid., May 19, 1900; see also Franklin County Incorporation Book, 10–11; and numerous entries in the Franklin County Commissioners' Minutes.

4. Apalachicola *Times*, Aug. 30, Sept. 6, Dec. 30, 1902.

5. For the graduation exercises see ibid., Dec. 24, 1898.

Another good omen occurred in 1899, the dedication of a statue to Dr. John Gorrie, the town's most prominent historical figure. Numerous people contributed funds, but the major donors were members of the Southern Ice Exchange, many of whom gave their proceeds from the sale of one ton of ice.[6]

The interlude of optimism was short lived. In the summer of 1899, a hurricane wrecked or stranded three schooners off Saint George Island. The strange storm, only twenty to twenty-five miles wide at any place, hit on August 1. The greatest destruction occurred at Carrabelle, where five people were killed, thirteen seagoing vessels were driven ashore, and a train was blown from the track.[7]

Tropical disturbances and plummeting temperatures were minor annoyances compared to the great fire of 1900. Mrs. George Broughton, like other citizens of Apalachicola, dreaded to see spring end and summer begin. By late May the heat had set in. Mrs. Broughton had reason for discomfort because she cooked dinner on a wood stove. Her typical southern household ate its main meal at noon. On Friday, May 25, about twelve o'clock, a fire broke out in Mrs. Broughton's kitchen.

The blaze could not be confined and quickly spread to the nearby Methodist church. Witnesses remembered the church bell pealing as the roof caved in. Blown by winds from the south, flames swept through the opera house, armory, and various homes. Then the wind changed, and, blowing from the west, drove sparks and cinders before it. Patton's butcher shop, the Knights of Honor lodge, Cone's barber shop and laundry, Nick Swain's tailor shop, Tony Spano's fruit store, and other businesses were consumed. Ironically, the town's fire engine, which had been purchased to replace the old "bucket brigade," fell victim to the flames before it could be used. Furniture and bedding were carried into the streets,

6. For more on the Gorrie statue see undated newspaper clipping in the Fred Sawyer, Sr., scrapbook. It is one of several containing valuable data on Apalachicola.

7. *Weekly Tallahassean*, Aug. 10, 1899; Wreck Report, Apalachicola Customs Office, 22, in possession of Dwight Marshall, Jr., of Apalachicola. See Apalachicola *Times*, Mar. 4, 1955, quoting Henry Lewis Mattair of Carrabelle, who survived the hurricane of 1898.

heaped into hills on canvas sails, and dragged away quickly by mules.

Several sections were dynamited as the fire raged toward the river. Weary fire fighters hauled buckets of water from the Apalachicola but could not save seven barrooms or prevent Grady's warehouse from blowing up. The fire burned itself out at the river. Six city blocks, practically all of the town's business section, were wiped out. Some seventy-one buildings, most of them insured inadequately or not at all, were lost. Embers smoldered for days, and a night watch was kept. Damages were estimated at over a quarter of a million dollars, but rebuilding was soon begun. Local residents concluded somberly that the new century was certain to be better than the closing years of the old one.[8]

Most of the county remained little concerned with who held legal title to Saint George Island. It was there in the bay where it had always been, a familiar bit of geography. Passengers on the launch *Sadie J,* the *Empress,* the steamer *Lottie,* or the popular *Crescent City* were treated to a view of Saint George Island not vastly different from that seen by Narváez, Cabeza de Vaca, and the lost Spaniards of 1528. In 1903, more people were concerned that Captain Andy Wing repair the bayside wharf (he did) than gave thought to the island's future.[9]

Paul and Steppie King, the newest owners, leased Saint George Island to George W. McCormack. He announced plans to stock it with hogs, goats, and sheep and to engage in fishing and planting oysters.[10] Forced to mortgage Saint George Island twice in 1904, the Kings were extended to their financial limit. Finally, they sold the island in 1905 to two Franklin County businessmen, W. F. Farley and W. E. Montgomery. The two men assumed the mortgages and took possession. They also became owners of the island's livestock except for one boar hog owned by lessee McCormack. The Kings got a check for $3,500.[11]

As new proprietors, Farley and Montgomery moved to secure their property. In September 1910, Lemuel K. Humphries, his

8. Apalachicola *Times,* June 9, Nov. 24, 1900; Aug. 1, 1903; May 24, 1938.
9. Ibid., May 30, June 13, July 11, 1903.
10. Ibid., Mar. 19, 1904.
11. Franklin County Deed Book L, 662–65.

wife, Nellie, and Ida Lee Humphries (probably their daughter) sold a claim to Saint George Island to Farley and Montgomery for three dollars. At the same time and for nominal sums the men made similar deals with Marion and Virginia Humphries Long and with G. G. and Helen Humphries Hensler.[12] Without doubt Montgomery and Farley hoped their property could become a part of the reactivated and flourishing shellfish industry. By 1907 so many visitors were going to the island that establishing a boat line was suggested.[13] Here was another way that the island could be made profitable. The tax appraisal for Saint George Island in 1907 was raised from $1,350 to $2,010 and, indicating rising prosperity, to $2,625 in 1910.[14]

One man who saw possibilities in Franklin County was George Washington Saxon of Tallahassee. Born in 1848, Saxon ended his formal education with grade school. He worked hard, and in the post–Civil War decades established a grocery store on Monroe Street in the capital city. The business was successful and soon was expanded into a dry goods store. By 1889, he operated a private bank as part of his store, and G. W. Saxon & Company quickly became a respected institution. The business was incorporated as the Capital City Bank in 1895.

Saxon established a branch of the bank at Apalachicola in 1897, to be managed by T. F. Porter, a native of New York state. He had been in the cotton brokerage business in Savannah and had raised oranges in Sanford, Florida, before moving to Apalachicola in 1895. Samuel E. Teague, another prominent local man, became cashier. Saxon's bank operated until 1906, when local businessmen bought it out.[15] Porter became its new president.[16] The change of

12. Ibid., Book R, 5–7; 7–9; 9–11.

13. Apalachicola *Times*, Jan. 30, 1907; May 30, 1908.

14. Franklin County Commissioners' Minutes, July 5, 1907; July 7, 1910.

15. John Ausley scrapbook; author's interview with Susan Ausley, Oct. 7, 1977. Several important scrapbooks relating mainly to Tallahassee and Leon County are in the possession of Mrs. John (Susan) Ausley of Tallahassee. For sketches of Porter see Apalachicola *Times*, Jan 14, 21, 1911. Apalachicola's other financial institution was the First National Bank, established in 1902. It was converted to a state bank in 1911. See Apalachicola *Times*, July 30, 1921.

16. Apalachicola *Times*, July 21, 1906.

ownership was smoothly accomplished. Saxon retained and extended his friendship with the leaders of Franklin County.

Devoted to his wife, Sarah Ball, and to his family, Saxon was a small, redheaded man with a fondness for cigars and an eye for business. On his frequent trips to Apalachicola, Saxon regularly checked in at the Franklin Hotel, consulted his friends, and found out how things were going.[17] His business acumen, somehow suggested by his quick-gaited, no-nonsense, slightly slue-footed way of walking, led him to make several investments. The bankrupt Kimball Lumber Company sold its property to Saxon in 1904. For the purchase price of one thousand dollars, Saxon obtained several wharf lots and numerous city lots in Apalachicola, a sawmill and its equipment, and timberland amounting to almost eight thousand acres.[18]

He made other investments in Franklin County, and at one time he was president of the Carrabelle Ice Company. He and Sarah Ball Saxon had holdings in what became known as Lanark Village— then called variously Lanark on the Gulf and Lanark Springs.[19] Located on the coast of Saint James Island some six miles east of Carrabelle, the community began as part of a promotion plan carried out by the Georgia, Florida, and Alabama Railroad, which owned the land, and became a fashionable resort for people in nearby counties. A two-story hotel with a broad veranda was erected facing the sound. Safety-conscious guests swam in an area enclosed by wire where they did not worry about the presence of sharks. By 1905 the railroad's industrial agents had persuaded a number of Georgians to buy lots and build summer cottages at Lanark.[20]

Saxon hit on the idea of promoting Saint George Island commercially. The sustained success of Edward G. Porter's summer cottage on Little Saint George Island was one inducement, and Saxon's own

17. Ibid., July 4, 1906.
18. Franklin County Deed Book L, 218. Author's interview with Mrs. Julian (Sarah Ball) Proctor, granddaughter of Saxon, Aug. 31, 1977, and with Palmer Proctor, great-grandson of Saxon, Aug. 31, 1977. Both are residents of Tallahassee.
19. Franklin County Incorporation Book A, 85–90; Franklin County Deed Book M, 367–68; V, 187–88, 349–50.
20. Apalachicola *Times*, May 20, 1905.

investments in Lanark Village further influenced his decision. He also knew of his fellow Tallahasseeans' interest in Saint Teresa, a well-established enclave on Saint James Island. Settled in 1875, Saint Teresa owed its existence to the stringency of the times. One of its founders, the dignified and bearded Dr. Phavious Augustus Byrd, wrote: "For a little community our society is hard to beat. It is composed mostly of families who *have been* very wealthy and were accustomed to taking trips during the summer to the Springs in North Carolina and Virginia or to some watering places at the North, but in these times are not able to spare the—time. Having determined to find some cheaper place of resort they have all ex- erted themselves to make St. Teresa as pleasant as possible and I do not think any one who has spent any time there will say that they have failed in their attempt." [21] In short order, ten homes were built and others were added yearly. Saint Teresa thus became a much- favored place that was pleasant, inexpensive, and accessible.

Besides Lanark Springs and Saint Teresa, Saxon had the example of Panacea Springs to convince him that a resort could be profit- able. A more recent success story, Panacea Springs was east of Saint Teresa where the Ochlockonee River flowed into an arm of Apala- chee Bay. Originally called Smith Springs, the numerous sulphur outpourings were well known to the Indians and early settlers and were prized for their curative powers. The completion of a railroad from Tallahassee to Carrabelle in 1893 brought access to the me- dicinal waters within miles of the track. From there it was a pleas- ant journey by stage to Panacea (later a tram line utilizing horse and mule power was opened). The springs officially became a spa with the opening of a hotel in 1898. Panacea maintained its popu- larity down to the 1920s. [22]

Finally convinced, the cautious banker tried his hand as a devel- oper (although that term did not gain wide usage until after World War I). Saxon decided to form a corporation, and he was able to persuade a number of Atlanta people to invest. The Georgians were

---

21. Dr. Phavius Augustus Byrd to "Dear Cousin Kate," Nov. 16, 1874. Letter in possession of Emilie Blackburn of Tallahassee.

22. Apalachicola *Times,* June 6, 1903; May 2, 1914. See also Burke G. Van- derhill, "The Historic Spas of Florida," 69–70.

primarily associated with the Atlanta Bank and Trust Company. In August 1910, two of the Atlantans came to Apalachicola at Saxon's invitation. After being given a tour of Saint George Island, they announced their willingness to invest in the island's future.[23] By the fall of 1910, the St. George Island Company was formed. That October a Mr. Bliss, one of the Atlanta stockholders, registered at the Franklin Hotel. He announced that the new company planned to build a large wharf at the island and begin construction of vacation homes and a $40,000 hotel. His statement impressed the editor of the *Times,* who looked "forward to Saint George being made the most popular resort on the Gulf coast."[24]

Saxon knew precisely how to set the company up. In November 1910, he purchased the island from Montgomery and Farley. He paid ten dollars to the owners, executed a mortgage for the remainder of the purchase price, and took over as trustee for the St. George Island Company.[25] A month later he executed the trustee's deed, turning the island over to the corporation. The St. George Island Company then mortgaged the property to secure an indebtedness of $19,600 to Montgomery and Farley.[26] With that the company became sole possessor of seven thousand acres, all fishing and oyster rights, all the island's cattle, hogs, and goats, and one horse.

Saxon served as president of the company, C. R. Porter as general manager, L. A. Porter as secretary, and S. E. Teague as assistant secretary. With capital amounting to $50,000, the St. George Island Company planned to engage in every activity its members considered appropriate, among them real estate and constructing, owning, and operating hotels, boardinghouses, bathhouses, bowling alleys, skating rinks, swimming pools, billiard parlors, poolrooms, and shooting galleries. The corporation proposed to build and operate gas and electric plants, waterworks and laundries, powerboats and sailboats, fish- and oysterhouses and canning factories; to deal in seafoods both fresh and canned; to own, raise,

23. Apalachicola *Times,* Aug. 20, 1910.

24. Ibid., Oct. 1, 1910.

25. Franklin County Mortgage Book E, 593–95.

26. Franklin County Deed Book R, 63–66; Franklin County Mortgage Book E, 604–9; Franklin County Mortgage Satisfaction Record, A, 332. Payment was made in five promissory notes at 6 percent; by 1912 payment was completed.

and sell livestock; to operate livery stables and garages, opera houses and other places of amusement; and to own, stock, operate, and control game preserves and sell membership and license privileges to shoot on them.[27]

Tangible prosperity, much of it achieved since 1900, made the citizens of Apalachicola confident. The promise of the future seemed to have arrived in the present. Their town had taken on many aspects of a city, not the least being the opening of the New Pace Vaudeville Theatre in 1909. Featuring comedy sketches and vocal and instrumental music, the Pace was only briefly successful. It was surpassed in popularity by the Dreamland, the town's first movie house, opened in 1910. It played to capacity audiences, and its five-piece orchestra alone was said to be worth the price of admission.[28] If a picture show was not progress enough, stockholders in the St. George Island Company met in December 1910 and announced their intention to push construction on their island hotel. Tourist dollars would flow through the economy. "Soon the sound of the saw and the hammer will be heard on the Island," the *Times* predicted.[29]

If and when Saint George Island prospered, the owners were prepared. In 1910 part of the island was surveyed by S. J. Ruff. What would endlessly be referred to later as "Ruff's survey" was accomplished either by Farley and Montgomery, who became principals in the company, or by the company itself. The firm was determined to exercise close control. It would lease a lot or lots (based on Ruff's survey) to an individual for ninety-nine years. The lease could be canceled; it could also be transferred with the company's approval but never to a non-Caucasian. The lessee was free to build the type of house or structure he or she desired so long as it was never "used for a place for gambling or for a saloon, or for any immoral or disorderly purpose." Leasing the land carried automatic membership in the St. George Island Club. The organiza-

27. Franklin County Incorporation Book A, 103–4.

28. Apalachicola *Times,* Feb. 4, 1911. See ibid., Dec. 19, 1908; Jan. 9, 1909; June 7, 21, 1910.

29. Ibid., Nov. 12, 1910.

tion was owned and operated by the company and was subject to the same restrictions.[30]

Streets were laid out if not built; the main thoroughfares were named Saint George's Avenue and Gulf Promenade. A bayside wharf was constructed, and sometime late in 1911 a small hotel fronting the Gulf of Mexico was built by the company. In the winter of 1912, Atlantans A. J. Smith and his wife stayed at what came to be called the Club House. With the aid of a talented black cook named Nancy, they gave a dinner party for forty people.[31] The Club House never functioned regularly as a hotel, but for several years C. N. Fuller managed it during the warm months. Meals were provided and sleeping accommodations were available. A bathhouse was built near the beach, and Fuller, an accomplished fisherman, rented bathing suits and boats.[32]

By 1912, H. L. Oliver, an Apalachicola businessman, became interested in Saint George Island. He and several associates wanted to build a fifty-room hotel where the Club House stood, widen the pier to accommodate automobiles, and extend it all the way across the island. Despite periodic progress reports, he never enlarged the Club House.[33]

Oliver leased all the growing pine timber on the island from the company. He was given exclusive rights to "turpentine" Saint George Island for six years.[34] The contract was more demanding than its clauses indicated. J. T. Brogdon, a naval stores operator, was one of Oliver's associates. Brogdon was a woodsman long used to avoiding bad-tempered reptiles, but in 1913 his experience was tested: Near the gap separating Little Saint George Island from Saint George Island, he encountered and killed a large alligator.[35] Another hazard the company encountered was the tension resulting from hard work. In 1913 a gambling argument between two

30. Franklin County Incorporation Book A, 103–4.
31. Apalachicola *Times*, Feb. 24, 1912.
32. Ibid., Aug. 10, 1912; May 17, 1913.
33. Ibid., Sept. 21, Nov. 2, 1912.
34. Franklin County Deed Book S, 43–45.
35. Apalachicola *Times*, May 31, 1913. The alligator's reported length of 22 feet was no doubt exaggerated.

black workers at Oliver and Brogdon's turpentine camp resulted in the shooting and death of one of the men.[36]

After 1915 Oliver entered into a partnership with George M. Counts, Sr., a philosophical businessman of Apalachicola. Tall, thin, and enterprising, Counts would have a close relationship with future events on Saint George Island. During much of 1916–18, he lived on the island in quarters at Nick's Hole on the bay side and directed a black work crew in its turpentine operations.[37]

After paying off the mortgage, Saxon decided that he wanted more direct control. In December 1913 he had the St. George Island Company convey the property to him by warranty deed. The price was five hundred dollars as well as "other valuable considerations," and the exceptions were those lots in Ruff's survey already leased or deeded by the company to various individuals.[38]

During these years the company and, on occasion, the Saxons as individuals sold or leased island lots to some twenty or more people. Purchasers usually bought single lots in Ruff's survey, rarely paying over $250 per lot.[39] A number of Atlanta people spent vacations of several weeks on the island, and several announced plans to build cottages.[40] Yet the corporation did not realize even minimally the grandiose plans trumpeted in its charter. Counts recalled that not more than two or three cottages were built.[41]

The Club House remained popular. Numerous dinner parties were hosted for local and out-of-town groups. The island continued as a desirable destination for excursionists and as a favored locale for hunters and fishermen. For those fortunate enough to own an automobile, Saint George Island offered a new diversion.

36. Ibid., July 5, 1913.

37. Author's interview with George M. Counts, Sr., July 28, 1978. Now deceased, Counts resided at Winter Haven, Florida.

38. Franklin County Deed Book S, 245–47. Each time Saint George changed hands, the new owner obtained the livestock as well.

39. The various sales have been identified by the author and are noted in a 1952 action to quiet title. There is no individual listing of sales except where they figure in subsequent events and litigation.

40. Apalachicola *Times,* Nov. 23, 1912.

41. Author's interview with George M. Counts, Sr.

After 1910 it became fashionable to drive cars along the beach at low tide, both in the daytime and by moonlight.[42]

Predictions of a coming war in Europe were noted by Apalachicolans but with little alarm. The Balkans might be the powder keg of Europe, but they were a hazy geographical concept to many Americans. Besides, there were so many local matters: the newly formed Apalachicola Lawn Tennis Club was building a court; the Chamber of Commerce had been organized; the recently formed Citizens' Band was giving concerts in newly established Battery Park; Allen's Negro Minstrels came to town.[43] The Dreamland Theatre was renovated and a cornet player and traps drummer were added to its orchestra. Even those improvements did not prevent Dreamland from being surpassed in popularity and eventually taken over by Alexander Fortunas's Dixie Theatre.

Opened in April 1913, the Dixie Theatre was a stunning addition to the town: the front glowed from fifteen white and a hundred colored electric lights; admission tickets were purchased at a conical ticket office with glass windows; inside were a main hall with 360 folding opera chairs and a sunken pit for the orchestra opposite the heavily curtained stage; to the right and left of the 140 chairs in the horseshoe-shaped balcony were roomy private boxes; noiseless rubber carpets covered the aisles, and the auditorium was cooled by fourteen oscillating fans.[44] There was nothing like the Dixie Theatre on the Gulf coast from Pensacola to Tampa (*illustrations,* Group 2).

Apalachicolans approved a new charter in 1914 establishing the city commission form of government. A local Mardi Gras festival was held in February and Oyster Day was celebrated in September. When war broke out in the summer, the *Times* recorded the event, and many citizens went to the Dixie Theatre to see a reel produced by Pathé Daily News showing "pictures from the world war now

42. For numerous trips to the island see Apalachicola *Times,* July 1, 1911; May 31, June 21, 28, 1913. Ibid., June 17, 1911, described an outing by S. E. Rice, Jr., his wife, and guests in a Ford.

43. Ibid., July 26, Aug. 16, 30, Oct. 4, 18, Nov. 8, 22, Dec. 13, 1913; Jan. 3, 1914.

44. Ibid., Mar. 22, 1940.

raging in Europe."[45] Dances, dinners, picnics, card parties, swimming—all the allurements of Saint George Island were frequently enjoyed.[46] The winter Mardi Gras of 1915 achieved a high level of interest as the aviator W. S. Luckey and his Curtis aeroplane made daily exhibition flights. Luckey remained airborne for forty minutes, and his plane probably made the first takeoff and landing in Apalachicola's history.[47] King Retsyo I ("oyster" spelled backwards) reigned over the proceedings.

All the activity in Apalachicola pleased Saxon because it meant increased business for his enterprises. Saint George Island was the exception. The Club House brought in few substantial returns, and the sale of lots had almost ceased. An extended outing on the island by a group from Atlanta in July 1915 resulted in just that, an outing with no down payments on land. Then two months later a hurricane from the West Indies raked the island and caused considerable damage in Apalachicola.[48] Saxon reevaluated his investment. The St. George Island Company's financial base was a bond issue. As early as 1911 the company had executed a trust deed to the American Bank and Trust Company of Rome, Georgia. First mortgage bonds in denominations of five hundred dollars each were issued, amounting to $50,000. Yet little had come of the venture; by 1916 Saxon had decided to sell Saint George Island.[49]

Before accomplishing the sale, Saxon needed uncontested ownership. He dutifully appeared at the Franklin County Courthouse and filed a bill of complaint in the circuit court to "quiet the title." The almost poetic phrase was legal terminology for the complicated process of clearing a plaintiff's possession of a particular piece of property with previous owners. The defendants were the American Bank and Trust Company and the State Bank of Rome. After considering a mass of documentary evidence and testimony, Judge E. C. Love quieted the title. Possession of Saint George Is-

45. Ibid., Aug. 22, 1914.
46. Ibid., June 6, 27, July 25, Aug. 1, 14, 29, Sept. 5, 1914.
47. Ibid., Jan. 16, 30, Feb. 15, 16, 1915.
48. Ibid., July 3, 10, Sept. 11, 1915.
49. Franklin County Mortgage Book G, 25–38; Franklin County Chancery Order Book G, 67–81.

land was now restricted to lands held by the company and to those held by Saxon in March 1919.[50]

Even after the tedious, drawn-out business of gaining full legal ownership, the soft-spoken banker was obliged to use all of his business guile and all of his patience. Saxon proved equal to the task, although the strain was considerable. The cause of business-man Saxon's upcoming frustrations was a man whose personality and acts challenged credulity. Accustomed to dealing with like-minded businessmen, Saxon now confronted William Lee Pop-ham, a person who was the banker's exact opposite in every way.

In July 1916 the *Times* mentioned that a "gentleman" had vis-ited Apalachicola and Saint George Island and had talked of buy-ing the property and establishing a "colony" there. The next month a land-seekers' excursion arrived from Montgomery, Ala-bama, chartered a boat, and went across to Saint George Island. There the Alabamians examined the lots offered for sale as cottage sites.[51] The unidentified developer and guide was Popham, a name familiar enough in other locales but not yet well known in Franklin County.

Popham had been preceded to the area in 1916 by William H. Roat, a gifted man with an unusual personality. Roat moved to Saint George Island, quickly acquired the title "the Island Man," and announced that he and his family were there to stay. Roat was an architect and a contractor. Employed by Popham, he described his status as that of resident agent, and by October was exhibiting drawings of three different bungalows scheduled for construction. Promising big things, the engaging and eccentric Roat penned letters to the *Times* boosting Saint George Island and the whole of Franklin County. Sometimes he expressed himself in poetry that Editor Johnston obligingly placed on page one of his newspaper. One unlikely poetic effort was a request for the return of two jack-asses stolen from him at a planing mill.[52]

People were puzzled by Roat until it turned out that he was affili-

---

50. Ibid.
51. Apalachicola *Times*, July 22, Aug. 26, 1916.
52. Ibid., Oct. 28; Nov. 11, 18, 25, 1916; Feb. 17, 1917.

ated with the even more colorful and imaginative Popham. Some Apalachicolans had heard of the Reverend William Lee Popham, Baptist preacher, Chautauqua lecturer, and author. They soon learned that he was also president of the Saint George Island Development Company.

Popham's first public appearance in town came in January 1917, when he preached at the local Methodist church. Despite Popham's Baptist credentials, W. T. Brantley, his host and pastor of the Methodist Church, wrote, "We trust that all the people of our city will give him a large and representative congregation." They responded, and Popham did not disappoint. He took as his text the familiar John 3:16: "For God so loved the World, that He gave his only begotten Son, that whoever believeth in Him should not perish, but have everlasting life." Popham spoke to a "very attentive audience," one that "was very highly pleased." He was asked to return soon.[53] Popham not only returned, he became the most controversial man in the town's history. His impact on Saint George Island and Apalachicola is still felt and still debated.

53. Ibid., Jan. 13, 20, 1917.

9

William Lee Popham, Esquire

No ONE knows me but God," William Lee Popham told his first and sole biographer. The biography was published in 1910, and Popham, only twenty-five years old, had already written eight books of poetry, essays, sermons, and fiction and was busy writing others. The author of the uncritical study was Maude Miller Estes, a young and stylish native of Kentucky. A year and a half younger than the subject of her book, she would later become Popham's wife. At the time she considered herself merely one among the thousands of his admirers.[1]

If one wished to discover the details of Popham's brief but jam-packed career, it was necessary to search them out in Estes's book. The table of contents, unlike the usual listing of chapter titles, offered no clues, advising the seeker instead to "turn to the pages and pick the kernels out." In the ninety-two pages that followed this direct instruction, the author (although rarely specific other-wise) revealed that Popham was born April 14, 1885, in Hardin County, Kentucky.

---

1. Maude Miller Estes, *Love Poems and the Boyhood of Kentucky's Poet, Being the Life-Story of William Lee Popham,* 7. Without doubt, Popham approved the dedication of his biography: "To Every Optimist Who Believes In Giving Flowers Of Praise To The Living Instead Of Placing A Wreath Upon The Grave Of The Dead This Volume Is Respectfully Dedicated." For Maude's age see California State Registrar of Vital Statistics, Sacramento, Certificates of Death.

In England the prominent Popham family had been active in the seventeenth-century explorations of the Virginia Company. The first Popham to settle permanently in America came to Virginia in 1708. After the American Revolution, one branch of the family went into Kentucky and others scattered north and south.[2]

Virgil Popham, William Lee's father, was a farmer-nurseryman who specialized in fruit and fruit tree production. On his hundred-acre tract a few miles from the rustic village of Big Clifty, Virgil grew apples, peaches, pears, and plums. The elder Popham's orchard and nursery business shipped fruit and plants all over the country and established its own post office, New Fruit, Kentucky. Besides devoting himself to his business, Virgil had also been a schoolteacher and country merchant. He was hard working but "had no poetic talent or unusual intellectual gift."[3]

William Lee's redheaded mother, "while uneducated, was a gentle kind and dutiful wife and mother." Clara had four children: Arthur Cobb, Elizabeth, William Lee, and Flora Ann. A fifth child, Albert, died at birth. William Lee, the future evangelist, lecturer, and writer, was said to have inherited his flamboyance and speaking ability from his mother's people. He possessed "a voice of melody—which at will becomes eloquent and commanding." But there was no explaining his literary talents. That gift was "born of heaven in his own soul."[4]

In a unique manner Popham was to direct these talents toward promoting and developing Saint George Island. As a salesman nonpareil in the 1920s, he was easily the equal of Miami's frenetic developers.

Young William Lee received a common school education at a log

---

2. Author's interview with Mrs. Claire Tillman Stanton, Oct. 3, 1977. Mrs. Stanton, who lives in Orlando, Florida, is the daughter of Popham's sister, Flora Popham Tillman; Popham's nephew, Arthur C. Popham, Jr., of Kansas City, Missouri, kindly provided information about the family in a letter to the author, Oct. 26, 1979. More information was provided by R. R. Popham of Darien, Connecticut. He is the grandson of Joseph Squires Popham, who was the brother of William Lee's grandfather Virgil. Letter to author Dec. 20, 1979. See also Estes, *Love Poems and the Boyhood of Kentucky's Poet*, 6.

3. Estes, *Love Poems and the Boyhood of Kentucky's Poet*, 6.

4. Ibid.

schoolhouse. In his early teens, according to his biographer, he entered East Lynn College, a small Kentucky school. Never graduating, he returned home and in 1897 persuaded his parents to move to Louisville, sixty miles away. There Popham continued his studies with private teachers, but he was nevertheless largely self-educated. The youthful Popham got a job as a messenger boy for a private company, and later he became a special delivery messenger for the post office. During that time he went to night school. Between working hours he enrolled as a student at the Southern Baptist Theological Seminary in the city and attended lectures for two years. Like everything else about him, Popham's educational experience was not the standard one. As he explained, "I did not take the courses, or the examination, for the simple reason I had to work during the day a great deal, and I could only attend those lectures between the hours I worked."[5]

From early boyhood Popham was a dreamer, and throughout his life he remained an incurable romantic. He was touched with a soaring (and frequently uncontrolled) imagination and perhaps with genius. His books were sentimental and pietistic potboilers, and his poetry was embarrassingly bad, but Popham had a flair for composition and an excellent, inquiring mind. Much of his knowledge was based on observation, and his insight was considerable and intuitive. In future real estate schemes, Popham's restless mind never remained satisfied, no matter how structured and detailed the plan. Always he shifted, rearranged, and embroidered. Never doubting that his original idea was without flaw, Popham would still amend it. In some undefined way, Popham knew what he was doing, but his acts and motives were frequently unclear to others.

Yet he was, as Maude Miller Estes claimed, a person who pored over books, a man of insatiable curiosity. Intellectually confident,

---

5. The quotation is taken from testimony given by Popham before Edgar Blessing, a solicitor for the Post Office Department. The hearing was conducted in Washington in October 1923. The testimony is conveniently included in U.S. Circuit Court of Appeals Fifth Circuit, No. 4698, William Lee Popham, Appellant v. United States, Appellee Transcript and Brief. See 1088 (1) to 1088 (130). (Hereinafter cited as Popham testimony, in this case, Popham testimony, 1088 (2). Testimony of others in this case is hereinafter cited simply as *Record*.)

he could turn adversity to his advantage. What would be grounds for bleak despair in others only opened new vistas for Popham. Years later, in 1982, his only son and namesake remembered that his father had a "reservoir of wit and humor" and a "dynamic . . . outspoken personality."[6] Popham's niece, Claire Tillman Stanton (daughter of his sister Flora), recalled that he was given to "grandiose gestures" and had a "flair for the dramatic"[7] (*illustration, Group 2*).

Popham was profoundly affected by his rural upbringing, and the influence was plainly evident in his writing. Some of his early poems were composed in the cornfield while he let his plowhorse rest, others in the pasture where he tended his father's sheep. Growing up, he had few intimate friends, although he was extremely close to his family. Clara Popham's place in the life of her son equaled that of his wife. He idealized Clara and Maude with deference and devotion that were lifelong.

If Popham had few intimates outside the family circle, he had many admirers. Arthur, his brother, graduated from the University of Louisville law school and became a prominent attorney in the city. He later moved to Kansas City, Missouri, and became one of the area's famous trial lawyers. Popham's affection for his brother was openly acknowledged and enduring.

At an early age, William Lee discovered that he could dazzle any gathering with his oratory. He soon combined that talent with his drive and ambition. Maude Miller Estes claimed that at the age of eleven Popham had a fourteen-verse poem, "The Babbling Brook," published in a London newspaper.[8] What the British thought of its verses is unknown. It was probably not much worse than the poems written in Popham's maturity. Once he attained the competency to compose verses that rhymed, Popham developed no further.

As he grew older, Popham continued to write maudlin poems,

6. A resident of California, Popham's son, who changed his name, has provided much information on family matters; William Lee Parker to author, Jan. 31, 1982.

7. Author's interview with Mrs. Claire Tillman Stanton.

8. Estes, *Love Poems and the Boyhood of Kentucky's Poet*, 15. Arthur C. Popham, Jr., to author, Oct. 26, 1979, noted that his father's law firm in Kansas City was Cowgill and Popham.

some composed idly, for relaxation, the way other young men whittled sticks. He could also write at reckless speed, and among his efforts were "My First Sweetheart," "Because the Violin Had a Bow," "Kiss the Cook," and "Memory Gallery." The years of poetic apprenticeship made it easy later for Popham to use his skills in verses about Saint George Island and even poems about the improbable and less romantic subject of oyster culture. Still in the future were such vintage poems as "The Golden Sunset Sinking o'er the Florida Sea," "Consider the Oyster," and "I May Live in Florida." Few men other than Popham could have written as he did in his "The Oyster Harvest Moon" that

> Beneath the oyster harvest moon
> Serene from all alarm
> Where harvest time is coming soon
> Is our Florida oyster farm;
> And here, a hundred thousand barrels
> Where, Winter rivals June—
> Our planted oysters thrive and grow
> Beneath the harvest moon.[9]

At the age of seventeen Popham became an evangelist and a lecturer on the Chautauqua circuit. He was an instant success. The slim youth who addressed overflow audiences had small, piercing, blue eyes and was of medium size. A photograph taken at the time revealed his straight, black hair, high forehead, rather broad face, and almond-shaped eyes that gave him a slightly oriental visage. He was well dressed without being dapper (he never lost his fondness for conservative but neat clothing) and handsome and had a look of utter sincerity. By his late twenties Popham had a thinner face; his long nose, wide and tilting upward, was more dominant, and his hair had begun to recede. As a mature man, he saw his hair's retreat become almost total. He gained weight, and the added pounds on his slightly less than average height gave him the appearance of being stout.

The Chautauqua circuit took William Lee many places across

9. *Record,* 670–71.

the United States and most definitely into the South, where love of oratory was part of life. Popham stated that he "lectured from 1907 and previous to 1907 probably a year or so, to 1912." Asked where he had lectured other than in Kentucky, Popham replied, "Scores of other places."[10] At one time his repertoire included thirty-four topics. Standing ovations were commonplace for his "Fools, Follies, Fibs, and Fancies," "Lovers in the Garden of Eden," "Kings Who Wear No Crowns," "Men and Swine, Women and Wine," and "Can God Kill the Devil?" If he faced a hostile audience, as he rarely did, Popham simply hauled out his unassailable lecture, "Mother, Home and Heaven."[11] His niece remembered that Popham always "talked reams around you."[12]

For a brief period he edited a magazine in Louisville called *Happy Home and Fireside*.[13] Gaining in popularity and reputation, Popham determined to promote himself and his work more profitably. He decided to publish his sermons, homilies, and speeches as well as his poems and fiction. With a few exceptions the future oyster king's publisher was the World Supply Company of Louisville. Some of his books were copublished by the Broadway Publishing Company of New York City. It is not certain that Popham had a financial interest in the World Supply Company, but considering his future propensity for spinning several projects off one main endeavor, it is probable that he did. All of Popham's books were copyrighted in his own name.

William Lee's first book appeared in 1905. Its title, not an exercise in modesty, was *The Road to Success / The Best Book in the World*. The book sold for twenty-five cents as an introductory offer, while its regular price was fifty cents. The author's object was to make clear the road to success. As the publisher's introduction explained, "The moral lessons taught herein are plain to comprehend, expressing golden thoughts and sentiments in language of the greatest simplicity. . . . Every sentence is not only decorated with entertaining language, but clothed with thoughts that breathe, and words that burn." The book was a grab bag collection of philo-

10. Popham testimony, 1088 (2–3), in *Record*.
11. *Record*, 340.
12. Author's interview with Mrs. Claire Tillman Stanton.
13. Popham testimony, 1088 (15), in *Record*.

sophical thoughts, pep talks, and pious admonitions. One section called the "Alphabet of Success" ranged from "A—Attend carefully to details and mind your own business" to "Z—Zealously labor for the right. Push forward, and never backward, in ascending the mountain of life, and the road to success is yours." [14]

Among the offerings were brief discussions of such topics as "Novel Reading," "Will Obeying the Ten Commandments Alone Gain a Home in Heaven," "Greatness," "Mother and Child," and "How to Prevent a Boy from Leaving Home." Even then his talent as a promoter, which he refined to a high art with Saint George Island, was burgeoning. Popham hit on the idea of a "Premium Badge Offer." To obtain a badge of honor one had to sell a dozen copies of *The Road to Success* and send the three dollars collected to Popham in Louisville: "No street or number is needed to reach him." The badge, to be worn on the coat, had three circular parts: a rose with the word "Honor" emblazoned on it, a picture of Popham, and an open book lettered with the words "The Road to Success." The badge, Popham wrote (ungrammatically), "is worn and appreciated by self-respecting people from ocean to ocean and is indeed! an honor to those whom honor deserves." [15]

Popham was even more effective as a speaker than as a writer—because he talked better than he wrote and because his Southern audiences liked the spoken word better than the written word. His voice rang with earnestness, and while he usually said the obvious he did so with absolute conviction. In print he was less persuasive, but without doubt he reached and convinced a large audience with such sentences as "profaneness is a brutal vice. He who indulges in it is no gentleman. I care not what his stamp may be in society; I care not what clothes he wears, or of what education he boasts." [16] And few would dispute that "There is no higher inspiration to manhood than a pure love for a pure woman." [17]

The truth was that Popham believed what he wrote. All of the people who knew him during his days of triumph and defeat in

14. William Lee Popham, *The Road to Success: The Best Book in the World*, 13–16.

15. Ibid., 89. See also 5.

16. Ibid., 139.

17. Ibid., 96.

Apalachicola recalled that he was gentle in language and never cursed. Despite his limited literary creativity, Popham became a master at composing advertising inducements. Among the devices he perfected was the abundant capitalization of key words in a promotional tract. He knew how to get the potential customer's attention. Ending explanations of "can't miss" projects with an exclamation mark or, increasingly, with multiple exclamation marks was a technique freely indulged by Popham.

From his initial success as an evangelist-lecturer, Popham polished his talents in the years that followed. He also continued his prolific outpouring of books. In 1910, *Love's Rainbow Dream* appeared under Popham's copyright but without the imprimatur of a publisher. The hardbound sixty-two page book sold for fifty cents and established a story line that Popham used in every work of his fiction: the triumph of true love. *Love's Rainbow Dream,* like all the books that followed, was poorly plotted, peopled by only a few characters (rarely more than four or five), and replete with stilted, moralistic conversations that sounded more like memorized speeches than real talk. The basic plot never varied from that of a young man and a young woman falling in love, facing some kind of conflict, triumphing over it, and living out their days in untroubled bliss. To his credit, Popham gave his characters mockserious but vivid names. The heroine of *Love's Rainbow Dream,* for example, was La Verne Sunbeam.

Also appearing in 1910 was Popham's *She Dared to Win.* Again, no publishing house claimed production credit. Selling for fifty cents, the seventy-six page book contained an autobiographical plot device that William Lee resorted to frequently. The hero was a lecturer-poet, in this case, Lincoln Burton, who finally won over Millicent Mordeaux, "the only daughter of a French millionaire cologne manufacturer."

Two books, even brief ones, might be taken as sufficient proof of a good year's work by any author. But standard measures of achievement did not apply to Popham. He continued his productivity in 1910. *The Valley of Love* (sixty pages long, fifty cents a copy, no publisher) and *The Village by the Sea* (fifty-six pages long, fifty cents a copy, no publisher) were additional works of fiction.

Both books were deliberately aimed at their readers' tear ducts. One of the two heroines in *The Valley of Love,* Una Nelson, died bravely at the end, while the more fortunate Princess le Roy of *The Village by the Sea,* after a shaky start, presumably lived a long life. Offered to readers at the same time was *A Tramp's Love,* a brief story, bound in cloth, that sold for fifty cents. The entire plot— how a nonproductive citizen became infatuated—was revealed in the book's title.

Not content with fiction, Popham published two other works in 1910. The first, *Silver Gems in Seas of Gold,* appeared simultaneously from the houses of the Broadway Publishing Company of New York and the World Supply Company of Louisville. It contained 250 pages and sold for $2.50. The book's blurb described Popham as an author, evangelist, lecturer, and poet and furnished a brief biography: "Born in 1885 on a farm in Kentucky, William Lee Popham has risen from a plow-boy to public life—and to-day, by the strokes of his pen and the delivery of his lectures, commands the attentions of anxious thousands. He spends his time in giving expression to beautiful sentiments and helpful thoughts to calm the waves in life's great sea." The book was divided into three parts. The first was devoted to essays, character sketches, and miscellaneous prose. Lectures, addresses, and sermons comprised part two, and the last section contained short love and character stories. According to the publishers, "Every subject has a noble lesson. . . . It should inspire millions of human lives to high aspirations and bless millions yet unborn." [18]

Among other things, Popham revealed his thoughts on "Fast Young Men," "Good Literature in the Home," "A Mother's Love," and "Low Wages." As for the use of tobacco, "If every cigarette is a coffin nail, some of our boys are getting pretty well boxed up." [19]

"You just ought to own a copy." Such was the publisher's admonition applied to *Nutshells of Truth,* still another Popham-authored book of 1910. The work sold for one dollar and contained short sayings, toasts of wisdom, common sense, and beauty,

18. See preface to William Lee Popham, *Silver Gems in Seas of Gold.*
19. Ibid., 115.

and sentence sermons. It bore a striking resemblance to *The Road to Success* and *Silver Gems in Seas of Gold.* In some cases identical passages were lifted from the previous two works.

The dedication of *Poems of Truth, Love and Power,* another of Popham's bountiful year of 1910, was not only sweeping but all-inclusive. As William Lee expressed it, "To all persons who appreciate the baby's smile, the mother's lullaby, the wind's whisper, the wavelet's music, the bird's song, the lover's love, childhood's laugh, humanity's affection, nature's beauty, home's enchantment, our country's flag, God's care and the Savior's grace, this volume is respectfully DEDICATED by the AUTHOR." The price was $1.50. None of the poems rose above mediocrity in quality, most were bad, but their unrelieved earnestness gave them a certain fascination.[20]

The man who would later bill himself as Florida's Pioneer Oyster Developer obviously did not devote much time to the writing of any single book. Yet the sheer volume of his work is proof of considerable time expended in writing.

As a lecturer and traveler Popham usually visited ordinary places, but he also toured sites of historic and geographical significance. He knew that many people were addicted to fiction, and he correctly concluded that they were fascinated by exotic natural wonders. William Lee decided to capitalize on these common interests. He would make them fit a single design by writing books that would combine the appeal of light romance and travel. Embellishment, making the attractive more attractive, always stirred some inventive urge in Popham. Just as he would later offer a package combining the profits from oysters in Apalachicola Bay with the pleasures of owning land and living on Saint George Island—all for the price of one—Popham devised a literary package in 1911. He began what he called his "Seven Wonders of the World Series (American)." Appearing between 1911 and 1913 were seven short books: *Yosemite Valley Romance, Mammoth Cave Romance, Yellowstone Park Romance, Garden of the Gods Romance, Grand*

20. William Lee Popham, *Poems of Truth, Love and Power.* This was the only book by Popham published exclusively by the Broadway Publishing Company. For the poems "Selfishnes," "Love's Thoughts," "August," and "It Will Do No Good to Whine," see 84, 152, 166.

Visitors to St. George Island around the turn of the century enjoyed the Gulf
waters and the sand, but they carefully protected themselves from the rays of the
sun.   HERBERT BROWN COLLECTION / FLORIDA PHOTOGRAPHIC ARCHIVES

David H. Brown and his family of Eastpoint on an outing to Saint George Island in 1904. The capture of a sea turtle was a rare event.

Facing page: Edward G. Porter owned Little Saint George Island and was the lighthouse keeper there. The resourceful Porter raised garden vegetables, raised and slaughtered cattle and hogs on the island, and was the first man, in 1912, to use the island for commercial purposes. He appears here in his formal "keeper's" uniform.   PEARL MARSHALL

The *Crescent City* made a daily run carrying mail and supplies from Apalachicola to Eastpoint and to Carrabelle. The boat was also popular for excursions to Saint George Island and remained active to the 1930s.

HERBERT BROWN COLLECTION / FLORIDA PHOTOGRAPHIC ARCHIVES

Facing page, top: Citizens of Apalachicola, Franklin County, and the surrounding area celebrated when the Apalachicola Northern's first locomotive crossed the trestle to steam into town on April 30, 1907. APALACHICOLA *Times*

Facing page, bottom: Whist was the most popular card game of the 1890s and early 1900s. Here an Apalachicola foursome (three intent, the young lady obviously thinking of something or someone else) are closely watched by two kibitzers. APALACHICOLA *Times*

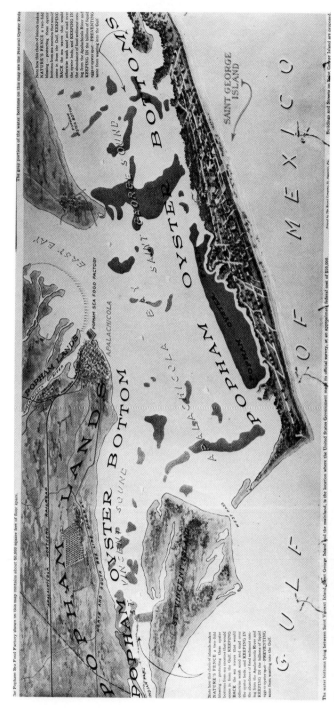

The Popham Sea-Food Factory shown on this map contains about 60,000 square feet of floor space.

The gray portions of the water bottoms on this map are the Natural Oyster Beds

Note how this chain of islands makes NATURE'S FENCE a two-fold blessing — protecting these oyster bottoms from sea erosion that would come in from the Gulf. KEEPING BACK the sea waves that would otherwise wash sand and mud over the oyster beds, and KEEPING IN the abundance of food settlement coming from the Apalachicola River and KEEPING IN the billions of liquid eggs or oyster-spat — PREVENTING same from wasting into the Gulf.

Note how this chain of islands makes NATURE'S FENCE a two-fold blessing — protecting these oyster bottoms from sea erosion that would come in from the Gulf. KEEPING BACK the sea waves that would otherwise wash sand and mud over the oyster beds, and KEEPING IN the abundance of food settlement coming from the Apalachicola River and KEEPING IN the billions of liquid eggs or oyster-spat — PREVENTING same from wasting into the Gulf.

SAINT GEORGE ISLAND

GULF OF MEXICO

The water bottoms lying between Saint Vincent Island, Saint George Island and the mainland, is the location where the United States Government made its official survey, at an approximate federal cost of $10,000.   Buildings and Streets on Saint George Island are colored.

Printed by The Record Company, St. Augustine, Fla.

Promotional map of William Lee Popham's lands and oyster bottoms. PRINTED BY THE RECORD COMPANY, SAINT AUGUSTINE

An early photograph of William Lee Popham
used in several of his books written when he
was in his twenties. This one is from *Washington Monument Romances* (Louisville,
1911).

A bird's-eye view of Apalachicola in 1906.   APALACHICOLA *Times*

William Lee, Maude, and William Lee, Jr., pose in Apalachicola in 1919. Popham's promotional activities were just getting well under way on Saint George Island.
ATLANTA *Journal Sunday Magazine*, July 13, 1919.

Canyon of Arizona Romance, Natural Bridge Romance, and *Niagara Falls Romance.* A trip to the District of Columbia convinced him that man-made structures could rival nature's handiwork, and so he wrote the *Washington Monument Romance.*

Scarcely distinguishable from one another, none of the books contained over 120 pages. Each began with an adjective-laden tribute to the site. Popham, who had visited all of the locales, would then sketch in a brief description of what, for instance, Niagara Falls looked like. Next came the chance meeting of the principals. Romance, conflict, and resolution followed.

Yosemite Valley Romance included excursions to Long Beach and descriptions of California's giant sequoias and Santa Catalina Island. The plot centered around the activities of Miss Dixie Darlington, "A Winsome Tourist of the West"; Chester Oakland, "The Handsome Flirt"; and Thelma, Annetta, Edna, Estelle, and Hazel, "Former Sweethearts of Chester Oakland." The book ended with Chester saving Dixie's little brother Robert from drowning. Dixie's grateful father, who had been suspicious of the flirt's intentions, said to Chester, "Mr. Oakland, we'll shake hands! You have saved my child's life. You are both gallant and heroic." He turned to Dixie, placed her hand in Chester's, and continued, "I have no objections to a son-in-law like you. Dixie is yours—she is a queen—treat her as such—and may the union always be a happy one—may God bless you—my son—my daughter." [21]

All of the books in the Seven Wonders series contained Popham's usual cast of characters with pseudo-comic names. *The Garden of the Gods Romance* (dedicated to an inanimate object, the State of Colorado, and containing, somewhat strangely, descriptions of Utah and Salt Lake City) was his finest creative effort. Masie Mayflower, "A Young Widow"; Garland Waterson, "Ex-Sailor-Capitalist"; Miss Ola, "The balance of her name to be made known in the story"; and Miss Blossom Illbeen, "Appearing only in the latter part of the story," populated the book.

The *Washington Monument Romance*—besides recounting the activities of Bildad, a farmer from the mountains; Daisy Sun-

---

21. William Lee Popham, *The Yosemite Valley Romance,* 119.

flower, a restaurant cashier; and a pawnbroker, otherwise known as "The Man with a Voice like a File"—briefly updated Popham's biography. The book mentioned that William Lee was "a graduate of the school of the plow-handles" but was "now a roamer—occasionally attempting to write a poem, create a book, preach a sermon and deliver a lecture."

How well Popham's books sold is not known, but it is doubtful, despite his claims, that he made much money from them. Although his writing talent was superficial, he made the most of it. In the future Popham would draw up a bewildering set of contracts and agreements relating principally to Saint George Island. In doing so he brought into play a facile writing style and made what are ordinarily dull, legalistic documents witty, lively—and unique. The most farfetched and outrageously romantic plots of his books were plausible, even rational, when compared to the actual events that followed in Popham's own life. In 1912 he was ready for adventures in Florida (*illustration*, Group 2).

10

Frenzied Finance

WILLIAM LEE and Maude began their married life under bizarre circumstances. In the late spring of 1912 he conducted a series of lecture-revivals at Baptist churches in Buford, McDonough, and other Georgia towns close to Atlanta. At the conclusion of one meeting, the evangelist decided that he had been a single man long enough. Popham could have waited until he returned to Kentucky, but, always the activist, he sent Maude a telegram asking her to marry him. He wanted her to drop everything and come to Georgia. She accepted and left Louisville on a train bound for McDonough. When Maude reached the small town, she and Popham obtained a license and went to the redbrick courthouse in the center of the business district. There they presented themselves to A. G. Harris, judge of the ordinary court for Henry County. He performed the marriage ceremony on May 11, 1912.[1]

The couple planned to go to Florida for their honeymoon but not until Popham had completed his lecture-revival engagement. Anxious to experience life in the city, they went to Atlanta one night and registered at the Terminal Hotel. Popham explained later that "we decided from purely romantic motives to keep our wedding a secret, that is, not to announce our marriage until after the

1. Henry County Marriage Record, 1903–27, 241. See also Popham testimony, 1088 (3–4), in *Record*.

close of the lecture engagement, until we were really free and ready to go on the honeymoon in Florida." They registered under separate names and were assigned adjoining rooms but used only one of them. Popham was getting dressed early the next morning to catch a three-o'clock train when there was a knock at the door. The unexpected visitor was the night watchman. He demanded that Popham come out, informing the startled poet-minister that he was going to report him, and that he had to go to police court to answer a charge of being in a lady's room. In the American South, the Victorian Age did not end with the queen's death in 1903.

William Lee and Maude packed their bags, checked out of the hotel, and, accompanied by the night watchman, took a taxi to the police station. Having been told by their "captor" that their bond would not amount to much, they decided to keep their marriage a secret. Confronted by the judge, the couple did not deny the charges. They posted bond (six dollars each) and were assured that the episode would not appear in the newspapers. The Pophams hurriedly went to the depot and managed to catch an early train. The next day as the newlyweds rode along to the upcoming lecture, a newsboy came through the car. Popham bought a newspaper and quickly came across a lurid story: "Preacher and author found in lady's room at Terminal Hotel."

The horrified couple got off the train at the next station. Popham wired a cancelation of his engagement, and they returned to Atlanta. Registering at the same hotel, the Pophams summoned reporters and told them what had happened. The newsmen checked with Judge Harris at McDonough, and the whole business was explained in a follow-up story. After remaining in Atlanta for a few days, the couple went to Florida for their belated and slightly tarnished honeymoon.[2] Despite the comic opera aspects of the episode, Popham was a deeply moral man, and among the future charges that would be lodged against him, marital infidelity was never included.

The Pophams were so impressed with the Sunshine State (he had been there before on the Chautauqua circuit and even had a prepared lecture called "Magic Florida—The Land of Flowers") that

2. Popham testimony, 1088 (4–6), in *Record*.

they bought a hundred-acre farm about fourteen miles from Tampa on the Alafia River. Besides the initial price of $4,800 for the wildwood property, Popham claimed that he spent $10,000 improving, fencing, and clearing the land. He planted orange groves and built a grape arbor. The entire effort was financed from money he saved from lectures and from the sale of his books. Popham named the sylvan spot Poet Eden, and soon he was buying and selling property in and around Tampa. As early as 1912, Popham purchased land from a man named James J. Abbott. Later Abbott acted as Popham's agent in selling land, and, still later, the two men became close associates in the Byzantine activities related to Saint George Island.[3]

In 1916, Popham first learned of Saint George Island from a casual conversation with a Tampa real estate agent. The man commented on Popham's well-known love of the outdoors. "There is one place in Florida you ought to see," he told Popham, describing the island. "If once you saw this place, you would buy it."[4]

Later in 1916, Popham ran in the June primary as a candidate for commissioner of Hillsborough County. There were four men in the race in District 5, and although Popham barely campaigned he finished second, losing by forty-six votes.[5] Shortly afterward, Popham remembered his conversation with the realtor. Since he was not going to be burdened with the responsibilities of public office, he took Maude on an outing to Franklin County. They inspected Saint George Island (George M. Counts, who was "turpentining" the island, recalled that the Pophams were stylishly dressed in outfits of matching khaki) and liked it so much that they returned home by way of Tallahassee. There the couple talked to Saxon about buying the island.[6] The Tallahassee banker, painfully aware that his St. George Island Company's sales were progressing slowly, was willing to sell.

As a result of the first meeting and subsequent communications, Popham accepted Saxon's price of $30,000. Saxon agreed to take

3. Ibid., (7–8).
4. Ibid., (8).
5. Tampa *Tribune*, June 9, 1916.
6. Popham testimony, 1088 (8–9), in *Record*; author's interview with George M. Counts, Sr., July 28, 1978.

as security the copyrights to all of Popham's books. The banker wrote to the publishers and was assured by them that the book copyrights were worth at least $10,000. Saxon was convinced that he had a substantial down payment, although it is difficult to believe that he actually read *Nutshells of Truth* or any of Popham's other works. Saxon agreed to let Popham sell lots on the island provided that 75 percent of the purchase price be placed in the Capital City Bank. Once the $30,000 was paid, a warranty deed would be released to Popham. In the meantime, the first 25 percent of the purchase price would be paid directly to Popham. He would use the money to stake off lots, send out literature, and promote the island as best he could. For his part, Saxon carried out a promise to obtain a clear title to the island.[7] "I hope you will make big money out of this enterprise and that we all may be well pleased with the outcome," Saxon wrote Popham in September 1916.[8] The indefatigable evangelist-turned-promoter was already in action.

The winter of 1917 started out much like other winters. As it had for centuries, the barrier island of Saint George lay as a silent guard to Apalachicola. Oyster boats bobbed in the bay, and the shrimpers made their way to the open sea. Apalachicolans walked more briskly due to the cold weather. They met in the streets, in cafes, at church, and they talked. The casual conversations ran heavily toward the weather, the ferry service to Eastpoint, and the complexities of everyday existence. National and global affairs did not go unnoticed, especially in April, when World War I changed from a European abstraction to an American reality. The United States was now at war, and doughboys from Franklin County would soon be overseas fighting with the Allies in France.

The Apalachicola *Times,* which kept the citizens informed about worldwide events, did not neglect local news of marriages, births, deaths, parties, and revivals. But always beyond the printed pages were the conversations. Like people in other small towns, the Apalachicolans talked to each other and they talked about each other. Word-of-mouth rumors flew quickly around town about the stem-winding preacher, William Lee Popham, who had

7. Popham testimony, 1088 (9–12), in *Record.*
8. Ibid., (11).

delivered such a powerful sermon the year before. It was said that he had big plans for Saint George Island.

As early as February 1917, Popham made an agreement to sell a thousand acres of land, bay to Gulf and adjoining the Ruff subdivision on the east. The prospective buyer, a Florida corporation called the Florida-Canadian Farms Company, was to pay $65,000. President Sidney E. Trumbull of Lakeland, Florida, agreed that the company would pay $20,000, subdivide the property, and have a plat made. Lots would be sold, and, as the money came in, the corporation would pay off the rest of the debt.[9] Popham did not have proper title to the island, but he had owner Saxon's permission to proceed with sales.

The next month, March 1917, Popham sold another thousand acres to Dr. George A. Lassman of Tampa for $65,000, payable $16,000 down and the balance six months later.[10] Unfortunately, the terms were never complied with, and the Lassman deal fell through. Meantime, what were called "breaks in the seawall" caused the Florida-Canadian Farms Company to become dissatisfied with its arrangement. Almost offhandedly the poet-promoter agreed to take the property back and give the company another thousand acres. The new grant was for land lying on the west of Ruff's subdivision. The company agreed to complete work on the hotel or Club House.[11]

By the spring a new organization, the Saint George Company, had been formed at Lakeland. It was made up of Trumbull and three other Lakeland residents: W. Steeves, president; Helen Brooks Smith, secretary; and John Malcolmson, treasurer. In April, Popham met with several officers of the Saint George Company at Apalachicola.[12] By October Trumbull had sold the Florida-Canadian Farms Company's two contracts to the new company. That the Saint George Company was a reorganization of the old one was evident by the transfer price of one dollar. Vice-president Trumbull

9. Franklin County Deed Book T, 157–60. The company was to pay $5,000 within thirty months and guarantee a payment of five dollars at the end of every twenty-four months.

10. Ibid., 162–63.

11. Ibid., 224–27.

12. Apalachicola *Times*, Mar. 31, Apr. 28, 1917.

and the others were equal partners with twenty-five shares each. With capital stock of $10,000 (a hundred shares at $100 per share), the company was chartered to deal in real estate. It proposed to operate mainly in Franklin County with headquarters on the "Island of Saint George by the Sea."[13]

The negotiations between Popham and the Saint George Company were largely the work of Helen Brooks Smith. Visiting Saint George Island in January 1917, she was impressed with its natural beauty and further convinced by the superlatives put forward by Popham. The secretary returned to Lakeland and persuaded her partners to invest. Mrs. Smith was an impressive woman; tall and large-framed, she had a distinctive white streak through her hair. John Malcolmson, a Canadian with a gray goatee, was equally striking. Always called "Captain," Malcolmson had twenty years' experience operating hotels at Georgian Bay and at Saint Catherines in Ontario, Canada. The new investors included a lease of the Club House in their purchase. "Island Man" Roat improved and enlarged the hotel, and Mrs. Smith renamed it The Breakers. The company purchased a thirty-two-foot boat, also named *The Breakers,* which would be used to transport up to sixteen passengers. Mrs. Smith and Captain Malcolmson urged Lakeland residents to build vacation cottages on Saint George Island, and it was hoped that by the summer of 1917 a new town would be well under construction there.[14]

A number of Lakeland residents announced plans to construct bungalows, and the Saint George Company was off to a good start. Editor Johnston of the *Times* wrote that Saint George Island was an excellent place "for the busy man of affairs to own at least a cottage where he can rest his tired nerves while basking in soft sunshine and warm breezes of the Gulf." At the same time he could be "enjoying the sea baths or maybe angling for the finny tribe, shooting ducks and geese or birds on the wing."[15]

13. Franklin County Deed Book U, 96–97; Franklin County Incorporation Book B, 219–22. Florida-Canadian Farms in all likelihood was dissolved.
14. Apalachicola *Times,* Mar. 10, 1917; author's interview with Homer Marks, July 7, 1978. Marks, now deceased, was a lifelong resident of Apalachicola.
15. Apalachicola *Times,* Feb. 24, 1917.

Popham himself organized a company in 1917. Known as the St. George Island Company, it was identical in name to the one established in 1910 by Saxon. Popham's company started slowly, partly because his purchase agreement with Saxon was not made formal until March 1918. No doubt Saxon felt better about the shaky literary collateral once Popham had paid $500 down and promised to pay $500 a month at 6 percent interest.[16]

The St. George Island Company was the result of Popham's salesmanship in Tallahassee. Among its principals were several state officials and employees. As it turned out, even Popham found island investors hard to come by. People were more concerned with the war and its effect on their lives. Even Roat settled his accounts in Apalachicola and left Saint George Island to work for the government for the duration.[17] Popham attempted to broaden his base by launching a campaign in Jacksonville. People had money, but the prospect of owning an island retreat did not fit the temper of the times. Nothing worked out, and the St. George Island Company was a failure. Later (and to his credit), Popham returned the original subscribers' investments, including 8 percent interest for three years.[18]

The ambitious projects of the Lakeland group's Saint George Company also stalled as the war came to Franklin County. There the response to President Woodrow Wilson's call for patriotism was overwhelming. The county had thirteen hundred men of draft age. As it turned out, compulsory conscription was not needed. Volunteering for service in the army, navy, marines, and coast guard were 174 whites and 74 blacks. The total of 248 made Franklin one of three counties in the entire country whose volunteer enlistments exceeded its quota in the first two drafts. Apalachicola observed lightless nights; the county went far past its quota in a Liberty Loan drive. Everything seemed to be happening at once. A large crowd watched in September 1918 when two hydroplanes from the Pensacola Naval Air Station "lighted" in the river

16. Franklin County Deed Book T, 463–67. The exceptions were lots in the Ruff Survey already sold or owned by the Saxons.

17. Apalachicola *Times*, Jan. 1, 1918.

18. Popham testimony, 1088 (13–14), in *Record*.

opposite Apalachicola. The town suffered an outbreak of Spanish influenza and was thrown into mourning when popular young Lieutenant Willoughby C. Marks was killed in action in France. Before the armistice, eleven other county residents died in the service, and two were wounded. Expressing a heartfelt mood, the *Times* declared, "The main business of this country is to lick the Kaiser, and it is your duty to get busy."[19]

Saint George Island ceased to attract investors, but its potential was not forgotten by Popham. He simply deferred to the exigencies of a wartime economy. Meanwhile, A. S. Mohr's steamer, the *Lottie,* stayed busy, as did the *Camp of Palms,* carrying people on brief outings to the island.[20]

With his plans temporarily interrupted, Popham had to readjust. Maude was pregnant, and a steady income was needed. Economic opportunities seemed better in North Florida, and the family moved from Tampa to Duval County. For some reason the Pophams were in Tallahassee during the holiday season in 1917. On Christmas Eve, Maude gave birth to a boy named William Lee, Jr., the only child the Pophams would ever have. In 1917–18, the St. Johns Shipyard in South Jacksonville, just across the river from their home, was booming and paying high wages. Popham had done manual labor before, and he, Maude, and their newly born son moved into a houseboat on the St. Johns River. Popham worked first as a painter, was promoted to safety man (which entailed inspecting scaffolds and ladders), and, finally, once his identity became known, to publicity man. In that capacity he edited a weekly publication known as *Hun Hammer.* In it Popham urged the shipyard workers on to greater productivity, pleaded with them to buy Liberty bonds, and fanned the fires of patriotism.[21]

Supporting his family on a fixed income limited Popham's ability to speculate. He was unable to meet the terms of his contract with Saxon. The banker still wanted to sell Saint George Island, and, in

19. Apalachicola *Times,* Aug. 31, 1918; see ibid., Jan. 1, June 15, July 27, Sept. 7, Oct. 26, Nov. 23, 30, 1918. For the enlistment figures see ibid., Apr. 26, 1930.

20. Ibid., June 15, 29; July 6, 24, Sept. 14, 1918.

21. Popham testimony, 1088 (15–16), in *Record.* William Lee Parker to author, Jan. 31, 1982.

the midst of wartime prosperity and inflation, decided to up the asking price from $30,000 to $35,000. He and Popham remained friendly associates. Throughout 1918, the evangelist retained the banker's authorization to sell and, on occasion, took prospective buyers to see the island.[22]

Popham's desire to promote Saint George Island had, if anything, intensified. The problem was how to do it. Once he took some of his fellow workers on a tour of the island, and, without exception, they all expressed a desire to move there. But for the shipyard workers, standing on the white beach sand and gazing out on the Gulf of Mexico, actually living on Saint George Island seemed no more likely than an invitation to Buckingham Palace. To them it was just a pleasant outing. But his coworkers did not know Popham. After considerable thought, he hit on a plan.

What became the St. George Co-Operative Colony, Unincorporated, was partly a business proposition and partly the product of Popham's newly found desire for a classless society. He wanted to establish an industrial colony based on a mutual sharing of investments and profits by its members. His would be a practical, workable utopia. The idea was derived from a number of sources—from the Bible to the colony that Harry C. Vrooman had attempted to create at Eastpoint—and given the unique touches of Popham. It was not difficult to rationalize the communal idea with his Christian beliefs. Nor was it inconsistent that the plan included handsome profits for himself as the promoter. If that made him a capitalist in disguise, at least he was no robber baron, and others would benefit as well.

The St. George Co-Operative Colony, Unincorporated, would have five hundred members who would pay two hundred dollars each. After making a small down payment, the member paid monthly or weekly installments. In return, an investor would receive four lots in the city that would be established on the island and a five-hundredth interest in the colony's holdings and operations. There would be, as Popham explained later, any number of ventures, and all profits would be shared. From the first, members

22. Popham testimony, 1088 (21), in *Record;* Apalachicola *Times,* Nov. 16, 1918.

of the St. George Co-Operative Colony, Unincorporated, would draw incomes because they would build the city themselves and be paid five dollars a day for their labor.[23]

Colonists and prospective members held regular meetings on Sunday afternoons at the Labor Temple on Riverside Avenue in Jacksonville. W. W. Anderson, a longtime municipal judge, was elected president, and among the several officers was Charles N. Hampton, who served as secretary. Like J. J. Abbott, Hampton would become a close associate of Popham's. The officers and nine other elected men made up a thirteen-man board of directors, which included Popham. The poet-evangelist and brief convert to the role of shipyard worker was once again in his element, and it was Popham who became the featured speaker at the Labor Temple gatherings.[24]

The new venture remained active and controversial throughout its existence, from its informal beginnings in July 1918 till December 1920. When World War I ended in the fall of 1918, Popham wasted no time. According to his interpretation, Saxon had given him permission to sell some ten thousand acres of Saint George Island. The primary purchasers would be the colonists, and Popham got the St. George Co-Operative Colony, Unincorporated, to agree to pay him $65,000 for eighty-five hundred acres. The future oyster king explained that he had already sold the Saint George Company a thousand-acre plot in the island's center. It was there that The Breakers and a boardwalk had been built. Since Saxon was only asking $35,000 for the island, Popham stood to make a profit of $30,000.

Popham, Abbott, and others busied themselves making sales in both Jacksonville and Tampa. Money began to come in, and President Anderson and the board of directors remained active. After several communications with Saxon, Anderson and others discovered that the banker's price was a far more attractive business proposition than buying the island from Popham. The board of directors held an emergency meeting. Hampton, who had been a

23. Record, 176–79.

24. For meetings of the Colony, Unincorporated see Jacksonville Times-Union, Jan. 16, 20, 25, 1919; Feb. 1, 2, 1919.

traveling salesman before he became a shipyard worker, was directed to perform his duties as secretary and inform Popham of the meeting. Busy selling memberships in Tampa, Popham received Hampton's telegram, boarded the first train out, and hurried to Jacksonville for the session.

Popham did not control the board of directors, and he had to accept the decision that was reached. The officials decided to buy from Saxon, not Popham. The promoter would be paid $13,000 as a commission for his work and to cover $2,000 he had spent furnishing the island's hotel and building an annex to it. Popham was reduced in power to the position of a salaried employee at thirty dollars a week.[25]

Temporarily defeated, Popham continued soliciting memberships, and "auxiliaries" were established at Tampa, Jacksonville, and Apalachicola. Once the goal of five hundred members was achieved, Popham went with Anderson to Tallahassee to make a down payment of $5,000 to Saxon. Then in February 1919, Saxon sold the island to the St. George Co-Operative Colony, Unincorporated, for $30,000. Payments were to be $500 a month, and a general warranty deed was deposited in escrow at the Capital City Bank. Saxon was protected by a clause declaring that if the payments lapsed, the contract was forfeited.[26]

In the next few months, Popham maneuvered successfully to have the colonists reduce their board of directors from thirteen to seven, most of whom were loyal to him. Among the new directors was William H. Collier—recently discharged from the navy, a prospective law student, and for the moment an avid Popham follower. Collier would join Abbott and Hampton as Popham's chief lieutenants. The board elected Abbott president and general manager, and Popham was unopposed for vice president.[27]

News spread of the St. George Co-Operative Colony, Unincorporated. On a visit to Atlanta in July 1919, Popham was interviewed by Ward Green of the Atlanta *Journal* and featured in that newspaper's Sunday magazine. The story was remarkable. Popham

25. Brief for Defendant, 7; Popham testimony, 1088 (21–24), in *Record*.
26. Franklin County Deed Book U, 202–6.
27. Popham testimony, 1088 (21–24), in *Record*.

supplied the reporter with a series of truths, half-truths, and out-right fabrications. Yet he revealed a compassionate philosophy far in advance of the times, an imagination with few limits, and a romantic showmanship that was both his blessing and his curse.

Green simply did not know what to make of Popham's proposal: a utopian settlement, self-supporting and self-governing, whose watchwords were equality, democracy, and cooperation. William Lee explained how he had purchased Saint George Island and lived on it in a self-built bungalow for seven years (all of the details of possession and residence were false). "Then," Popham added, "I got to thinking about it, and I decided I was very selfish. I decided I ought to give others the chance to enjoy the life perfect even as I was enjoying it. And so I decided to found a city by the sea." Popham noted that he went to Jacksonville and interested others and then provided an elaborate discussion of how the St. George Co-Operative Colony, Unincorporated, would operate. Each colonist was approved by the board of directors, who put the $200 membership fee in a common fund. Every member was responsible for building his or her own bungalow, but it was expected that each would get help from other members. Various trades and professions would be represented: shipbuilders, ministers, lawyers, cooks, fishermen, hunters, chauffeurs, and more. No outside labor would be hired. Members would raise their own food and livestock, saw lumber from their own sawmills, refine sugar, build a fleet of oyster boats and schooners, run cooperative laundries, theaters, and utilities. Periodically a member would transfer from one job to another, always receiving five dollars a day. All money brought in would go to a common fund. There would be no competition, and the major source of income would be the fishing industry.

Some of Popham's enthusiastic statements were not true. He told Green that the St. George Co-Operative Colony, Unincorporated, had an exclusive contract to furnish its products to the U.S. government as long as the world food shortage existed. There was no such contract. Besides owning a factory that would can oysters, shrimp, fish, and other seafoods, the members would engage in the porpoise industry. Without doubt Popham had stood on the sand beaches of Saint George Island and watched schools of uninhibited porpoises roll by. He easily envisioned putting them to commercial uses. Explaining to the Atlanta journalist his design for a special ship that would capture the intelligent mammals, Popham next outlined an arrangement for a slaughtering pen. Up to 1919, porpoises had not been considered a food fish. But that did not matter. Popham would educate Americans to the pleasures of eating dolphins. Beyond that, in the colony's tannery, dolphin hides would be tanned and converted into the finest shoestrings in the world.

On the island proper, the members would have cattle, hogs, and poultry. Popham mentioned the abundant wildlife on Saint George Island, both beasts and birds. He counted six freshwater lakes full of freshwater fish that did not exist (Saint Vincent Island, however, did have some freshwater ponds). Equally nonexistent was the $220,000 steel bridge built by the government to span the bay from Apalachicola to Saint George Island. Not until 1965 would a bridge connect the mainland (from Eastpoint) with the island. His claims of state and federal hard-surfaced roads crisscrossing the island were interesting but untrue. The loquacious minister mentioned plans for a fifty-mile racecourse for cars around the island and a streetcar system that would split it down the middle.

Leisure time was good anywhere, but it was especially good on Saint George Island because there was always something to do. Life on the island, according to Popham, was one long dream of "fishing, hunting, and wooing to the sweet song of the sad sea waves." Popham's utopia would be exactly that. There would be racing, boating, hunting, and fishing. Picture shows and theaters would be readily available, but they would be censored, as Popham said, to make sure no vampire movies or sex plays were presented. Because colonists were on their own to obey the law, there would be no jail or police force. There would be no bill collectors. The only rule in effect was the golden rule. Members had to agree in advance that if they broke the peace, expulsion from the island would follow.

Not only would labor be shared and rotated, no one could work over eight hours a day. "Our main crop," Popham declared, "will be children." Children could not be employed or forced to labor. "We shall give them a happy childhood that will be followed by a useful manhood," he said. "A big industrial school will be established on the island, together with other schools that will supply all the best of modern education, from the grammar grades to a university training." At some point Popham planned to have Saint George Island attain the legal status of a colony which, apparently, would function something like a county.

The Atlanta *Journal* included several pictures of Saint George Island. Another photograph showed William Lee standing erect, balding, well-dressed with a watch chain hanging prominently from his coat pocket, and wearing a jaunty bow tie. Maude stood at his side, buxom, slightly regal, her ever-present pince-nez glasses on display. Between them was a smiling and obviously healthy William Lee, Jr. (*illustration,* Group 2). Green, like many others, was impressed by his subject. "It is not so much Mr. Popham's eloquence—though few young men can out elocute him when it comes to subjects of love, romance, and the light that never was on land or sea." It was not so much that, Green wrote; it was more his simple statements of how democracy could work.[28] The Atlanta writer's problem was understandable. How could one explain a man who, on the one hand, seriously offered an outrageous scheme to market porpoise shoestrings and, on the other, so staunchly opposed child labor?

Upset by the article, colonists Hampton and Anderson sought to downplay some of Popham's more farfetched claims. They were more concerned than the Apalachicola *Times,* whose editor found the interview amusing and was glad that no accidents had occurred on Popham's steel bridge.[29] Hampton and Anderson dispatched a long letter of denial to the *Times* and the Atlanta *Journal.* The St. George Co-Operative Colony, Unincorporated, had such a bright future, they contended, "it is not necessary to make exaggerated statements concerning it." The Apalachicola Chamber of Commerce also sent a letter to the *Journal* deploring the erroneous publicity.[30] Popham was not fazed by the brief controversy.

For all his conversion of the Saint George Island Company to a

28. Ward Green, "Where Everybody Gets $5.00 a Day," Atlanta *Journal Sunday Magazine,* July 13, 1919.
29. Apalachicola *Times,* July 19, 1919.
30. Ibid., July 26, 1919.

colony, Popham still had to deal with the determined Helen Smith and the Saint George Company. To secure his own position, Popham appealed to his old associate W. H. Roat to move from Jacksonville to Apalachicola and serve as resident agent for the St. George Co-Operative Colony, Unincorporated. Roat, a stockholder in the venture, complied and on his return began issuing optimistic statements of certain profits.[31] Freed from wartime restraints, Mrs. Smith and her associates also became busy. As a kind of subsidiary, they formed the Saint George Packing Company. Besides engaging in canning shrimp and oysters, the Saint George Packing Company projected a hog and poultry ranch, a shipyard, and a concrete block plant. Mrs. Smith worked at developing an oyster cocktail for commercial uses. The company bought a boat, named it *The Governor,* and used it in express service to and from the island.[32]

Popham and his board of directors countered by visiting Apalachicola in March 1919. At a public meeting they explained how the colony would benefit Franklin County. Popham emphasized that the papers transferring the island to the St. George Co-Operative Colony, Unincorporated, had been signed.[33] Even so, the relationship with the Saint George Company was unclear.

When the warm weather began in May, Mrs. Smith announced that The Breakers was open for the season. Bridge parties and pre-ordered fish suppers were house specialties, and *The Governor* lay at Marks's dock in Apalachicola waiting for patrons to board.[34] An angry Hampton wrote from Jacksonville that Saxon had released Saint George Island to the St. George Co-Operative Colony, Unincorporated. *The Breakers,* he promised, would soon be enlarged and would operate under new management.[35] Mrs. Smith, with the backing of Captain Malcolmson, replied that her company had a lease to operate The Breakers for several years and that she intended to carry it out.[36] Even though Saxon upheld Popham—he

31. Ibid., Feb. 1, 15, 1919.
32. Ibid., Feb. 1, 22, 1919.
33. Ibid., Mar. 29, 1919.
34. Ibid., May 3, 1919.
35. Ibid., May 24, 1919.
36. Ibid., May 31, 1919.

wrote a letter stating that he had sold the island to St. George Co-
Operative Colony, Unincorporated, and had never leased any of
it—Mrs. Smith continued to operate The Breakers throughout the
summer.[37] Litigation followed, and after several decisions and appeals, Mrs. Smith was forced to relinquish the hotel.[38] The Saint
George Company itself withdrew from any further attempts to develop the island.

Even while the dispute over the hotel was in progress, the St.
George Co-Operative Colony, Unincorporated, was busy on the island. By July, Popham had Captain D. T. Brown driving piles for a
new dock and a fish- and oysterhouse at Nick's Hole. J. P. Webster,
a stockholder and temporarily local manager, oversaw a work crew
of ten that repaired the boardwalk across the island. *The Mayflower* was purchased to haul freight and passengers, and Webster
ordered large stocks of lumber from local mills to build cottages.[39]
A few colonists arrived in Apalachicola and caused a boom among
renters. Popham could be forgiven for his expansive statements to
the Atlanta *Journal.* Stockholders were in and out of town constantly. By September the Pophams and the Abbotts became permanent residents. The St. George Co-Operative Colony, Unincorporated, rented an office at Coombs's wharf (plans were made to
erect a cold storage plant next to it). The fish- and oysterhouse began operation under the management of Lonnie Meyers. A Captain Lloyd commanded *The Mayflower,* but it would soon be used
for shrimping and another boat, the *Edna,* would carry island passengers. Few doubted the need for the *Edna.* Transportation would
be essential for the occupants of the cottages soon to rise on Saint
George Island.[40]

After the hotel dispute was settled, Mrs. Smith moved to Sara-
sota. Some women members of the St. George Co-Operative Colony,
Unincorporated, made brief attempts at managing the hotel, but
the duties were finally turned over to Mrs. J. W. Reeves. The name
was changed to the Reeves Boarding House (although it was al-

37. Ibid., June 14, Aug. 9, Sept. 20, 1919.
38. Ibid., Sept. 27, 1919; Franklin County Deed Book U, 96.
39. Apalachicola *Times,* July 5, 1919.
40. Ibid. Oct. 18, 1919.

ways popularly called the Club House), and she ran it as a commercial venture. Good food, it was promised, "will abound under her careful and experienced management."[41] Mrs. Reeves headed her menu one Saturday with a fifteen-pound raccoon.[42]

Although his title "resident agent" brought him no pay, Roat repaired and enlarged the Club House and the bathhouse. He was supposed to lay out divisions for a town, but never did, although he surveyed the island. Roat's daughter, Naomi, then and in the future, was employed as an organizer and officer in various Popham enterprises.[43] The Club House was widely used, and one swimming, dining, and dancing party came from the mainland with its own all-black orchestra. Apalachicolans marveled at it all.[44]

The St. George Co-Operative Colony, Unincorporated, appeared to be in a good position, but it was torn by internecine conflict. Some members opposed Popham's freewheeling ways and were dissatisfied. There were arguments over whether to cut and sell the island's timber. Periodic reports, although standard procedure in most business ventures, were rarely issued. Particularly disturbed was Mrs. A. M. Jones, who was defeated for secretary-stenographer in the reorganization struggle. She instituted a suit in federal court against St. George Co-Operative Colony, Unincorporated, and it eventually went into receivership. Before the receivership was ordered, the colonists had paid Saxon about $8,000 of their $35,000 indebtedness.

Aware of the difficulties, Hampton, Collier, and Abbott decided to incorporate the enterprise and expand it. Accordingly, they applied for a charter as the St. George Co-Operative Colony, Incorporated. They asked the members of the unincorporated venture to shift their membership to the new one. In truth, the founders merely expanded the old plan. Capitalization was at $100,000 divided into five hundred shares valued at $200 each. As it turned

41. Ibid., Nov. 15, 1919; see ibid., Oct. 25, Nov. 1, 1919; May 8, 1920.
42. Ibid., Nov. 29, 1919.
43. Brief for Defendant, 5–6. At one time Roat and Popham discussed forming yet another company to be called the Florida Board of Trade. Roat was to be president, but the idea was abandoned.
44. Apalachicola *Times*, May 15, July 17, 24, Aug. 14, 1920.

out, the company soon had 770 subscribers. Mrs. Jones, far from giving up, raised a counterpetition and presented it to the governor, who finally refused to grant the charter. Later, in December 1919, the company was incorporated in Delaware.[45]

After the St. George Co-Operative Colony, Unincorporated, went into receivership, it defaulted on its payments, and, once again, Saxon found himself in possession of the island. There seemed to be no way that he could rid himself of it. Yet the newly formed St. George Co-Operative Colony, Inc., was interested in gaining title. The accommodating Saxon agreed to sell Saint George Island to the corporation for $27,000 (as previously mentioned, the St. George Co-Operative Colony, Unincorporated, had paid some $8,000 to Saxon). The sale was made on June 26, 1920. Officials of the St. George Co-Operative Colony, Inc., agreed to pay $6,000 by August 5 and the balance at $500 a month.[46]

With Abbott as president and Collier as secretary, the St. George Co-Operative Colony, Inc., acquired new office space in Apalachicola. Like its unincorporated predecessor, the company had large ambitions. It proposed to deal in real estate, develop a town, and service it with utilities. Then there would be fisheries, sponge operations, fertilizer factories, boat construction, hotels, parks, bathhouses, moving picture theaters, public halls, restaurants, electric railways, streetcar lines, and tramways. The company would own, operate, lease, and hire automobiles, taxis, and trucks. Also planned were electric power, gas, and ice plants; cold storage, bakeries, and general stores; various factories, tanneries, livestock and poultry, apiaries, and various kinds of agriculture. The company began modestly with a thousand dollars, but it was given a look of visible prosperity when Abbott bought and put in service a fast boat named the *Broadbill*.[47]

45. *Record*, 412–13; Popham testimony, 1088 (25), in *Record;* Brief for Defendant, 13.

46. Franklin County Deed Book V, 222–25. Certain lots in the Ruff Survey were excepted. In November 1919, as the Colony was striving for incorporation, it mortgaged the island to secure an indebtedness of $1,500 to William Darby. See Franklin County Mortgage Book J, 34–37.

47. Franklin County Incorporation Book A, 239–48; Apalachicola *Times,* Sept. 4, 1920.

For once, Popham stayed out of a promotional enterprise. He bought but quickly sold a certificate or share in the St. George Co-Operative Colony, Inc., and he never had an official connection with it. Still, he wanted Saint George Island as badly as Saxon wanted to dispose of it. Moving to Apalachicola in the fall of 1919, Popham had become the best known man in town. One either read about him in the paper or, almost as frequently, read something by him. In November 1919, he placed his first poem in the *Times* (many were to follow). It had forty-eight lines and was entitled "The Golden Sunset Sinking o'er the Florida Sea." Editor Johnston commented that "Poetry is as natural with Mr. Popham, as song is to a mockingbird."[48]

Popham's status automatically gave him a position that commanded respect. If he could only gain legal title to the island, he would have a base from which to launch a number of activities. When the St. George Co-Operative Colony, Inc., had difficulties with what later generations would call cash flow, Popham got his chance. He loaned the new corporation $6,000 but protected himself by attaching a provision that permitted him the right to prevent the purchase contract from lapsing. The St. George Co-Operative Colony, Inc., further gave Popham ten acres of land and fifty unimproved lots adjoining the Ruff survey on the west.[49]

Despite the financial assistance, the company was unable to meet its obligations to Saxon, and Popham made several payments to the banker out of his own pocket. Popham testified later that because it made no sense for him to meet the company's obligations, "I notified the St. George Co-Operative Colony Incorporated, and Mr. Saxon that I did not intend to make any more payments at all."[50] When the installments ceased the contract lapsed, and in the fall of 1920 Saxon found himself still the owner of a familiar albatross, a sliver of land in Apalachicola Bay.

The physical presence of Saint George Island and Apalachicola Bay were beguiling attractions for Popham. In 1920 he devised a plan to exploit for profit the bay's natural resources. The ancient

48. Apalachicola *Times*, Nov. 15, 1919; see ibid., Nov. 1, 22, 1919.
49. Franklin County Deed Book V, 112–15.
50. Popham testimony, 1088 (29), in *Record*.

oyster industry, he decided, was moribund but could become a lucrative business. Various government surveys of the oyster beds had been made, the latest in 1916. Poring over the published report, Popham was dazzled by the reproductive capacity of oysters. He went into action. On October 1, 1920, William Lee and Maude established the Oyster Growers' Co-Operative Association, an unincorporated enterprise operating under a declaration of trust. Simply put, the company planned to plant, harvest, handle, and process oysters. Quickly issued and, as it turned out, quickly sold, were a thousand shares or certificates of beneficial interest in the business. Large advertisements promoting the company were inserted in such newspapers as the Tampa *Tribune*.[51]

Popham tied the future of the Oyster Growers' Co-Operative Association to acquiring Saint George Island. Before that, he succeeded in making the association well known. "Apalachicola Is Good Enough for Me" established in poetry Popham's affection for his adopted town, and Editor Johnston, who published the poem, remarked that it "is worth a place in your scrapbook." One verse called attention to William Lee's new interest:

> Like sea gulls, the oyster boats
> Make this port their home—
> And like the pelican that floats
> O'er the rolling foam
> This enterprising fleet
> And boatmen worry-free,
> Make Apalachicola
> Good enough for me.[52]

A week later he dedicated a poem, "At the Rainbow's End," to members of the Oyster Growers' Co-Operative Association. In August 1921, Popham had no less than four poems in the *Times*: "Down in Florida on Our Oyster Farm" (there was no subtlety in its verses); "The Game of Chance"; "Here's to Florida"; and "The

51. Franklin County Deed Book V, 144–52; Apalachicola *Times*, Nov. 27, 1920, quoting Tampa *Tribune*.
52. Apalachicola *Times*, July 23, 1921.

Land of Childhood" (accompanied by an advertisement extolling the association). "The Game of Chance" was a clever kind of limerick in the style of the Burma-Shave signs that would not make their appearance until 1925:

> A fair young girl of sweet sixteen
> Wanted to ride in a new machine;
> The young couple sat beneath the trees—
> He proposed to the girl on bended knees;
> He lost his heart and lost his head;
> Bought a Ford and they were wed;
> He wrecked his Ford and broke her arm,
> And lost everything but his oyster farm.[53]

By the late summer of 1921, Popham claimed that the association, capitalized at $425,000, had over seven hundred members in forty-eight states. He said that a score of boats and crews were engaged in planting five hundred acres; shells were planted in piles of fifty barrels and on top of that another fifty barrels of coon oysters were being planted. The first harvest was over two years away, but he said that the association had $255,000, owned river lots where modern factories would rise, paid its debts in cash, and did not owe a penny. Signs of the evangelist-promoter's affluence were seen in his new Ford and new boat, the *President*.[54]

Newspapers around the state ran stories about the association, and at long last Popham was solvent enough to talk terms with Saxon.[55] Gone forever, it seemed, were the days when Popham would have to offer copyrights on his books to secure a loan. That was just as well because a warehouse fire in Louisville destroyed most of Popham's book inventory. He estimated the loss at $10,000, but some of the volumes were saved and he donated a copy of each book to the library in Apalachicola.[56]

53. Ibid., Aug. 20, 1921; see also ibid., July 30, Aug. 13, 27, 1921. Frank Rowsome, Jr., *The Verse by the Side of the Road*, 14–15.
54. Apalachicola *Times*, Aug. 20, 1921. Coon oysters have thin shells and grow in clusters in shallow waters.
55. Ibid., Nov. 5, 1921, quoting Tampa *Tribune*, Oct. 23, 1921.
56. Apalachicola *Times*, Nov. 5, 1921.

In late July, Saxon had conveyed the island by warranty deed to his Capital City Bank. The St. George Co-Operative Colony, Inc., now a shambles, remained incapable of buying the property, and on December 7, 1921, Saxon got Saint George Island back by a quit claim deed.[57] His action was necessary because on the same day he sold the island to Popham. Paying $5,000 down, Popham agreed to supply the remaining amount owed by the St. George Co-Operative Colony, Inc. Popham also agreed to be bound with Saxon in any judgments growing out of lawsuits involving the two cooperative colonies.[58]

Popham had achieved fame for his efforts to revitalize the oyster industry. When he journeyed to Tallahassee to close the purchase with Saxon, the visit became news. Reporting the new owner's plans for the island, the *Daily Democrat* dealt in understatement: "It is the intention of Mr. Popham to develop it as a great pleasure resort."[59] The purchase made banner headlines in the Apalachicola *Times*. Popham's poems, such as "Consider the Oyster," were now accompanied by advertisements that discussed Saint George Island as well as the association's dealings in oysters. A delighted Popham gave all the preachers, blacks and whites, and their families, a turkey and cranberries for their Christmas dinner.[60] At long last, Popham owned Saint George Island.

As for Saxon, after receiving numerous promises and partial payments, he finally had a valid check for $22,224.50.[61] The banker liked Popham, but he looked forward to future business dealings that were more conventional.

57. Franklin County Deed Book V, 82–86, 86–87.
58. Ibid., W, 82–86. A Bill of Complaint had been filed in the District Court of the United States for the Northern District of Florida. Popham, Saxon, and the Colony, Incorporated were defendants in a suit asking the cancellation of certain contracts and an accounting of all transactions. See Franklin County Les Pendens Record A, 149–51. No disposition was given.
59. Tallahassee *Daily Democrat*, Dec. 7, 1921.
60. Apalachicola *Times*, Dec. 10, 24, 1921.
61. Popham testimony, 1088 (29), in *Record*.

11

The Florida Co-Operative Colony and Apalachicola Land & Development Company

As Apalachicola and Franklin County moved into the 1920s, Popham's unusual air of great expectations was at least partially matched by the mood of the populace. Even the stolid annual report of the State of Florida Department of Agriculture rang with accounts of rich, natural oyster reefs and abundant shrimp in Saint George Sound and beyond. On the mainland, according to the official estimate, "the streets of Apalachicola are filled with life and business activity": the "roar and clamor of sawmills, the shrieking whistles of tugs and steamers towing logs and barges of lumber," "the daily arriving and departing of steamers from points on the river and gulf, the whistles of canning factories, planing mills and sash, door and blind factories [all] tangible evidence of prosperity."[1]

People's attention was caught by such things as, in the spring and summer of 1921, Rudolph Marshall's boat, powered by a two-hundred-horsepower Curtis airplane engine, which he had built for Rice Brothers, and Eric von Stroheim's performance in "Blind Husbands" at the Dixie Theatre.[2] One constant topic of conversation was the attempt to enforce the Eighteenth Amendment. On a dark night a boat put out from a schooner; it was quietly rowed ashore at Saint George Island, where its crew worked quickly to

1. Florida Department of Agriculture, *Seventeenth Biennial* . . ., Part 1, 1921–22, 95.
2. Apalachicola *Times*, June 4, Sept. 10, 1921.

bury several crates before returning to the schooner. The crew's movements were observed but not by the law. For a few days people talked about thwarting the rumrunners and boasted quietly about how fine it was to drink good liquor again. There was silent admiration for W. A. Maxwell, a moonshiner who was arrested at his still, taken before a jury, and fined three hundred dollars. Because he couldn't pay, he was sentenced to six months' hard labor. Unremorseful, Maxwell vowed to return and improve the quality of his product.[3]

With William Lee Popham in town, life was even more exciting. He delayed promoting the Oyster Growers' Co-Operative Association by devoting his energies to a smaller venture. Lying indirectly across from the waterfront of Apalachicola in the river's deep channel was a narrow strip of land about five miles long. The island (to give it an undeserved geographical dignity), covered with marsh grass, was slightly above sea level. On the west it bordered the Apalachicola River and on the east the St. Marks River; the Little St. Marks River ran through it. At extremely high tide it was covered with a foot or more of water. The Porter family had owned the island for over sixty years, but since the marshy expanse was of little value, it had done nothing except pay taxes on it. "I didn't use it for anything but snipe hunting; it was fine snipe hunting," R. G. Porter said later. "The island never had any name."[4] But to the visionary Popham, the location conjured up no less a parallel than Venice. He envisioned the island criss-crossed with canals like the Italian city, bustling with activity and economic importance.

Popham discussed the possibilities with his associates Abbott and Collier, who became caught up in the poet's enthusiasm. Nor is it difficult to imagine Porter's pleasure when he told his wife Steffie that Popham had offered him $2,000 for the 2,720 acres that made up the island.[5] People in Franklin County and Apalachicola were growing accustomed to Popham's extravagant schemes, but they were incredulous at his spending so much money for an island that disappeared periodically.

3. Ibid., Sept. 25, 1920; June 25, 1921.
4. Testimony of R. G. Porter in *Record*, 352–59.
5. Franklin County Deed Book V, 226. Porter was allowed to keep the timber on the island for twenty years.

The Florida Co-Operative Colony was organized in April 1920. It bore an obvious kinship to previous colonies and was set up under a declaration of trust signed by Popham, Abbott, Collier, Rupert Smith of Arcadia, and D. B. Dickson, a large property owner and merchant of Lakeland. Duly filed with the clerk of the circuit court, the document committed the Florida Co-Operative Colony to "take over, hold, own, conduct and manage the business of planting, cultivating, harvesting, shucking and marketing shell fish in Apalachicola Bay, St. George Sound, and St. Vincent Sound," and "to act as agents to survey and stake for individuals, citizens of Florida, water bottoms, which they may hold, not exceeding twenty acres, under leases from the State of Florida, and to plant, cultivate, harvest and market shell fish as such agent."[6]

Popham began the pleasurable task of composing promotional literature. Early in February 1920, he sent out pamphlets and brochures soliciting members (even though the Florida Co-Operative Colony was not formally organized until September). Brushing up on his poetic skills, Popham combined art with economics in one pamphlet by interspersing verses with the explanations of how the Florida Co-Operative Colony would operate. One tract was entitled "A Little Book of Florida Poems." He used this method of juxtaposing verses with technical information in other booklets.

Popham's rhymes complemented his plans for the land he had acquired from Porter. William Lee had the unsound stretch surveyed and platted and gave it the historic name of Venice Island. A deed was executed to the Florida Co-Operative Colony for $60,000 and put on deposit in the American Exchange Bank at Apalachicola. The deed would be held in escrow and turned over to the colony on payment of the money. Since the promoter had only paid $2,000 for Venice Island, the government would later interpret the transaction as a scheme by Popham to steal $58,000.

To join the Florida Co-Operative Colony one put $25 down and paid the balance of the $80 fee in monthly installments. In return, the investor received forty 26-by-40-foot lots, one a business lot fronting the Apalachicola River and the remainder stretching in an

6. Ibid., 17; testimony of I. M. Fink and advertisement in Tampa *Sunday Tribune*, July 18, 1920, quoted in *Record*, 500.

unbroken tract further back. The member then had a right to acquire twenty acres of oyster bottoms from the state. The bottoms would be surveyed and planted by the Florida Co-Operative Colony for $55, bringing the total membership price to $135 for the lots and oyster lease. Popham explained the benefits: the lots would shortly be worth $200 each (or $8,000 for all forty); after the fifth year the oyster farm would be producing sixteen thousand barrels of oysters, and at a dollar a barrel the yield would be more than $1,300 a month.[7]

The new company secured business space in the offices of the earlier Oyster Growers' Co-Operative Association. Newspaper advertisements announced the project and, like the pamphlets, contained coupon applications that could be mailed to the company with a membership fee that was soon reduced to $10.[8] Membership was limited to 770 persons. Yet the promotion was so convincing that 700 Floridians and 142 non-Floridians subscribed, and it was ultimately claimed that 912 investors signed up. The astonishing success was achieved by Popham's salesmanship and the aid he got from his coworkers, especially Abbott. One of Popham's poems engaged in laconic boosterism and reflected on current trends:

> Lovers are the thickest,
> Grass widowers the slickest,
> And they marry the quickest
> In Florida
>
> 'Near beer' is the nearest
> And the price is the dearest—
> In Florida
>
> The sucker's getting wiser
> To the profiteer and miser

7. Brief for Defendant, 18; testimony of F. B. Wakefield and I. M. Fink quoted in *Record*, 532, 910. Many sales were in the names of the Pophams and the Abbotts. See Franklin County Deed Book V, passim.

8. Florida Department of Agriculture, Shell Fish Division, *Second Bi-Ennial Report*, 1915–16, 17, 19–22.

And damns 'em with the kaiser—
In Florida

Business is the hummest,
Rum-shops are the rummest,
And politics are the bummest—
In Florida

Red-bugs have a relish
And a bite that's hellish
In Florida

The cost of living's higher,
'Wet goods' getting dryer,
In Florida.[9]

The poem went on for twenty-nine verses, but for those who disliked poetry, there was Popham's prose. Smooth as the tupelo
honey that abounded in Franklin County, Popham's sentences read
like patent medicine claims. To be a member of the Florida Co-
Operative Colony required no extended labor: "Nature's hand
works for you while your sleep." The oyster season, from October
1 to April 15, left "five months and fifteen days' vacation by the
sea every year, where fishing boating, hunting, and pleasuring are
good the year around." Oysters were amazingly prolific, and Popham gave added authority to his claims by citing productivity and
profit possibilities from the 1915–16 biennial report of the State of
Florida Department of Agriculture's Shell Fish Division.[10]

Prospective investors were reminded that privately leased
grounds or artificial beds of riparian owners had no season and that
the restriction of using hand tongs to remove oysters did not apply.
A private oyster farmer could harvest with a scraper and dredge
attached to the rear of a powerboat, greatly decreasing the labor

9. *Record*, 501–14, 527–28, quoting pamphlet. The map showing the oyster
bottoms in Franklin County, prepared in Washington by the Bureau of Fisheries,
was included in the Florida Department of Agriculture, Shell Fish Division, *Second Bi-Ennial Report*.
10. See *Record*, 515–40.

involved. The poet-developer also cited figures from the governmental survey of 1916 that had mapped Apalachicola Bay's oyster bottoms. He called the attention of potential buyers to Apalachicola's fifteen oyster packinghouses and four canning factories employing a thousand persons and to the two hundred boats located just opposite the island on the waterfront. In Popham's metaphor, it was a "liquid gold mine." There was the added bonus of distance from the tensions of city life. "Can you beat it—beneath or on the topside of God's round earth?" There were sea breezes in the summer and sunbeams in the winter and, by a stretch of Popham's imagination, evergeen orange trees bending with yellow gold (a few county residents raised satsuma oranges).

It was not necessary to move to Apalachicola to join the Florida Co-Operative Colony. The initial membership fee was to be forwarded to the colony's address over Tibbett's Corner in Tampa. Monthly payments would be sent to the American Exchange Bank in Apalachicola, where cashier F. B. Wakefield held the deed in escrow. Still, it would be difficult to resist moving to Florida. Where else were there mockingbirds, waving palms, sighing pines, and blooming magnolias, not to mention ocean music and sea breezes?[11]

No matter what his plan, Popham liked to enlarge and rearrange it. Whatever the theme, there were inevitable variations. The Florida Co-Operative Colony was no exception. In another pamphlet the entrepreneur began with a poem and then explained the benefits of owning a "liquid homestead." He suggested that the 770 owners employ a reliable and experienced salaried manager to look after their interests full time, with himself as overseer. All the investors neeeded to do was pay an extra ten cents a week and Popham would handle all of the details.

Bordered at its upper end by the railroad bridge that spanned the river, Venice Island had a connection with the mainland. But even Popham admitted that, for all its glories, Venice Island, was not an ideal place for homes. Once he got control of Saint George Island in 1921, Popham tried to turn his ownership to advantage by changing the terms of joining the Florida Co-Operative Colony. Now, a member paid five dollars down, ten dollars a month at

11. National Archives, Record Group 28.

6 percent interest, and upon reaching one hundred dollars received the forty lots on Venice Island plus a 50-by-100-foot lot on
Saint George Island for a residence. Popham and his associates
agreed to donate $5,000 from their own profits toward the con-
struction of an oyster packinghouse on Venice Island and a lot to
build it on. Another possibility, in case a buyer was not interested
in an oyster farm, was to invest ten dollars in the packinghouse
and have equal ownership in it.[12]

The Florida Co-Operative Colony's existence was threatened in
the spring and summer of 1921 by personality clashes and legal
difficulties. Popham was frustrated in his attempts to secure leases
from William A. McRae, the commissioner of agriculture. On numerous trips to Tallahassee, William Lee always seemed to find the
commissioner out of town. Equally frustrating, he encountered
negative opinions from the attorney general. As a result, neither
the Florida Co-Operative Colony nor any of its members was
granted leases.[13] Even so, Popham assured the membership that he
was fighting for their rights.

A rift developed between Popham and his associates. Although
Abbott and Collier were closely involved with him in the Florida Co-Operative Colony, they became instrumental in forming a
new organization, the Apalachicola Land & Development Company. Begun in March 1921 (a four-column front-page advertisement in the Times heralded its arrival), the company did nothing
to discourage the idea that it was incorporated. It was actually organized under a declaration of trust.[14] Abbott, as secretary and
general manager, and Collier, as assistant secretary and treasurer,
had begun to issue subscription blanks and promotional booklets
by July. The company was capitalized at $1 million and its shares
were $100 each (a fourth of the shares would be issued to the pub-
lic). The owners planned to purchase land from several prominent

12. Brief for Defendant, 32; *Record*, 106–16; Franklin County Deed Book V,
252–60.

13. National Archives, Record Group 28; Apalachicola *Times*, Mar. 12,
1921.

14. Brief for Defendant, 32; *Record*, 106–16; Franklin County Deed Book,
252–60. At a March meeting in Lakeland, Florida, Popham resigned from the
Florida Co-Operative Colony at the request of the members.

men in Apalachicola and to engage in the oyster and shrimp business.[15]

Collier and others maintained that the area's oyster bottoms belonged to the abutting property owners, not to the state. They argued that the Forbes Purchase was not in the conveyance of Florida by Spain to the United States in 1821. Since it was assumed that land in the Forbes Purchase had already been disposed of to private individuals, the government had never surveyed the land and had no general plat of it. Reducing its claims of sovereignty, the Apalachicola Land & Development Company conceded to Florida and the United States jurisdiction over the land. Yet the company's officers declared that the conveyance by deed from the crown of Spain to Forbes gave them control of submerged lands and riparian rights. Such logic was in keeping with other real estate manipulations taking place in Florida during the 1920s.

Putting would-be action to theory, the Apalachicola Land & Development Company's officers purchased considerable acreage on the mainland. They advised likely investors that each share of stock included an undivided interest in some sixty thousand acres of water bottom, nine thousand acres of bayshore land, a $30,000 packinghouse, a $10,000 dredge boat, a $40,000 ice plant, a $10,000 fish scrap dryer, and about four hundred feet of riverfront in Apalachicola. Inspired by Popham's example, the managers promised enormous profits.[16]

Popham was angered by the apostacy of his colleagues, particularly Abbott's. In an article published in the *Times* in March 1921, Popham accused the rival company of trying to sell the natural oyster beds to prospective customers. Although he tempered his tirade with a poem, "The Land Where the Oyster Grows," he was irate at claims by Abbott's group that they owned Saint George Island. A few days later Popham made a public retraction. He explained that he had talked with the company's board of trustees and had been convinced that their sale of stock in the natural beds was contingent upon winning a suit instituted against the state. He endorsed the trustees as honorable men and resigned as president

15. *Record*, 494–95; Brief for Defendant, 32.
16. Franklin County Deed Book V, 263–66; Brief for Defendant, 33.

of the Florida Co-Operative Colony. The Apalachicola Land & Development Company permitted members of the Florida Co-Operative Colony to transfer their interests to the new endeavor, and many took advantage of the offer.[17] In the weeks that followed, Popham and Abbott used the *Times* to explain their positions, although they clarified little. At one point Popham replied to a full-page exposition by Abbott by purchasing three columns of space and leaving them blank.[18]

Of greater importance was the case brought by the Apalachicola Land & Development Company against the state. Lawyers for the plaintiff argued that the tracts granted first by the Tallapoosa and Seminole Indians in 1804 and 1806 to Panton, Leslie and Company and second by the Lower Creek and Seminole Indians in 1811 to John Forbes and Company included the rights to submerged lands. According to the directors of the Apalachicola Land & Development Company, the Indian-Spanish grants were confirmed in 1835 by *Mitchel v. the United States* and passed directly to them. The company cited volume four of the *American State Papers* as its authority but ignored such important qualifying statutes as the Florida Riparian Act of 1856. In any event, the argument continued on appeal from the circuit court to the Florida Supreme Court, which ultimately ruled against the company in 1923. The court heard extensive arguments before finally concluding that the Indian-Spanish grants did "not include submerged lands or tide lands."[19]

Popham had seemingly forsaken the Florida Co-Operative Colony and had stamped his approval on the work of the Apalachicola Land & Development Company. But things were rarely what they seemed with Popham. In October 1920, he had formed the Oyster Growers' Co-Operative Association with himself as president. The new company, as mentioned, was organized under a declaration of trust with William Lee and Maude as the trustees.[20] In the spring of 1921 he asked members of the Florida Co-Operative

17. Apalachicola *Times*, Mar. 3, Apr. 4, 1921.
18. Ibid., Apr. 9, 16, 23, 1921.
19. *Florida Reports* 86 (1923): 397. For the full case see 393–465.
20. Franklin County Deed Book V, 144–52.

Colony to join him in a reorganization, agreeing to assume the difficulties and expenses of setting up the company practically single-handedly. "I am serving you in this capacity," he declared, "because your welfare and my honor are at stake, although at a great sacrifice on my part, in giving this matter my time and personal attention." [21]

While all this maneuvering was going on, the state legislature passed the important Butler-Lindsay Riparian Act, named for its sponsors, Senators B. H. Lindsay of Bonifay and J. Turner Butler of Jacksonville. Collier and the Development Company took much credit for lobbying the measure through. Especially to the company's liking was the provision awarding the ownership of oyster bottoms to the property holders whose land they abutted. Yet Popham, who had been assured of a lease to five hundred acres of oyster bottoms by Commissioner of Agriculture McRae, was also active in the capitol. Finally making contact with McRae and others, Popham claimed victory for his own lobbying: the natural oyster beds and planting bottoms were state-controlled, and the state had the right to lease them for oyster culture. Since the Apalachicola Land & Development Company had not leased a single acre of oyster bottom from Florida, Popham now declined to recommend it as a sound investment. [22] His friend Roat soon obtained a permit to oyster five hundred acres in the bay and planned to plant oysters for both himself and Popham. [23]

The "Oyster King," a name frequently applied to Popham by newspapers, quickly sold all one thousand shares of his new Oyster Growers' Co-Operative Association. The Apalachicola Land & Development Company was eclipsed, indicating that Abbott and Collier were better followers than they were commanders. Their organization made a few sales, but by January 1922 it had conveyed its land to Popham, who agreed to pay off the company's mortgage. Popham paid the ill-fated concern only ten dollars, and

21. *Record*, 532–40. Popham testimony, 1088 (13), in *Record*, shows that he resigned from the Colony completely in 1921, and afterwards he had no connection, direct or indirect, with it.

22. Ibid., 541–47; *Laws of Florida* 1920: 1228–31; 1921: 332–35.

23. Apalachicola *Times*, Apr. 2, 1921.

at the same time Abbott turned over his share of Venice Island to William Lee for one dollar.[24]

The Apalachicola Land & Development Company's existence had been brief. Its formation was based on Popham's ruptured relations with Abbott and Collier. "No vain attempt will be made . . . to fathom the motives behind this manipulation" was the helpless statement of federal attorneys later.[25] In 1923, Popham paid $6,000 to N. H. Hays, S. E. Teague, and H. L. Oliver, the men from whom the company had bought its land.[26]

It was not long before Abbott and Collier rejoined Popham. As for the Florida Co-Operative Colony, it vanished as though it had never existed, which it had not except on paper. No oysters were planted, cultivated, or harvested. The initiation fees that averaged ten dollars disappeared as completely as Venice Island at high tide. Some of the money deposited in the American Exchange Bank was probably transferred to the Apalachicola Land & Development Company, to the Oyster Growers' Co-Operative Association, or even to new schemes that Popham devised later. For the time being, Popham was pleased with his new organization. He was now free to develop Saint George Island and to build an oyster kingdom.

24. Franklin County Deed Book W, 88–91; Brief for Defendant, 17–18.
25. Brief for Defendant, 34.
26. Franklin County Deed Book W, 430–34, 438–40. The payment was for city lots, but it was probably also for nine thousand acres of land that the company had contracted to buy.

12

Popham Triumphant (Temporarily)

FROM 1920 through 1924, Popham engaged in a number of deals and promotions. Primarily, he concentrated on making a success of the Oyster Growers' Co-Operative Association. During those years he was also beset by difficulties that threatened the crazy quilt that was the Saint George Island—oyster empire he had erected but kept rearranging. On the promotional side, Popham and his confederates—Abbott, Collier (only twenty-eight), Hampton—never stopped speaking, writing, or selling. The handsome Collier married eighteen-year-old Percis B. Buck in 1920. The marriage, which took place at the Baptist church, joined an outsider with a prominent local family. Collier took his place in town life and developed into a convincing salesman.[1]

The *Oyster Farm News,* three to four leaves of quality paper, with Popham as sole owner and editor, was mailed monthly to some four thousand investors in the Oyster Growers' Co-Operative Association and later in the Million Dollar Bond Plan. "I want to tell you he was some talker" was how one Franklin County person remembered Popham. Not only was he "a downright talker," he was "a natural born promoter."[2] Tracing Popham's activities reveals him in what he, if not his detractors, considered a period of triumph.

1. Franklin County Marriage Record Book 3 (1919–1922), 349. Mr. and Mrs. L. G. Buck were the bride's parents, and the marriage was performed by the Rev. James L. Folsom. Author's interview with Homer Marks, July 7, 1978.
2. Author's interview with George M. Counts, Sr., July 28, 1978.

In 1921 he contracted with the Acme Packing Company (founded in 1917 to deal mainly in canned oysters and shrimp) to purchase oyster shells. The multipurpose shells would be used for road construction on Saint George Island, and they would also be planted on the oyster bottoms that Popham was leasing. To further the plan, Popham bought from his old employee, William H. Roat, his lease of five hundred acres of oyster bottoms. Roat, who had become county surveyor, had been assigned the bottoms by Florida Secretary of Agriculture McRae. The lease was located approximately in front of West Gap off Saint George Island.[3] Popham purchased back from Roat two lots on Saint George Island and signed a rent contract, with option to buy, on certain lots the surveyor had leased in Apalachicola.[4] By 1921, Popham had planted one hundred thousand barrels of live oysters and shells on the bottoms.[5]

Popham also began extensive advertising of the Oyster Growers' Co-Operative Association. When the Georgia Securities Commission questioned the authenticity, and thus the legality, of the more elaborate claims, Popham responded with newspaper advertisements. He reprinted tributes to his oratory and business acumen from papers across the country. From Palatka, Florida, came the *Morning Post*'s statement that the developer's work was "enduring and constructive, safe and sane as well as remunerative to his investors." According to the Atlanta *Georgian*, Popham was "the young Narcissus, poet-laureate and love singer of the ages." Popham emphasized his affection for Georgia and Georgians but denied violating that state's laws. "I stand on . . . common law, equity and freedom as given and assured by the constitution of the world's greatest nation whose flag of blood-red, lily-white and sky blue has never been dragged into the mud by either the Huns of Germany or any American peanut politician."[6]

---

3. For the purchase of oyster shells see Franklin County Deed Book V, 364. For the deal with Roat see Franklin County Deed Book W, 1. The transaction cites Record of Leases, Book 2, 310, Mar. 29, 1921. See also Apalachicola *Times*, Dec. 23, 1922.

4. Franklin County Deed Book U, 156. The rent was thirty dollars a month with a purchase price of three thousand dollars. See Franklin County Deed Book V, 390–91. The property was owned by J. H. Cook.

5. Apalachicola *Times*, Mar. 11, 1922.

6. Ibid., Nov. 5, 1921.

Popham was busier than ever in 1922. In that year he bought two lots from John and Maude Marshall and still another one from William Moore.[7] Additional workers were hired to plant more oysters; the *Crescent City* brought in twenty-eight thousand pounds of wire mesh to be placed on the bottoms to hold the scattered oyster shells and prevent them from sinking or floating off with the current. In speaking engagements in Tampa, St. Petersburg, and Jacksonville, Popham announced plans to build three oyster factories: at 11-Mile Road on the bayshore, on Saint George Island, and at wharf lots 7 and 8 at Apalachicola.[8]

The oyster promoter liked islands, even semi-islands. He paid John G. Ruge and his wife, Fannie, $150 for Upper Tow Head, an island of 150 acres located in the Apalachicola River. He also paid them fifty dollars for half interest, about forty acres, in nearby Tow Head Island.[9] Perhaps he intended to use those islands in connection with the Venice Island project. After the transaction, relations between Popham and Ruge worsened. Frequently mentioned as a civic leader and widely known for his work with oyster production, Ruge considered Popham an economic rival. But the two men moved past being business competitors and became deep personal enemies.

In 1923, Popham paid J. H. Cook $2,600 for the historic Alvan W. Chapman house in Apalachicola. Constructed in the 1840s, the home of the renowned botanist was a two-story frame house with a hipped roof, a typically modest example of the Classic Revival style. He spent $12,000 improving it. He built a garage apartment and had the grounds planted with handsome palms, shrubs, and flowers.[10]

Popham's parents occasionally visited Apalachicola. When the

7. Franklin County Deed Book U2, 174; W, 252; Apalachicola *Times*, June 17, 1922.

8. Apalachicola *Times*, Apr. 8, June 17, 1922.

9. Franklin County Deed Book W, 248–50.

10. Ibid., U2, 232. See also Florida Master Site File, Historic Site Data Sheet, Florida Department of Archives, History, and Records Management, Tallahassee. The recorder was Phillip Werndli, Survey Date 7502–7506. The Pophams lived in the Chapman house before they bought it, even advertising several unfurnished rooms for rent. See Apalachicola *Times*, Sept. 10, 1921; May 12, 1923.

elder Popham died in 1922, Clara moved into the Chapman house with Popham, Maude, and William Lee, Jr. Also a resident was James, "Silent Jim" Estes, Maude's mentally retarded but harmless brother. He lived in the garage apartment, performed yard work at the Chapman house, and sometimes went over to Saint George Island, where he fashioned coat hangers from cedar trees cut on the island. For all his limitations, Estes was a man of surprising wit and independence. Mostly he walked the streets of Apalachicola, carrying a package of tobacco under his arm, forever filling his pipe and talking to himself. Usually dressed in khaki trousers and white shirt and wearing a hat, Jim Estes became a town character. When town youths teased him, Jim would seize his pipe like a pistol and pretend to shoot them. Asked why he talked to himself so much, he replied that he liked to converse with someone who was intelligent.[11]

The Pophams purchased furniture and fixtures at fine stores in Jacksonville. More visible evidence of prosperity was Popham's car: a four-door, seven-passenger Willys-Knight, painted red with matching red upholstery. Purchased in 1923, the car replaced Popham's Ford, which he had wrecked. Although Popham was thrown against the windshield, his stiff new straw boater saved him from injury, and no one was hurt in the accident. Many considered Popham's Willys-Knight more elegant than John G. Ruge's Studebaker, even though the latter's car had once been used to drive President Warren G. Harding around Columbus, Georgia. The comparison of cars, while small, did not improve relations between Popham and Ruge.[12] Popham had a part-time chauffeur, but he enjoyed taking his family for drives around Apalachicola, espe-

11. Author's interview with Mrs. Tilla Sheally and her sister, Mrs. Tessie Mecoen, June 29, 1977 (Mrs. Sheally is a resident of Apalachicola and Mrs. Mecoen lives in Orlando); author's interview with Homer Marks; author's interview with Charley Brown, June 29, 1977 (Brown lives at Apalachicola); author's interview with Pat Hays, Nov. 24, 1976 (Hays is a resident of Apalachicola); author's interview with Frederick Sawyer, Jr., Nov. 24, 1976 (Sawyer lives at Apalachicola). In 1921, Popham's parents lived in Kansas City, Missouri. See Apalachicola *Times*, Feb. 26, 1921.

12. Author's interviews with Charley Brown, Mrs. Tilla Sheally, and Mrs. Tessie Mecoen; Apalachicola *Times*, Dec. 10, 1921; Aug. 26, 1922; Apr. 21, 1923. The question of who owned the most prestigious car was thrown into con-

cially at night when the car's interior lights were turned on and the occupants could be seen playing cards. On mornings when he drove his son to school, Popham often stopped and picked up other children, who were delighted to ride in the fancy automobile.[13]

Stylish and attractive, Maude Popham was also buxom and given to wearing diamonds and wide hats. Easily distinguished by her pince-nez glasses attached to a gold chain, Maude was often seen walking around town in an attempt to reduce. She liked to dance. Although dancing—like drinking, smoking, and cursing—was taboo for the former evangelist, Popham had no objections to Maude's indulging and even hired a man to take her to dances at the armory.[14]

In 1923, Popham activated some of his pronouncements of 1922. He bought wharf lots 7 and 8 in Apalachicola from N. R. Hays for $5,000.[15] The purchase was in anticipation of the need to handle the oysters that would be harvested from the bottoms obtained from Roat. Expanding his company's holdings, Popham bought land from L. G. and Terry Buck opposite the productive oyster grounds known as the Porter bar.[16] Even more important was his purchase of valuable land at the 11-Mile oyster landing. Popham was pleased and so were H. L. Oliver, S. E. Montgomery, and C. L. Shepherd, partners in the Acme Packing Company, who received $8,000.[17] In November, Popham got an option from O. C. Hoppe to buy about 150 acres and the submerged land adjacent for oystering. The land bordered Saint Vincent Sound and the bottoms were called Hoppe Sound. Hoppe died shortly after selling Popham the option, but Popham negotiated the sale of the property with Helen G. Hoppe, the widow, for $10,000.[18]

Under any circumstances the Pophams were gracious hosts, but

fusion in 1923 when local distributor E. S. Wefing sold a Cadillac to S. E. Rice, Jr. See Apalachicola *Times*, Apr. 14, 1923.

13. Author's interviews with Charley Brown, Mrs. Tilla Sheally, and Mrs. Tessie Mecoen.

14. Author's interview with Francis Lovett, Aug. 25, 1977; Lovett resides at Apalachicola. Author's interview with Homer Marks.

15. Franklin County Deed Book U2, 221.

16. Ibid., 195.

17. Ibid., W, 434–37.

18. Ibid., X, 300–301; 301–2; 302–3.

in 1923 they particularly enjoyed entertaining William Jennings Bryan. The Great Commoner had adopted Florida as his home and had been to Apalachicola previously. Bryan's appearance in May had to do with raising funds for a Young Men's Christian Association building at the University of Florida. Acting as official host, Popham met Bryan at Carrabelle and brought him to Apalachicola in his speedboat. Maude provided the Democratic party leader with a meal of oysters and fish, which he pronounced delicious. Bryan spoke on Saturday night at the Dixie Theatre. After William Lee's opening remarks, Bryan, who knew a kindred spirit when he heard one, said that it was difficult for him "to come down to earth after such a flowery introduction."[19]

Promoting Saint George Island, developing the oyster business, and entertaining party statesmen did not occupy all of Popham's time in 1923. Launching new ventures, Popham began selling land for other people and briefly considered planting satsuma oranges on a large scale. Popham received so many inquiries about land that he added a real estate department to his Oyster Growers' Co-Operative Association. For a 5 percent commission, he listed property for people in Franklin and surrounding counties. "No tract of land is too large, and no tract of land is too small," Popham wrote, "to be easily and quickly handled in the real estate department of his office."[20] Interested in the production of citrus crops, Popham joined the Satsuma and Fruit Growers' Association. He apologized for being unable to attend the organization's annual meeting and declared that "the satsuma is a commercial gold mine for north and west Florida beyond any doubt whatever. I contemplate planting ten thousand acres of satsumas and hope to increase to one hundred thousand acres."[21] He never got beyond the point of contemplation. The year ended on a promising note when Popham cleared up a minor detail regarding his ownership of Saint George Island.[22] He was ready for whatever 1924 had to offer.

The Florida land boom was a wonder of the modern world.

19. Apalachicola *Times*, May 19, 1923. See ibid., May 12, 1923; William Lee Parker to author, Jan. 31, 1982.

20. Apalachicola *Times*, May 5, 1923.

21. Ibid. Feb. 17, 1923.

22. Franklin County Deed Book X, 323. Popham paid one dollar for William Darby's mortgage from the old St. George Co-Operative Colony, Unincorporated.

Popham, despite troubles that could no longer be deferred, was his usual confident self, wheeling and dealing. The balding, heavy-set man, as conservatively dressed as a preacher or a banker, inspired confidence just by his appearance. "He was a fine, well-built man. What you'd think would be a gentleman," one of his employees remembered over fifty years later.[23] Soft-spoken and completely convincing, William Lee had no trouble attracting investors. Another man who knew Popham, Homer Marks (then in his early twenties), remembered that Popham once talked about gaining economic control of South America, or at least Brazil.[24]

Popham's most spectacular transaction in 1924 concerned almost forty thousand acres of land in Franklin and Liberty counties. R. D. Fryer of DeSoto County, Florida, owned the land, which was mortgaged for $20,000. Popham agreed to assume the mortgage and pay an additional $130,000—$3,000 by February 1925 and $3,000 a month thereafter.[25] He called his new venture the Florida Wholesale Land Company, Inc.

Adding to his chain of almost-islands, Popham bought a marshy stretch bounded by North Channel, Crooked Channel, and Apalachicola.[26] Next the promoter made three purchases from Mrs. Joseph Porter, who owned Little Saint George Island. She sold him the right to take fish from that island and from Sand Island; she also sold Popham her rights to bottom lands, where he had a lease from the state to plant oysters (between Little Saint George Island and the channel of Saint George Sound). In addition, Popham paid her for submerged lands around Little Saint George Island and Sand Island.[27]

Two plots of seventeen and ten acres on the mainland opposite the Porter bar became Popham property after he paid the heirs of

23. Author's interview with Leland Williams, Aug. 18, 1981. Williams and his wife reside in Apalachicola.

24. Author's interview with Homer Marks.

25. Tampa *Times*, Oct. 2, 1924; Franklin County Deed Book Y, 361–64; author's interview with Francis Lovett. See also Liberty County Deed Book T, 354.

26. H. L. Grady and Charles G. and Elizabeth Parlin of Ocean Springs, Mississippi, were paid two hundred dollars for the island. See Franklin County Deed Book X, 357.

27. Ibid., 363, 359, 370.

E. W. Vause $1,000.[28] Popham paid the Lewis State Bank and the Capital City Bank of Tallahassee $1,000 for wharf lots, six lots in Apalachicola, and two hundred acres in Franklin County.[29] The entrepreneur's property evaluations reflected his economic activities: wharf lots 7 and 8, appraised at $2,000 in 1922, were appraised at $12,000 in 1924.[30]

No one wondered where the money to buy all the property was coming from. The Apalachicola post office was deluged with mail to the Oyster Growers' Co-Operative Association. No ordinary box was large enough, and a special container was installed to handle the sacks of envelopes that Popham received. Harry Cummings, then a young man in his teens, worked for Popham in the company's mailing department. He remembered later how he used to enter the back door of the post office to pick up the packets containing payments from investors. Young Francis Lovett, engaged as a special delivery boy, heard rumors that as much as $25,000 a day came in.[31] In August 1923, the corporation received 1,306 pieces of first-class mail. A count of letters addressed personally to Popham on eight successive days in June 1923 revealed that he received 83, 96, 100, 87, 66, 76, 86, and 62 items.[32]

While engaged in making purchases, Popham was even more busily involved in making sales. Saint George Island had been surveyed again in 1921, this time by C. M. Dechant, and the sale of lots was proceeding with amazing success. Characteristically, Popham had already decided to change the organization and goals of the Oyster Growers' Co-Operative Association. In February 1922, the poet-promoter issued what became known variously as the New and Enlarged Plan or the Million Dollar Bond Plan.

28. Ibid., 366–68.
29. Ibid. Y, 56–57, 57–58.
30. Franklin County Commissioners' Minutes, Book 3, 296, 345.
31. Author's interview with Harry Cummings, Aug. 25, 1977; author's interview with Francis Lovett. For a typical letter of interest by a stockholder see Apalachicola *Times*, Sept. 30, 1922.
32. J. Farley Warren to E. J. Mansfield, June 9, 1923, Ralstad papers. Ralstad, now deceased, was at one time postmaster at Apalachicola. He kindly placed a valuable set of letters and records relating to Popham's postal operations with the author.

As the plan operated (or was supposed to operate), it seemed simple enough. Popham signed a John Doe bond binding him to a million dollars' worth of real estate. For $1,200 at 6 percent interest—ten dollars a month for twenty years—a person doing business with Popham would receive a warranty deed to a 50-by-100-foot lot in the Dechant survey. On the leased water bottoms, Popham would propagate a hundred thousand oysters for each investor and would build and operate a mammoth oyster packinghouse and factory to handle the annual market (*illustration,* Group 2).[33]

Taxes on the investors' homes and on the water bottoms and lands bounding them and all business expenses would be assumed by Popham. Profits from the sale of oysters would be distributed equally among the investors. Popham promised to advertise the plan in five thousand newspapers and magazines with a circulation of ten million readers. To underwrite his objective, Popham deposited a deed for a thousand lots on Saint George Island (worth $1 million at a selling price of $1,000 each) with H. G. Fannin, an employee at the American Exchange Bank at Apalachicola. Fannin put up one dollar on the ninety-nine year bond. Theoretically, an investor would have a homesite and a lifetime cash income from oyster culture.[34]

Members of the Oyster Growers' Co-Operative Association were asked to transfer their stock. In exchange each individual would receive a deed to a $1,000 lot and a Million Dollar Guarantee Bond—printed on bright yellow paper with red and blue seals. Later, in 1924, Popham got out a "Supplementary Contract and Agreement" to the Million Dollar Bond Plan, adding details concerning profit distribution and enlarging the enterprise to include fish, shrimp, and crabs.[35]

The Oyster Growers' Co-Operative Association's original thousand investors approved the new plan. They and the new recruits to the Million Dollar Bond Plan soon numbered four thousand and represented every state in the union. An examination of Frank-

33. Franklin County Deed Book W, 169, 171–75; see testimony of H. G. Fannin in *Record,* 970–75; and Apalachicola *Times,* Mar. 11, 1922.

34. Apalachicola *Times,* Mar. 11, 1922.

35. Franklin County Deed Book X, 453–58.

lin County deed books in the first half of the 1920s shows that Popham's name recurs far more frequently than any other.

Popham transferred his office from the waterfront to Market Street, the town's major thoroughfare. He rented the entire upstairs of a building owned by J. H. Cook. Dividing the space into eight rooms, he employed a staff of thirteen people: bookkeepers, assistants, and stenographers. The latest equipment was installed, including the town's only dictaphone and a machine called an "Addressograph." Harry Cummings remembered running the Addressograph for a dollar an hour.[36]

Collier developed into a good salesman. Abbott and his family became prominent in Apalachicola and he made frequent trips to South Florida promoting the corporation. Like Popham, Collier and Abbott worked out of the headquarters building in Apalachicola. Prominently displayed in the sales office was a two-thousand-year-old giant oyster shell that weighed 119 pounds and rang like a bell when tapped. Wide-eyed prospective buyers, who, as Cummings said, "didn't know if a oyster had wings or feet," never discovered that the shell did not come from Apalachicola Bay. Popham bought it in Jacksonville, although it was originally from Australia. If such fakery pricked the consciences of the officers, they rationalized that the shell was, after all, just a symbol. Like others who worked for Popham, one young woman, whose job was folding the *Oyster Farm News* and sealing copies in envelopes, recalled that William Lee was not only unfailingly kind and courteous but paid well.[37] The *Oyster Farm News* was begun in May 1922; a subscription cost a dollar a year. Printed in Tallahassee by T. J. Appleyard, Printer, it attracted a large number of subscribers.[38]

Usually dressed in a dark suit (with the added formality of a chain stretched across the vest), Popham was anything but the con-

36. Author's interview with Harry Cummings; author's interview with Tilla Sheally; Apalachicola *Times*, Apr. 7, 1923.

37. Author's interview with Harry Cummings; author's interview with Tilla Sheally; Apalachicola *Times*, Feb. 4, Dec. 9, 1922.

38. See notarized statement by Popham, Mar. 23, 1923; and Popham's application for a second-class mailing permit, in Ralstad papers. Appleyard himself bought a lot on Saint George.

servative businessman that his appearance suggested. The dull and awkward prose that normally described legal agreements and contracts was refreshingly absent from those drafted by Popham. Nor did his sense of how a business arrangement should be worded conform to standard procedures. Andrew Mellon, then secretary of the treasury, would have renounced the oyster king's penchant for eliminating contractual details simply because "All promises, like pie crusts, are easily broken." Further, the Philadelphia millionaire would have viewed as corporate anarchy Popham's concepts of organizational structure and chains of command: "Preventing an unequal distribution of honors and titles—as president, vice-president, treasurer, secretary, etc.," Popham wrote, "we will have no organization, and by having no organization, will save red-tape reports to state departments, corporation taxes, corporation income taxes, revenue stamps on certificates, fat fees to politicians in 48 states for admittance to do business in their states, tiresome board meetings, personal liabilities, or any possibilities of such liabilities, and a 100 other bothers incidental to any ORGANIZATION." [39]

Popham used the old business device that had worked in 1905 when he was promoting *The Road to Success:* readers who sold the book as a sideline were given a commission. Now, by clipping coupons from the *Oyster Farm News* and getting new subscribers, members of the Million Dollar Bond Plan were given credit for stock. Recognizing the effect of the profit incentive on most people, Popham simply steered it in his own direction.

For those who came to Apalachicola, and many did, to investigate Popham's proposals, the beauty of Saint George Island was a powerful lure. To get onto the island, a visitor landed on the bay side at a substantial 170-foot-long pier. From the pier, a six-foot-wide boardwalk made of cypress lumber led to the hotel, which fronted the Gulf. Nearby was a large bathhouse. The pier, boardwalk, hotel, and bathhouse had all been improved by Popham. The ten-room hotel had a screened porch running the length of the

39. Franklin County Deed Book Y, 442. See 441–44 for Popham's entire proposal. Drafted in 1921 but not recorded until 1925, the proposal was an early version of the Oyster Growers' Co-Operative Association.

building and across the back, and each room had doors that opened onto the west and east porches. A dining room that faced the Gulf was added, as was a kitchen off the east porch. Meals were prepared on a large wood cookstove, and steel army cots were stored (there were no beds) for use when needed.[40]

Leland P. Williams, a twenty-three-year-old veteran of World War I, was hired by Popham to look after the island. Williams, a native of Mississippi, and his wife, Lily Mae, from South Carolina, had moved to Apalachicola with their infant and Leland looked for work. Williams had been born on Cat Island off the Mississippi coast from Gulfport, and went to see Popham when he heard about the island enterprise. "I kept begging him for a job," he later recalled. Once he was employed, the family moved to a small cottage on Saint George Island. Cattle, hogs, and some goats roamed the island, and the turpentine men came and went. The only permanent people were the keeper and the assistant keeper at the lighthouse and their families. Leland and Lily Mae were busy showing the island to visitors and keeping the hotel and the bathhouse tidy, but much of the time they were by themselves. The seventeen-year-old Lily Mae had her family, but she was a long way from home ("I like Florida all right, but I was born in South Carolina," she explained in 1981). She could have endured the solitude, but there were other problems. The maddening insects pestered the family, especially the baby. Lily Mae could never get used to the morning trip to check the hotel and bathhouse. She and Leland made their way carefully along the boardwalk because it was covered by rattlesnakes, water moccasins, and less deadly reptiles sunning themselves. "You'd just take your time and they'd get off," she remembered. The Williamses lived on the island in 1923 and 1924, but Lily Mae finally persuaded her husband to move to the mainland.[41]

Popham understood the Williamses' decision. The truth was that not many cabins were built and the hotel was hardly worthy of the name. But Popham always blended the future with the present. He saw Saint George Island in the early 1920s as only a beginning.

40. Author's interview with Leland Williams.
41. Ibid.; author's interview with Lily Mae Williams, Aug. 18, 1981.

The illustrated literature that was sent out showed Popham's oyster beds along with a Saint George Island whose Gulf beach was rimmed with permanent cottages clustered around a glamorous hotel. It stated that the latter developments were in the planning stage.

As early as 1922, Popham announced plans to build a thousand-room hotel on Saint George Island, every room with a connecting bath. The million-dollar hotel would be built of concrete reinforced with steel, and the exterior walls would feature multicolored seashells. He also said that he planned to make the island a giant game preserve. But he promised more than a rainbow-colored luxury hotel and a ten-thousand-acre game preserve populated by deer, antelope, elk, Australian rabbits, squirrels, and practically all known birds, from coots to peacocks. All low places holding shallow water would be turned into artificial lakes and ponds (either salt- or freshwater, depending on users' preference) by means of flowing wells bored for that purpose. These would be stocked with native fowl, fish, and oysters. If a boiling spring could be bored, Saint George Island would develop into a health resort comparable to Hot Springs, Arkansas.[42] A street to be known as Broadway would run down the middle of the island. Homes would be built, and, as the local paper said, "To pin a flower to Mr. Popham's coat-lapel, instead of waiting to place it on his grave, we must say that if any man on earth can build on Saint George Island the city-by-the-sea, it is this promoter."[43]

As sales increased—the average price per lot was $250—so did Popham's oystering activities. The bay area produced so many fine oysters that even Popham's claims did not sound exaggerated. In his methods of planting oysters, Popham borrowed from an ancient Japanese practice. He sent crews, mostly young men between fourteen and twenty who were glad to get nine dollars a week, to

42. *Record,* 770–71, quoting Tallahassee *Daily Democrat,* Sept. 27, 1922. By 1923 the cost of the proposed hotel was two million dollars. See Tallahassee *Daily Democrat,* May 21, 1923. Popham also planned to have a quail preserve of nine thousand acres on the mainland. He inserted a notice in the local paper declaring Saint George off limits to hunting or shooting, although Franklin countians paid it no heed. See Apalachicola *Times,* Mar. 11, Sept. 23, 1922.

43. Apalachicola *Times,* Mar. 11, 1922.

Saint George Island early on Monday mornings. There they cut down scrub oaks eight or nine feet tall, trimmed the branches, and bound the branches together with wire. The bundles were dragged to the water's edge by mules or oxen. The *Oyster Farm News* reported that the sight of oxen snaking long strips of brush across the island "is as beautiful as it is unique." The oaks were then carried by boat into the bay and anchored at intervals to the bottom. Despite inevitable deterioration, they became ideal places for the spat to grow into oysters.[44]

Popham soon came into contact and conflict with the colorful State of Florida Shell Fish Commissioner, T. R. Hodges, who carried out his duties of enforcing shellfish laws, collecting license fees, planting oysters, protecting the natural beds, and supervising the state's fishing industry in a flamboyant manner. He had sailed around the state on an army vessel, the *Seafoam*, emerging at various ports of call wearing a uniform. Such trappings plus the commissioner's strict adherence to the law did not sit well with Florida's weathered shellfishermen. Nor had they sat well with Sidney J. Catts, the fiery transplanted Alabamian who had garnered enough Cracker votes to win an upset victory as governor in 1916. One of his campaign pledges had been to remove Hodges from office and the *Seafoam* from the high seas. Catts carried out his promise, but he was a one-term governor; his successor, Cary Augustus Hardee, reinstated Hodges.[45] When Hodges clashed with Popham, the shellfish commissioner was armed with the authority of his office and another boat, a submarine chaser borrowed from the U.S. government.

Hodges questioned Popham's methods. According to the commissioner, Popham's leases were on bottoms too deep to oyster easily with tongs. The bottoms themselves were too soft, and it was difficult to disengage oysters from the oak branches. Besides, in time the branches rotted.[46] Even so, Popham planted oyster shells

44. Apalachicola *Oyster Farm News*, July 1, 1922. Also author's interviews with Charley Brown, Pat Hays, Harry Cummings, Francis Lovett, and Homer Marks. See also Apalachicola *Times*, Mar. 11, 1922.

45. For the Catts-Hodges controversy see Wayne Flynt, *Cracker Messiah: Governor Sidney J. Catts of Florida*, 46, 58–59, 110, 129–30.

46. See testimony of T. R. Hodges in *Record*, 934–65.

as well as scrub oaks, and his methods worked. He also offered healthy employment to the young men who stayed in a 40-by-100-foot boardinghouse Popham had built on pilings at Nick's Hole. A big, redheaded man named Seber Russell cooked for them in the bayside building. The young men returned to town on Friday afternoons. The same barge that carried them to Apalachicola would be loaded with the next week's supplies purchased at the Marks Brokerage Company.[47] Popham claimed to have planted two hundred million live oysters and shells in 1921 and 1922.[48] Although Ruge and others had promoted oyster culture before him, Popham realized the industry's potential and attempted to dramatize it. The state itself soon was engaged in planting activities, utilizing oyster shells.

Although Popham was controversial, he made far more friends than enemies. Most people thought, like Leland Williams, that "he was a fine man."[49] Popham made frequent guest appearances in the pulpit of the Calvary Baptist Church. He declined an invitation to serve as its permanent pastor but agreed to be superintendent of the Sunday School. He reached his oratorical pinnacle in Apalachicola in 1923. Five years earlier he had preached his first sermon at the Methodist church. Now on Mother's Day he taught his Sunday School class at the Baptist church, then went to the Methodist church to preach at a special "Union," a gathering of the various local congregations. In addition to local churchgoers, people from Port St. Joe, Eastpoint, and Carrabelle crowded into the church. Popham was at his evangelical best, reading from his own poetry and preaching on the topic "A Mother's Love." It was reported that he used his "seemingly never ending vocabulary" and held "the audience charmed and spell bound from the time he spoke the first word of the discourse to the end."[50]

Popham became president of the Apalachicola Chamber of Commerce and also headed the Franklin County branch of the Automobile Association of America. On Wednesday afternoons when

47. Author's interviews with Charley Brown and Homer Marks.
48. Tallahassee *Daily Democrat*, May 21, 1923.
49. Author's interview with Leland Williams.
50. Apalachicola *Times*, May 19, 1923; see ibid., May 17, 1923.

businesses closed, he organized excursions aboard the launch *Empress* to Saint George Island (fifty cents for adults, twenty-five cents for children).[51] He bought a twenty-three-foot motorboat that was run by a ninety-horsepower Curtiss airplane engine. Named the *Lady Popham,* the boat was driven for its owner by Rudolph Marshall in Fourth of July races. Crowds lined the waterfront to watch Marshall contend against the Rice Brothers' *Miss Apalachee* and the Cypress Lumber Company's *Cyclo.*[52]

Besides impressive headquarters in Apalachicola, Popham maintained a sales office on College Avenue in Tallahassee. There the walls were adorned with murals of the Apalachicola Bay area, and as a customer entered the office, his attention was immediately claimed by a large aquarium with oysters growing in it.[53] Evidence of activity was at every hand: Popham bought Ford trucks, various insurance policies, four boats (the *J. Ed. O'Brien, Joe Mazzina,* the Peterses' boat, and the Williamses' boat), seven barges, numerous small boats and skiffs, a power dredge boat named the *Willie N. Johnson,* and all the equipment necessary to operate them. He had money on deposit in several banks.[54]

In 1923, Popham toured New England in the company of a consulting engineer to observe the latest packing methods. Then he employed Adolph Maddox to construct a two-story building of sixty-one thousand square feet on the waterfront. The oyster factory and warehouse were cooled by fans, heated by steam, equipped with modern machinery, and enameled inside with three coats of dazzling white. The building blazed at night with hundreds of lights and could be seen from Saint George Island. To celebrate the opening, Popham staged a huge dance in the building. Seaplanes from the Naval Air Station at Pensacola saluted the event, and that night people danced to the strains of Henry and Reva Cummings's

51. Author's interview with Tilla Sheally and Tessie Mecoen; Apalachicola *Times,* June 24, 1922.

52. Author's interview with Francis Lovett; Apalachicola *Times,* Mar. 24, 1923.

53. Author's interview with Frederick Sawyer, Jr.

54. File TT, Circuit Clerk's Office, Franklin County Courthouse, Mable L. Osborne, Complainant, v. W. L. Popham and Maude Popham (hereinafter cited as Complaint of Mable Osborne).

local orchestra.[55] Popham announced that in addition to oysters the factory would process fish, shrimp, and crabs. "He has done more for his investors than he at first told them he would do for them," the *Times* pointed out. "It appears that William Lee Popham is an unusual promoter, who is very different to promoters who have little or no regard for their promises."[56]

The Saint George Island promoter advertised by erecting on jetties in the bay oblong wooden signs made of pecky cypress. Stained green, the signs were adorned with the word "POPHAM" spelled out in oyster shells. Highways coming into Apalachicola were lined with similar advertisements, and most blocks in town had at least one. In all there were fifty to a hundred of them, and visitors arriving for the first time thought the signs referred to a soft drink. They soon knew better. Admiring citizens had only to look at the enameled warehouse and read: "POPHAM OYSTER FACTORY NO. 1," spelled out in oyster shells.[57]

Saint George Island was more popular than ever. A party held there in May 1923 could have served as the basis for a short story by F. Scott Fitzgerald. Hosted by Percis Collier and Lamar Bledsoe, a spirited group left Popham's dock "attired in khaki skirts and knickers, all ready for the fun. On reaching the Island the Vic was immediately put into action and never ceased." For several days the young couples swam, ate, and danced. An exhausted but happy participant wrote, "For those suffering from dyspepsia, diabetes, boredom or any other ailment, we heartily recommend old St. George. Let's all boost Mr. Popham in his enterprise."[58]

It seemed to many people that somnolent Franklin County had come wide awake and would never be poor again. Gazing across Apalachicola Bay at Saint George Island, they did not doubt that Miami Beach had a formidable rival.

55. Author's interviews with Harry Cummings and Frederick Sawyer, Jr. See also Apalachicola *Times*, Oct. 7, 1922; Feb. 24, Mar. 3, 1923.

56. Apalachicola *Times*, Mar. 3, 1923.

57. Author's interviews with Frederick Sawyer, Jr., Francis Lovett, Tilla Sheally, Tessie Mecoen, and Homer Marks. See also testimony of S. E. Rice in *Record*, 868–69; William Lee Parker to author, Jan. 31, 1982.

58. Apalachicola *Times*, May 12, 1923.

13

Tribulations—and Trials

POPHAM flirted briefly with politics in 1922 by seeking a seat in the Florida House of Representatives. In his reasonable, somewhat conservative platform, he promised low taxes consistent with efficient and necessary government, more state aid for county roads and federal aid for highways, cooperation with railroads, more funds for schools, and fair property assessments for taxes.[1] Anyone could announce similar goals, including his opponents S. J. Giles of Apalachicola and W. A. Register of Carrabelle, but no one could match the hyperbole of his announcement. Citing his desire to build up West Florida, Popham mentioned his special affection for Apalachicola and Franklin County:

> I love every acre of her sunny soil; I love every drop of sparkling water in the great Gulf that kisses her border; I love every drop of red water in her great river and its redness, resembling the gulf of her crimson sunsets; I love every grain of sand that helps to keep the waves within their own home; I love every shell from her liquid depths; I love every business man here, and want him to prosper in his business; I love every flower that nods its head o'er sparkling sands—sun-crowned, moon-lit and dream-kissed; I love every vine that hugs the wall of

1. Apalachicola *Times,* May 12, 1922.

217

home, fence or tree; and I love every man, woman and child in Franklin County, for whom there is not one that I would not rise from my bed at midnight and walk miles in the darkness to favor, or aid in time of need.[2]

Politicians in Apalachicola and Carrabelle had worked out an informal agreement concerning the Florida House of Representatives seat. Although there were exceptions, the usual order was to rotate the two-year seat between the towns. The arrangement did not apply to the Florida Senate seat because Franklin County shared it with neighboring counties. In 1918, E. R. L. Moore of Carrabelle won the house seat without opposition. An Apalachicolan, John H. Cook, had no rival in the June Democratic primary of 1920, but for personal reasons he bowed out of the race before the November general election. E. R. L. Moore thereupon stepped in and was again elected without opposition.[3] The Democratic party was so overwhelmingly in the majority that nomination in the Democratic primary was tantamount to victory in November. The ensuing triumph was so axiomatic as to render the general election practically redundant.

The election in 1922 was different. There were three Democratic candidates for nomination, and the usual gentleman's agreement was abandoned. The election was still decided in the primary but not without a struggle. Register asked his fellow citizens to support him as the candidate of the little man. He promised to work hard to reduce taxes, and, hitting at Popham, to "force the man who owns TWENTY THOUSAND acres of land to pay taxes in proportion to the small property owner."[4] He was young and inexperienced, but he reminded the voters that he had fought for his country five years previously and, at twenty-seven, was fit to fight for his constituents in the legislature. He directed his attack mainly against Popham. He attempted to tarnish the oyster king with the label of carpetbagger. "There is not a drop of Gypsy or Indian

2. Ibid., May 6, 1922.
3. Franklin County Primary Election Records, 1914–42, 16; Apalachicola *Times*, Sept. 25, Oct. 2, 23, 1920.
4. Apalachicola *Times*, May 12, 1922.

blood in my ancestry," Register's political advertisements declared. "I am not a wanderer or son of a wanderer. I am not an adventurer or son of an adventurer. I did not 'float' into Florida and I shall not 'float' out." In the legislature, Register promised, he would represent the people of Franklin County "instead of a Sea of outside IN-VESTORS, FLOATERS, ADVENTURERS, AND MONEY-HUNGRY SUCK-ERS FROM ALL OVER THE UNITED STATES AND KENTUCKY."[5]

S. J. Giles had served for a number of years as a judge in Wakulla County before moving to Carrabelle. He was a conservative and respected man.[6] All of the candidates pledged themselves to work for beneficial legislation to promote the oyster and seafood industries. The candidates faced each other twice in common rallies, and on one occasion Popham rented the Dixie Theatre for a speech. A large crowd attended, in part because Popham arranged for those who came to stay and see a movie free. Although he was a candidate, Popham did not campaign much. When he did he complimented his opponents and declared that he was too busy to stand around on street corners soliciting votes. The Apalachicola *Times* predicted a Popham victory.[7]

When the votes were counted, Giles received 214 votes, Popham 119, and Register 102. The victorious Giles had carried Carrabelle strongly, while Popham carried Apalachicola but lost enough votes to Register to ensure defeat. In the time-honored tradition, Giles was gracious in victory and Register was gracious in defeat, and, after waiting a few days, Popham issued a statement. Despite the advice of friends, he said, "I will neither ask for a re-count, nor will I contest the primary." He congratulated the winner and thanked the people of Apalachicola for their strong support.[8]

Losing his bid for the state legislature did not dim Popham's glitter. Yet despite his achievements, William Lee was in deep trouble. His professional differences with some individuals led to personal enmities as well. Besides Shell Fish Commissioner Hodges and John G. Ruge, Popham argued orally, in print, and physically with

5. Ibid., June 3, 1922.
6. Ibid., May 20, 1922.
7. Ibid., May 20, June 3, 1920.
8. Ibid., June 17, 1922; see also ibid., June 3, 10, 1922; Franklin County Primary Election Records, 1914–42, 22.

Paul H. Ploeger, a dealer in oysters and shrimp and owner of the Sea Food Products Company. In their newspaper exchanges, the originator of the Million Dollar Bond Plan referred to his adversary as Pudding Head Paul. On one occasion their differences led to fisticuffs.[9] Once Popham narrowly avoided a fist fight with a critic, and at another time he exchanged knockdowns with a man known as the Shankie Hot Shot. The encounter took place under a certain oak tree well known as the site where disagreements were thus settled.[10]

Popham also aroused the suspicions of the postal authorities. They conducted an intensive investigation with much correspondence—letters, notes, telegrams—between local Postmaster J. Farley Warren and E. J. Mansfield, an inspector for the U.S. Post Office assigned to the case. The central question was whether Popham's voluminous communications with his investors violated federal laws. Had Popham engaged in the illegal use of the mails to obtain money under false and fraudulent pretenses? Early in 1922, a federal grand jury at Tallahassee investigated various allegations (according to Popham, Ruge and Hodges were the only two witnesses against him other than postal employees who simply made factual statements) and returned two indictments. The charges against William Lee and Maude, as well as Collier and Abbott, were that they had violated Section 215 of the U.S. Penal Code: improper use of the mails in furtherance of fraud. In allegedly breaking a federal law, Popham had, by leasing oyster bottoms to nonresidents of Florida, also violated a state law.[11]

As the intricacies of legal embattlement unfolded, Popham and his staff had to go to Tallahassee in February 1922 to post bond for their appearance in court. Presumably, the trial would come up in January 1923. Acting as sureties for the accused were Popham's

9. See testimony of Paul Ploeger in *Record*, 639–44; author's interview with Harry Cummings. For the election see tracts and brochures in Ralstad papers.

10. See letter from J. J. Abbott to Apalachicola *Times*, May 1, 1926.

11. Popham detailed the history of his attackers and his own counterattacks in Tallahassee *Daily Democrat*, May 23, 1923. Warren had been postmaster before the Democrats took over under President Woodrow Wilson. Warren succeeded C. I. Henry, who had held the job eight years, in 1922. See Apalachicola *Times*, Apr. 1, 1922.

old business associate George W. Saxon and another Tallahasseean, D. M. Lowry.[12] On returning to Apalachicola, a seemingly
unbothered Popham declared, "The whole affair is a great big
NOTHING; with a tail to it."[13]

Because the leases were in his own name, Popham argued his
right to share the earnings with residents or nonresidents, as he
chose. In brief, the investors bought the profits but not the bottoms. "Yes, sir," the confident Popham stated, "I freely and frankly
acknowledge that I am absolutely guilty of the charge in the indictments to having issued shares to persons living in states other than
Florida, and I am glad of it; happy in having done so, were it to be
done over, I would do it again."[14]

The developer of Saint George Island openly complained that
Hodges was the author of his troubles. During his campaign for
the legislature, Popham had listed one thing he hoped to achieve:
"the death of Kaiserism and bigotry in our shell fish commission."[15] Popham issued a public challenge to Hodges and his
friends. William Lee would put up $10,000 and Hodges would put
up $1,000. If it could be proved that Popham had leased any oyster
bottoms to non-Floridians, he would forfeit the $10,000. If it
could not be proved, Hodges would lose his one thousand.[16] When
the shellfish commissioner ignored the challenge, his lack of action
was not interpreted as proof of Popham's innocence. State officials
were supposed to comport themselves properly and avoid the-
atrics. Still, the federal government delayed bringing the case to
trial, and, as time passed, Popham had a legitimate grievance in
seeking a speedy disposition of the charges.

Support for Popham in Apalachicola was widespread. The *Times*
compared him to Henry Ford and believed that his attempts to
combine the development of Saint George Island and the oyster industry were legitimate and honest. "Whether the wind blows

12. Scattered Recognizances for Appearances and other documents for the
January and February indictments and arrests are in the Federal Records Center
of the National Archives at East Point, Georgia.

13. Apalachicola *Times*, Feb. 25, 1922.

14. Ibid.

15. Ibid., June 3, 1922.

16. Tallahassee *Daily Democrat*, May 23, 1923.

North, East, South or West, Popham's great storm-proof wind mill
. . . is well anchored to a firm foundation," wrote Editor Johnston.
Popham, he noted, "this promoter of oyster culture . . . uses all
stumbling blocks as stepping stones—onward and upward to
greater success and power." [17] Over sixty years later, many people
in Apalachicola believed that Popham had been victim of a conspiracy. Leland Williams stated categorically, "That bunch here got
in behind him and railroaded him." [18]

In a letter to members of the Oyster Growers Co-Operative
Association, Popham implied openly that Hodges and Ruge were
his major opponents.[19] Members of the Calvary Baptist Church defended him. Dr. J. P. H. Feldman, the pastor, admitted a lack of
knowledge about laws pertaining to oysters, but he denied that
Popham was guilty of fraud. If anything, the law itself was uncon-
stitutional. What the Reverend Feldman did know was the nature
of the accused: "[I have] the highest opinion of the ability, integrity,
and wholesouled altruistic character of Mr. Popham." To the minister, Popham's claims seemed "founded upon truth and solid business righteousness." [20]

By May 1923, Popham still had not been tried. That month he
was hit by a new and double set of legal problems. First, he and
Maude were given notice of a tax lien by the Bureau of Internal
Revenue of the Treasury Department. The government claimed that
the Pophams owed $200,000 in unpaid income taxes and penalties
for the years 1920 through 1923. Similar tax liens, although for
considerably smaller amounts (the highest was $31,601.64) were
filed against them in 1924 and 1925. The Bureau of Internal Revenue placed all of the properties of the Oyster Growers Co-Operative
Association under temporary attachment. As it turned out, the
taxes were never paid and were wiped off the record in 1945 as
uncollectible due to lapse of time.[21]

The second difficulty, which shattered what remained for Pop-

17. Apalachicola *Times*, Feb. 25, 1922.
18. Author's interview with Leland Williams.
19. Letter in Apalachicola *Times*, Mar. 11, 1922.
20. Ibid.
21. See Record of Liens, Book B, Franklin County, 259, 261–65; Franklin
County Mortgage and Lien Satisfactions, Book C, 67, 69–72.

ham of the month of May's traditional charm, came when he and Maude, along with Abbott and Collier, were indicted again by a federal grand jury sitting in Pensacola. The new indictment elaborated on charges of fraudulent mail usage and included Popham's activities in advertising Saint George Island. Supposedly, Popham used funds collected from investors for personal expenditures.[22]

Popham wrote another letter to his investors, claiming that the grand jury's second indictment clarified the various charges and meant that he would soon get his day in court. Popham noted that he would be so occupied for the next sixty days that the letter would serve as an issue of the *Oyster Farm News*. He closed by taking heart from both the Old and the New Testaments: David slaying the giant (1 Samuel) and the Gospel according to Matthew, "Blessed are ye when men revile you."[23]

Hodges, whom Popham blasted in his letter, was not universally loved. The shellfish commissioner's clashes with Popham aroused public sympathy for the beleaguered promoter, particularly in Franklin County. In April, a month before Popham's second indictment, the Apalachicola Chamber of Commerce voted to ask the governor to remove Hodges from office or transfer him to another position. As president of the Chamber of Commerce, Popham cast a ballot supporting the removal of Hodges. Beyond that, a petition bearing a thousand names of Franklin County people connected with the seafood industry was drafted. It also demanded the ouster of Hodges. Popham was appointed a committee of one to carry the petition to Tallahassee and present it to the state legislature then in session.[24]

When Popham arrived in the capital in May, the indictment from Pensacola had been returned. Armed with the petition against Hodges, the verbose William Lee quickly became a favorite with the press corps. The legislature had just enacted an agricultural statute dealing with the acute problem of tick eradication. Popham told a reporter from the Tallahassee *Daily Democrat* that

22. Tallahassee *Daily Democrat*, May 15, 22, 1923.
23. Apalachicola *Times*, May 19, 1923.
24. Tallahassee *Daily Democrat*, May 21, 22, 1923; Apalachicola *Times*, May 19, 1923.

there were ticks in Hodges's politics. The owner of Saint George Island condemned the expensive and unnecessary maintenance of a submarine chaser. He charged the commissioner with using the boat for private as well as public purposes. It was, according to Popham, a war craft and a floating palace captained by Hodges, who dressed like a czar. Popham promised that before he left Tallahassee, he would preach a sermon on parasitic insects in state government.[25]

Popham adroitly tied the dispute between himself and Hodges to the shellfish commissioner's larger duties. "I do not blame the honorable T. R. Hodges for his kaiseristic methods and for his failure to get along with the toilers of the sea," Popham explained. In fact, "he is more to be pitied than blamed, because he can not change his natural disposition any more than a leopard can change his spots." The indicted developer seized the moment to expand his monetary proposal of 1922. He offered to put up $50,000 to the commissioner's $5,000 with the same outcome upon proof of his guilt or innocence. Popham proposed further to rent an auditorium in Tallahassee and meet Hodges in public debate concerning the charges.[26] Like Popham's earlier challenge, this one got no response from Hodges.

Stories circulated in Tallahassee that the shellfish commissioner would be replaced (he was not). At one point Popham offered to address the legislature. He was turned down because adjournment came at 6:30 in the afternoon and the solons were too tired to listen.[27] Yet Popham left the capital with the feeling that despite his own difficulties, he had scored points against Hodges. A young man in Apalachicola, George Core, who would become the long-time clerk of the circuit court of adjoining Gulf County, heard all the talk about Popham. He was not surprised that Popham's magic worked as well in Tallahassee as in Apalachicola. "I've never seen one like him," a retired Core explained. When Popham spoke "you automatically listened to it. He had the knack to hold your attention."[28]

25. Tallahassee *Daily Democrat*, May 21, 22, 1923.
26. Ibid., May 22, 1923; Apalachicola *Times*, May 26, 1923.
27. Tallahassee *Daily Democrat*, May 23, 31, 1923.
28. Author's interview with George Core, Mar. 1, 1980.

During the summer of 1923, Popham's legal problems remained in limbo, and he pushed his business enterprises. Sales of property on Saint George Island went extremely well. Popham's good reputation in Apalachicola was seen in a September primary when he was nominated without opposition to run for mayor.[29] But the respite from his troubles was short lived. On October 8, Popham was summoned to Washington to testify in a hearing before the Post Office Department. Accompanying him was his chief counsel, Philip Beall of Pensacola (in Washington, Popham's attorney was Eugene R. West). Also testifying was Shell Fish Commissioner Hodges. Solicitor Edgar M. Blessing conducted the closed hearings, but it was later revealed that they were animated and no one doubted what they were about. Although the hearings lasted nine and a half days and produced 1,938 typewritten pages of transcriptions, no immediate decision was reached. Popham returned to Apalachicola and Hodges to Tallahassee.[30]

In November, Popham was overwhelmingly elected mayor in the general election (his opponent received two votes). Yet he barely had time to savor the victory before catastrophe struck. On December 6, J. Farley Warren, postmaster at Apalachicola, received a telegram from Horace J. Donnelly, acting solicitor for the U.S. Post Office in this case, stating that the postmaster general had issued a fraud order and that all of Popham's mail was to be held. Assistant District Attorney Earl Hoffman, whom the developer would meet later in the courts, had been instrumental in building the case against Popham.[31] Warren and E. J. Mansfield were also active in assembling evidence. Since most of Popham's business activities were utterly dependent on the U.S. mails, his situation was desperate.

Although Popham complied with the fraud order, he fought

29. Tallahassee *Daily Democrat*, Sept. 12, 1923.

30. Ibid., Oct. 8, 17, 1923. The hearing, originally set for Sept. 19, had been postponed. See Records of the Post Office Department, Office of the Solicitor, "Fraud Order Case Files," File no. 4313, Record Group 28, National Archives, Washington, D.C.

31. Jacksonville *Florida Times-Union*, Dec. 8, 1923; Tallahassee *Daily Democrat*, Nov. 21, Dec. 7, 1923; Complaint of Mabel Osborne. See also Postmaster General Harry S. New's Order no. 9915, Dec. 6, 1923, and telegram in Record Group 28, National Archives.

back. One small victory came when eighteen men were arrested for taking oysters from Popham's leased Hoppe bottoms. The men, Popham charged, were encouraged in their acts by Hodges. Apparently the shellfish commissioner did not believe that Popham had legal control of the submerged lands. After the first offender was convicted, the others pled guilty, were fined twenty-five dollars each, and released.[32]

Abbott issued a statement from Popham, whom he called "the fighting lion," that appeared as an advertisement in the Apalachicola *Times*. Popham expressed confidence in his ultimate vindication and demanded a thorough investigation and speedy trial. The investors were given a moratorium on their payments until the charges were dismissed, although if they wished, the monthly funds could be sent by express.[33] Popham could still receive all but first-class mail, and the order did not prevent him from sending out mail.[34]

Public reaction, as reflected in the press, favored Popham. Frank Webb, editor and owner of the Tallahassee *Dispatch*, visited Apalachicola and interviewed twenty-five citizens, mostly merchants, businessmen, and dealers in seafood. The consensus was that if Popham were left alone the area would prosper; if not, "there would be no hope for future development." G. W. Shank, a packer and shipper of oysters, disagreed; he approved the fraud order: "it will be to the investors' advantage, because it will prevent Popham from getting any more of their money." Webb himself strongly supported Popham and was equally opposed to Hodges. That Popham's "development work should be retarded by such men as our Shell Fish Commissioner," Webb wrote, "is more than we can understand."[35]

32. Franklin County Circuit Court Clerk's Office, File GG 14; Tallahassee *Daily Democrat*, Dec. 7, 1923; Tallahassee *Dispatch*, Dec. 14, 1923, quoting Apalachicola *Times*.

33. Quoted in Tallahassee *Daily Democrat*, Dec. 12, 1923. For Popham's attempts to avoid the fraud order see A. S. Behymer to J. Farley Warren, May [?], 1924; E. J. Mansfield to J. Farley Warren, May 6, 24, 29, 1924. All in Ralstad papers.

34. Tallahassee *Dispatch*, Dec. 14, 1923.

35. Ibid.

When the Tallahassee *Democrat* asked Popham for some facts, he responded with a paid advertisement. "The whole trouble in a nut shell, is a bitter persecution started and kept up by State Shell Fish Commissioner, T. R. Hodges." Ruge was also excoriated as one of "those who by envy, malice and hatred, are trying to ruin a great and legitimate development of Florida's natural resources of sea foods, and the opening up of the Gulf territory." The progress on Saint George Island would be wiped out, and the investors would lose their money. All the charges were spurious, Popham contended, since he had made no claims other than those contained in bulletins issued by the U.S. government. His signature beneath the advertisement was followed by two words: "The Persecuted."[36]

Popham also issued a pamphlet defending himself. He was consoled by the knowledge that through the ages men of achievement had always faced opposition. He did not doubt that a mail fraud order would have been issued against Benjamin Franklin, Henry Ford, John D. Rockefeller, and the founder of Piggly Wiggly, a popular grocery chain that had been established at Jacksonville in 1918.[37]

Nothing seemed to go right for Popham. In mid-December it was reported that the state attorney general was about to enter suit against him for utilizing more oyster bottoms than the six hundred acres allowed by law.[38] After talking with Popham, one editor was amazed that he was not discouraged or his mood no worse than stoical. After all, Popham had pending against him two separate grand jury indictments; his bank accounts had been attached for nonpayment of income taxes; his mail had been stopped; and the state was threatening a suit. "He is very optimistic, however, and he is planning for bigger developments than ever."[39]

Popham and his attorneys had been pressing for trial since the original indictment in 1922. He finally got one, or so it appeared, in January 1924. Popham took time out to be sworn in as mayor of Apalachicola. He then assembled his witnesses and descended on

36. Tallahassee *Daily Democrat,* Dec. 13, 1923.
37. Publication quoted in *Record,* 837–40.
38. Tallahassee *Daily Democrat,* Dec. 15, 1923.
39. Tallahassee *Dispatch,* Dec. 14, 1923.

Tallahassee (because of distance and expenses, a change of venue had been granted from Pensacola). His entourage took over an entire floor of the Cherokee Hotel. For several days the former evangelist gave out interviews, predicted a verdict of not guilty, but declined to announce his candidacy for governor in the next election. If he ran, many thought he would win.[40]

Even before the trial began, a grand jury hastily assembled and impaneled in Tallahassee on January 7 returned new indictments against Popham. They involved the old charges as well as new developments brought on by the Million Dollar Bond Plan. Some of Popham's supporters wavered. It would take the best efforts of Philip Beall, who was assisted by John P. Stokes of Miami, State Senator W. C. Hodges, and Fred H. Davis and E. T. Davis of Tallahassee to win a favorable verdict for Popham. They were faced by District Attorney Fred C. Cubberly and his aide Earl Hoffman, the assistant U.S. attorney general who earlier had garnered evidence for the postal authorities' case against Popham.

To judge by the crowd that packed the courtroom, one would have thought a lurid murder trial was in progress. In addition to the "regulars" who showed up at all trials of any consequence, many curious Tallahasseeans were joined by numerous visitors from Apalachicola. Those from Franklin County came even though they had to miss the Dixie Theatre's presentation of Wallace Reid in "The Dictator" followed by "The Sign on the Door" starring Norma Talmadge. Movies took second place to the Popham trial.[41]

The defense lawyers got off to a good start by filing a plea in abatement alleging that the most recent grand jury indictments, those returned only a few days before the trial, were illegally constituted. Judge William B. Sheppard agreed. In a district where the population was less than three hundred thousand persons, two grand juries could not function simultaneously. The grand jury previously impaneled could make no effective rebuttal, and Judge Sheppard quashed the more recent indictment.

Next to be considered was the indictment returned in May 1923

40. Apalachicola *Times,* Jan 19, 1924; Jacksonville *Florida Times-Union,* Jan. 1, 1924.

41. Apalachicola *Times,* Jan. 19, 1924.

by the federal grand jury at Pensacola. Defense lawyers demurred to the indictment; after they were overruled, they announced themselves ready to proceed with the trial. At that point, Assistant District Attorney Hoffman asked for a continuance. He argued that the government was embarrassed by the quashing of the Tallahassee indictment. The government had intended to combine it with the Pensacola indictment, but now its whole case had been disrupted. Replying, defense attorney Stokes argued eloquently that Popham was ready to be tried. He had waited patiently and was entitled to defend himself. If the government was not ready, then the case should be *nol prossed*. Before making a decision, Judge Sheppard adjourned until two o'clock in the afternoon.

The principals and the crowd had barely reassembled when the judge, to Popham's consternation, granted the continuance. Next, Judge Sheppard made short work of the original indictments returned in the winter of 1922 against William Lee, Maude, and the others. Those charges were dismissed for the government's failure to prosecute them soon enough. Popham had clearly won the first round. All of the indictments except one had been dismissed, but to his disappointment, the most important charge, fraudulent use of the mails, which Judge Sheppard announced he would try in February, did not come up.[42]

Popham returned to Franklin County and got out a letter to his investors; it also appeared in the Apalachicola *Times*. He noted his appearance before the federal court and asked, "Why did they say in Tallahassee that they would not go to trial, after these two years of bitter, unlawful, unjust and unfair persecution?" The simple answer, according to Popham, was that his detractors had no case. He predicted victory, vindication, the restoration of his mailing privilege, and profits for his investors. Truth, he assured investors in the Popham Oyster Farm, would triumph. Meanwhile, they should remit monthly payments by express, free with all carrying charges paid at Apalachicola.[43]

42. *Record*, 33; Jacksonville *Florida Times-Union*, Jan. 1, 13, 15, 1924; Apalachicola *Times*, Jan. 19, 1924.

43. See Popham's letter dated Jan. 16, 1924; H. S. Roberts and E. J. Mansfield to J. Farley Warren, Jan. 15, 1924; in Ralstad papers. See also Tallahassee *Democrat*, Jan. 14, 1924.

In the spring of 1924, Popham still could not receive mail at his business office; the Bureau of Internal Revenue still had his funds attached; and he still had a federal indictment pending against him. Apparently the state did not pursue its case concerning Popham's alleged leases of oyster bottoms to non-Floridians. Popham decided that his and the investors' interests would be better served if the company went into receivership. He and Maude resigned as trustees on June 14.[44] A suit was brought by Mabel L. Osborne, a native of Louisville, Kentucky, who had earlier moved to Fort Pierce, Florida, and still later to Apalachicola. Attracted by Popham's various plans, Mabel, her mother, and her sister made investments and became permanent residents. According to Mabel, Abbott, acting in behalf of Popham, approached her about bringing suit. Mabel agreed, and even though Popham reconsidered later, she refused to withdraw the suit, which was filed June 21, 1924.[45]

Mabel's lawyer, William Fisher, presented the case: money was still coming into the company, the oyster operations were ongoing, and the services of a competent person to run them were essential. The amended declaration of trust of 1924 permitted trustees to designate their successors. Since William Lee and Maude had not done so, Fisher argued that the courts should appoint a receiver and designate a trustee. In that way the investors would be protected from the Bureau of Internal Revenue's claim that the company's assets were in reality the personal property of Popham. The court agreed, and on June 23, circuit court Judge E. C. Love appointed R. G. Porter as the trustee and S. E. Rice, Jr., as the receiver. The responsibilities of the two local men were complex. William Lee's several enterprises, including Saint George Island, now became legally known as the Popham Trust Estate.[46]

Popham, the Tallahassee *Dispatch* protested, far from commit-

44. Franklin County Deed Book Y, 613.

45. Complaint of Mabel Osborne; for various Osborne investments see Franklin County Deed Book X, 98–100.

46. Franklin County Chancery Order Book G, 34–38; see also Complaint of Mabel Osborne, Record 896–97, quoting Apalachicola *Times*, June 28, 1924. Popham disliked S. E. Rice, Jr.'s handling of the company's properties and advised his investors not to cooperate. He accused Rice of "konivering," a nonword invented by Popham. See Popham's statement of Sept. 2, 1924, in Ralstad papers.

ting any crime, had greatly helped Apalachicola. He was a man ahead of his time, but his fiercest opponents refused to recognize it.[47] The federal government lost its claim on Popham's assets. Later, in April 1925, a U.S. district court judge at Pensacola ruled that the Popham Trust Estate, not the Bureau of Internal Revenue, had a rightful claim to the company's properties.[48] Judging from the past, no one was willing to count Popham out, but it was obvious that he was down.

47. Tallahassee *Dispatch*, Dec. 14, 1923.
48. For the case see Franklin County Chancery Order Book G, 17–21.

14

The Verdict

BESET by legal troubles, Popham found needed diversion in the spring and early summer of 1924. Local elections were accompanied by a presidential race, and there was more than the usual interest in politics. Unsuccessful in winning a legislative seat in 1922, Popham decided to try again. He called forth the political custom in Franklin County of alternating the office of state representative between Apalachicola and Carrabelle. Since the retiring S. J. Giles was from Carrabelle, it was time for the county seat to be represented at Tallahassee. The tradition, broken in 1922, was broken again when former representative E. R. L. Moore of Carrabelle announced for the office.

Popham announced his own candidacy for the June 3 primary. Declaring himself a better known figure, he urged Moore to retire from the contest. When Moore declined, Popham issued a platform calling for a reduction of taxes. He offered to discuss the issues publicly with his opponent. The oyster king proposed renting the Dixie Theatre at his own expense, but the debate never came off. Moore well realized that the political advantage lay with him and that he could count on solid backing in Carrabelle. Popham had numerous foes in Apalachicola and could not command a solid bloc of voters. In any case, Moore was elected in a close race, 417 to 391. Popham, who had campaigned even less than in 1922, did not seem to mind.[1]

1. Franklin County Primary Election Records 1914–42, 26. See also Political

A brief but pleasanter diversion had come for Popham that April. His old friend William Jennings Bryan was touring Florida by car and speaking at every county seat. Unlike Bryan's appearance of the previous year, this visit was frankly political. With the blessing of state officials, the Great Commoner was seeking nomination in the primary to one of Florida's four delegate-at-large seats at the Democratic national convention. It was a situation made to order for Popham. As mayor of Apalachicola, he was responsible for welcoming Bryan who, despite three losses as a presidential candidate, was still a popular hero.

Popham was an expansive and considerate host. He ordered the town's streets closed to automobile traffic so there would be no distractions as Bryan addressed "a large and appreciative audience" for two hours. He gave Bryan his usual flowery introduction and urged the ex-Nebraskan's election. The sixty-four-year-old Bryan was in good condition physically and good form oratorically. He spent the night at Popham's home and the next morning enjoyed a big breakfast with Popham and local civic leaders. William Lee's skipper of the *Lady Popham* had an injured foot, forcing the slightly embarrassed mayor to send Bryan to Carrabelle by commercial transportation, the Wing line's *Jessie May*. Still, the visit was a success, and Bryan was elected a delegate-at-large.[2]

Popham forgot his problems briefly by immersing himself in a new business enterprise. As discussed, in 1924 Popham established the Florida Wholesale Land Company, Inc. He proposed to purchase forty thousand acres in Franklin and Liberty counties for development. Energetic as ever, he toured the state looking for even more property, speaking of developing three million acres. He issued periodic statements about having special agents and buyers throughout Florida. The company was founded on the Golden Rule, and its letterhead stationery explained, "Our Success Is Our Recommendation." Popham came up with an imaginative slo-

---

Tract dated May 5, 1924, and Political Brochure dated Mar. 26, 1924, in Ralstad papers.

2. Apalachicola *Times*, May 3, 1924; Louis W. Koenig, *Bryan: A Political Biography of William Jennings Bryan*, 619; Wayne Flynt, *Duncan Upshaw Fletcher, Dixie's Reluctant Progressive*, 137–38.

gan—"The Best Investment On Earth, Is The Earth Itself"—and even won approval from the postal authorities to send and receive mail.[3]

Next, Popham tried to expand the Oyster Growers' Co-Operative Association. He asked his investors for permission to purchase the Rice Brothers Packing Company, the Bay City Packing Company, and the Carrabelle Fish and Oyster Company, including its ice factory. S. E. and R. R. Rice, brothers and partners who had inherited their father's business, would be paid annual salaries and receive 1 percent of the profits for managing the new aspect of the company.[4]

Try as he might, Popham could not escape reality. His mild flirtation with politics ended in failure, and while it was flattering to entertain the Silver-Tongued Orator, that episode ended as Bryan disappeared from sight across Apalachicola Bay. Popham had to defer his plans for the Florida Wholesale Land Company, Inc. (but he would not forget the scheme), and enlarging the Oyster Growers' Co-Operative Association was impossible once it went into receivership. The former evangelist may well have thought of himself as a character in the Old Testament as afflictions continued to pour down on him.

At Pensacola, on September 8, 1924, Osgood H. Anson, foreman of a federal grand jury, returned a true bill to Judge William B. Sheppard presiding over the U.S. District Court for the Northern District of Florida. Indicted were Popham, Abbott, Collier, Charles N. Hampton, and Jefferson D. Kenney.[5] Hampton and Kenney were new to the list of alleged miscreants. According to Earl Hoffman, the indictments were a consolidation of previous charges. The five men were scheduled to be tried at Pensacola on November 4.[6] Popham retaliated with a flyer dated September 15, entitled, "Popham Ex-

3. William Lee Popham to Postmaster General Harry S. New, Aug. 2, 1924; William Lee Popham to J. Farley Warren, July 31, 1924; J. Farley Warren to William Lee Popham, Aug. 12, 1924; all in Ralstad papers. Apalachicola *Times,* Aug. 2, Sept. 30, 1924.

4. Copies of postcards Popham sent to his investors, in Ralstad papers; Apalachicola *Times,* May 3, 1924.

5. U.S. District Court, Northern District of Florida at Pensacola, Criminal Minute Book J, East Point Records Center, National Archives.

6. Jacksonville *Florida Times-Union,* Sept. 9, 1924.

plains the Prosecution." The flyer was addressed to each investor. He ripped into his opponents, including a new one, R. R. Rice, whom he called "Rip Ranter" Rice, and signed his apologia "Until death do us part."[7]

Popham and his compatriots were indicted on eight counts: seven for the violation of Section 215 (using the mails to defraud) and one for conspiracy. The conspiracy charge, which was a new one, held that the accused had violated Section 37 of the Penal Code. Kenney supposedly permitted the use of his name on mail that actually involved the machinations of Popham. After posting bond before a U.S. commissioner, the men asked for a transfer of the case to Tallahassee. As in the past, the request was based on geographical convenience and the expenses involved in obtaining witnesses. The plea was granted, and the trial was set for January 1925.

In December, the month before the trial, a group of citizens of Apalachicola, including Postmaster Warren, left a Chamber of Commerce meeting and held an indignation gathering of their own. Convinced that Popham's damaged reputation was hurting Apalachicola, they elected a new set of officers. Shortly afterward, Popham sent Warren a certified letter demanding that the postmaster forward all mail addressed "President of the Chamber of Commerce" to him. As for the rump meeting, Popham dismissed it as "a farce, a bluff, illegal, unlawful and a bag of wind."[8]

William Lee brushed aside his quarrel with Warren and concentrated on his upcoming trial. Preparing for a bitter battle, his defense team of Philip D. Beall, William C. Hodges, and Fred W. Davis added Jonathan P. Stokes and John M. Coe to their forces. The government's lawyers were Special Assistant Attorney General Arthur N. Sager of Washington and two familiar prosecutors, Earl Hoffman and Fred Cubberly. U.S. District Attorney Cubberly was in charge of the government's case. Presiding over the trial was W. I. Grubb, judge of the U.S. District Court for the Northern District of Alabama. He was present under special designation.

On January 12, Popham's laywers filed demurrers to the indictments. When the demurrers were overruled, the defendants pled

7. Copy in Ralstad papers.
8. William Lee Popham to J. Farley Warren, Jan. 9, 1925, Ralstad papers.

not guilty and the trial began. From January 12 to January 21, a large number of witnesses for both sides took the stand. Mansfield and his staff of postal inspectors, for example, had been staying at the hotel in Apalachicola. Now they shifted to Tallahassee.[9] Testimony and exhibits piled page after page into the record—1,187 pages of testimony from eighty-one witnesses and six hundred exhibits. For some reason Hampton was the only defendant to take the stand. He underwent only brief examination and cross-examination. The disappointed courtroom audience wondered why Popham did not come forward as a witness in his own behalf. If his lawyers could not prevail, surely the renowned Popham eloquence could sway a jury.[10]

The testimonies of Ruge and Hodges were devastating to Popham. Ruge pointed out that for Popham's four thousand investors to receive the promised hundred dollars a month income would require harvesting forty-eight million bushels of oysters a year, eighteen million bushels more than the entire production of the United States and more than the total output of the world.[11] "I have never had any altercation with Mr. Popham," witness Hodges declared. "But he has repeatedly said unkind things about me in the past and of course I have no very friendly feelings toward a man who would do that, but as far as any enmity is concerned, I have none." With that disclaimer, the shellfish commissioner then told the jury that Florida's varied fish industry yielded annually about $1.5 million, about a third of what Popham promised his investors from oysters alone. The mathematical calculations of Popham's opponents seemed incontrovertible.

The indictment for conspiracy was thrown out, and Judge Grubb directed the jury to find Kenney innocent of all charges. He simply had not been involved in any of the activities of the Oyster Growers' Co-Operative Association or the Million Dollar Bond Plan. He submitted to the Post Office Department an affidavit stating that Popham had used his name without permission.

On January 21, eleven days after the trial began, the prosecution and the defense rested their cases. After hearing Judge Grubb's

9. E. J. Mansfield to J. Farley Warren, Dec. 28, 1924, Ralstad papers.
10. For the testimony of Charles N. Hampton see *Record,* 1100–1109.
11. For the testimony of John G. Ruge see ibid., 910–19.

charge, the jurors retired. Ten hours of deliberation passed, but the members of the jury were unable to reach a verdict. They were locked up for the night at 10 o'clock but continued their efforts; they finally arrived at a decision, and at 9:30 the next morning, foreman George Y. Malone handed Judge Grubb the verdict. Abbott, Collier, and Hampton were declared innocent of all charges. Popham was found guilty on all seven counts and was sentenced to four years' imprisonment at the federal penitentiary in Atlanta.[12]

Stunned, Popham directed his lawyers to appeal the decision and make a motion for a new trial. The motion was denied, but the attorneys soon received a writ of error out of the U.S. Court of Appeals for the Fifth Circuit at New Orleans. Popham made bond to appear in February but was given a ninety-day extension to prepare.[13]

In the months that followed, Popham spent many days in Tallahassee conferring with his lawyers, going over every facet of his case. He did not seek reelection as mayor of Apalachicola. At one point he escaped the tension by taking his family for a quiet vacation in the North Carolina mountains. People still visited Saint George Island, oblivious to the anguish of the embattled Popham.[14]

Both sides filed their briefs, and to Popham's disappointment the decision of the lower court was upheld on March 17, 1926.[15] Neither Popham nor his lawyers gave up. He still had a chance. In April his attorneys' "Petition For Rehearing" was refused. Then in June Popham's counselors applied to the court of appeals for permission to present an extraordinary motion in the lower court for a new trial. The court of appeals, having already upheld the lower court and having denied the petition for rehearing, gave Popham until September 1, 1926, to file the application for a new trial. The motion was based on the claim of Popham's attorneys that several members of the jury believed that, after the other defendants were acquitted, Popham would be given a separate trial and found innocent. A letter to this effect had been mysteriously and improperly

12. *Record*, 41, 46–49; Jacksonville *Florida Times-Union*, Jan. 13–18, 20–23, 1925; Tampa *Morning Tribune*, Jan. 14–15, 17, 23, 1925; Apalachicola *Times*, Dec. 19, 1925.
13. *Record*, 60–61.
14. Apalachicola *Times*, July 4, Aug. 9, 15, 29, 1925.
15. *Record*, 60–61.

circulated among the jurors while they were deliberating. In addition, several members of the jury had complained that they had not seen all of the testimony.[16]

In the midst of his legal difficulties, Popham lost a valued friend. Following Popham's conviction and Abbott's acquittal, the former partners became completely estranged. In May 1926, Abbott was interviewed at length by the Apalachicola *Times*. He accused Popham of dishonesty and claimed that the promoter had manipulated the investors' money to his own personal uses. "Mr. Popham," Abbott said, "built for himself a mansion, clothed himself and family in sumptuous garments, furnished the mansion in an elaborate and expensive style and exalted himself to the position of a self-styled millionaire oyster king." In brief, Popham was guilty as charged.[17] "Vicious and untrue," Popham replied. The interview with Abbott was "an unwarranted attack." Vowing that his enemies were not going to take over his business enterprises, Popham was equally confident of avoiding prison. "Instead of being discouraged, bluffed and down and out as these men had hoped, I am one of the happiest men in Florida."[18]

More important than personal quarrels was the pressing problem of getting his conviction overturned. What if the court of appeals denied the application for a new trial? The defense lawyers had correctly anticipated such an event. When the motion was turned down on September 19, they got the denial mandate postponed for ninety days pending action by the Supreme Court for a writ of certiorari. If the writ were granted, the case would be reviewed.[19] Popham told the *Times*, "I am happy and content to have the high privilege to take my case to the highest court in the land, the United States Supreme Court at Washington." Popham had adopted a mood of religious fatalism. If he were innocent, he believed the Lord would have the court order a new trial. But "if I am

16. Apalachicola *Times*, July 3, 1926. The presence of the letter and their belief that Popham would go free in a second trial was later sworn to by several of the jurors. See Tallahassee *Daily Democrat*, July 9, 1933; William Lee Parker to author, Jan. 31, 1982.

17. Apalachicola *Times*, May 1, 1926.

18. Ibid., May 8, 1926.

19. Ibid., Sept. 11, 1926.

guilty of any dishonesty, I am fully certain that the high court will commit me to prison—where dishonest wrongdoers belong." It was in the hands of the Almighty; "I am not at all discouraged."[20]

There was, however, the truism that the Lord helped those who helped themselves. Popham had acquired two more lawyers: W. J. Waguespack of New Orleans and Robert H. McNeill of Washington. They got the Supreme Court to grant Popham's motion to stay consideration of his appeal for a writ of certiorari until a supplemental petition could be filed. The maneuver bought them time to bring in new evidence.[21]

Popham had been in Washington part of the time, but now he returned to Apalachicola to await the decision. On November 1, he heard from McNeill: the Supreme Court had refused to review his conviction. Popham wired the lawyer to do what he thought best and suggested bringing an injunction against the Supreme Court until a congressional committee could consider the case. Popham then went to Washington seeking an interview with Calvin Coolidge. Perhaps he could persuade the president to intervene.[22]

Whether he gained an audience with the chief executive is not known. Nothing was done to stay the original sentence and, as unthinkable as it was, William Lee had found no way out. He would have to go to jail.

In late November, Fred Cubberly and U.S. Marshall Millard Owens escorted several prisoners to Atlanta. Proceeding from Pensacola, the party was joined at Tallahassee by Popham. Cubberly and Owens noted that their newest prisoner was carrying an extremely heavy suitcase. Popham explained that it was filled with all the books he had written and that he intended to donate them to the prison library. Once they reached Atlanta, the library clerk, himself a former book publisher from New York, accepted the books with great pleasure.[23]

After a long struggle to stay out, Popham was now in the penitentiary. Even so, he went behind the walls in his own unique style.

20. Ibid.
21. Ibid., July 3, Oct. 23, 1926.
22. *Record*, 60–61; *U.S. Reports* 1926: 718 (Nov. 20, 1926).
23. Apalachicola *Times*, Nov. 27, 1926.

15

The Quest for Respectability—
and Profits

P OPHAM was crucified," Clifford C. Land, a business associate
of the oyster king, recalled many years later. Mrs. Alice Hodges,
a longtime resident of Apalachicola, agreed: "If they had left Mr.
Popham alone he would have made something out of the island
and out of the town."[1] In a larger sense the entire state was headed
for economic trouble. South Florida's land boom collapsed in
1925. Paper fortunes were wiped out, and speculators and promoters retired for the moment. Harder hit were the small investors
whose dreams of wealth became nightmares of ruin. The real estate
debacle in Florida made headlines across the country. Less heralded were the events in the northwestern section, where the many
people who had invested in one or more of Popham's plans could
only hope for some kind of return.

Following the suit introduced by Mabel L. Osborne, S. E. Rice,
Jr., was appointed receiver of the Popham Trust Estate. The appointment was important because the estate was extensive, with
mainland and island holdings totaling about twenty-two thousand
acres. Many moneyed combines were rumored to be interested:
DuPont was supposedly willing to pay $500,000, Jacksonville
bankers more than that, and an unnamed speculator even more. In

1. Author's interviews with Clifford C. Land, Aug. 5, 1977, and Mrs. Alice
Hodges, Aug. 18, 1981.

240

line with the wishes of some three thousand investors, the trustee was to sell the estate.[2] Rice remained as receiver until December 1, 1925, when R. G. Porter was appointed trustee. Porter's responsibility was to carry out the investors' wishes and Judge Love's orders to develop and sell the estate.[3]

False hope of resolving the complicated issues arose on March 6, 1926, when R. Lee Jarrell, president of Apalachicola Bay Shores, Inc., purchased the estate. Saint George Island was included with the exception of lots already sold in the Dechant and Ruff surveys and eight hundred acres on the western end.[4] On the day of the purchase, the corporation made arrangements to sell eight hundred acres on the island between West Gap and East Pass and to include certain lots in the Dechant survey.[5] The sale never materialized.

To secure their purchase, Jarrell and Apalachicola Bay Shores, Inc., executed a mortgage to Porter as trustee for $675,000 at 8 percent interest.[6] All of the confusion seemed to be over. Perhaps it would have been except that the corporation never got around to paying any of the principal or interest on its debt. In March 1927, when no payment had been made, Porter filed a bill of complaint in the Circuit Court, Second Judicial Circuit of Florida, to foreclose the mortgage. Three months later, a court decree ordered Apalachicola Bay Shores, Inc., to pay. W. P. Dodd of Apalachicola was appointed special master in chancery to sell the island and the rest of the estate.[7]

Popham, who had unsuccessfully applied to become receiver of

2. Apalachicola *Times*, Oct. 24, 1925.

3. At his death, Joseph Harper Hodges, a prominent businessman of Apalachicola in the twentieth century, left behind a miscellaneous collection of papers and documents dealing with the town and county. Considerable data pertains to Popham. Mrs. Alice Hodges, his widow, kindly permitted me the use of the Hodges papers. The citation above is to a note in those papers. See also Apalachicola *Times*, Dec. 5, 1925; Mar. 13, 1926.

4. Franklin County Chancery Order Book G, 39; Franklin County Deed Book Z, 193–95.

5. Franklin County Deed Book Z, 215–16; AA, 176–79.

6. Franklin County Mortgage Book K, 366–71.

7. Franklin County Chancery Order Book G, 200–204; see also Franklin County Les Pendens Record Book A, 200.

the estate, transferred much of his property to his mother or made other arrangements. It was difficult to determine exactly what the Popham Trust Estate consisted of. That Saint George Island was part of it was undisputed. Any investors who complied with the terms of the Million Dollar Bond Plan could claim their island lots.[8]

The brief interlude of new ownership ended on August 10, 1927, when Dodd executed a special master's deed for the estate back to Porter.[9] Acting as trustee, Porter was high bidder at $300,000. Administering the estate was a difficult, time-consuming, and thankless task. In June 1927, a large number of investors, represented by committees and individuals, met at Lakeland, Florida, and petitioned the court to appoint as trustee Greene S. Johnston, Jr., of Tallahassee. Their request was refused, but in 1928 (and after another petition), Porter stepped down, and the court designated Johnston as the trustee.[10] The owners of many lots on Saint George Island, as well as of mainland properties, had not paid their taxes. When the tax collector put their lots up for public sale, there were few takers. The county, like the estate, took in only limited amounts of money.[11]

Little Saint George Island was not a part of the estate, but it came into public notice in the 1920s. After E. G. Porter died in 1913, his widow, Joseph Charlotte, inherited Little Saint George Island. Following her death in 1924, the island was divided among her children, and John W. Wakefield was appointed executor. In 1925, L. B. Giddens, a Tampa businessman, expressed interest in buying Little Saint George Island for $110,000. With the collapse of Florida's real estate market, Giddens backed down, and the Porter family heirs stopped their efforts to quiet title to the property.[12] The island went on the market once more in 1929. As executor of the estate, Wakefield sold Little Saint George Island to a Florida com-

8. See note in Hodges papers.

9. Franklin County Chancery Order Book G, 200–204; Franklin County Deed Book AA, 193–96.

10. Hodges papers; Franklin County Chancery Order Book G, 258–59.

11. See notice of delinquent tax lands in Apalachicola *Times*, July 16, 1927.

12. Franklin County Deed Book Y, 524–26; see also Apalachicola *Times*, Sept. 12, Nov. 14, 1925.

pany known as Southwestern States Incorporated for $17,500.[13] For the time being, Saint George Island was no longer the property of Popham, and Little Saint George Island had passed from the ownership of the Porter family.

As the 1920s came to a close, the county enjoyed the second fight between Gene Tunney and Jack Dempsey in 1927 at Soldiers Field in Chicago; it came to Apalachicola by a special arrangement with radio station WJAX in Jacksonville. Except for inveterate gamblers, few people lost money by betting on Dempsey—funds were far too scarce to be squandered. In 1928 the nation's leading singer, Gene Austin, and his wife stopped briefly at Apalachicola. They left their yacht long enough for an admiring crowd to gather round, and Austin obliged them by singing "Ramona," "Then Came the Dawn," and his biggest hit, "My Blue Heaven." Abe Fortunas remodeled his Dixie Theatre in 1929, and an excited audience bought all available tickets in September to see the town's first talking picture. No one seemed disappointed with Metro-Goldwyn-Mayer's production of "The Broadway Melody," starring Anita Page, Bessie Love, and Charles King.[14]

Long used to economic adversity, even Franklin County was not prepared for the severity of the Great Depression. As if to emphasize the hard times, a powerful hurricane washed completely over Saint George Island in the fall of 1929 and damaged Apalachicola. Hard times were indicated by the number of Franklin County students who enrolled in college in 1929; there were only two attending the University of Florida, which put the county in a tie with Canada and Brazil. An important exception to the general economic decline was the opening in 1930 of the Intracoastal Waterway, which began in Corpus Christi, Texas. Eventually, the waterway was extended around Florida and up the Atlantic coast. Local

13. Franklin County Deed Book BB, 195–97; Franklin County Mortgage Record L, 434–36.

14. Apalachicola *Times*, Sept. 10, 24, 1927; Sept. 29, 1928; Sept. 9, 14, 21, 1929. The picture won the academy award as the best movie of the year. MGM's last silent movie, *The Kiss*, starring Greta Garbo, was also made in 1929. Al Jolson had appeared in the first "talkie," Warner Brothers' *The Jazz Singer*, in 1927, and the same studio produced the first all-talking movie, *Lights of New York*, in 1928. See Daniel Blum, *A New Pictorial History of the Talkies*, 11.

citizens also showed their perseverance in 1930. Like thousands of other Americans, they reflected their reduced circumstances by taking up the newest craze: miniature golf.[15]

In the Apalachicola Bay area the seafood industry, although greatly depressed, remained the chief means of livelihood. The state Shell Fish Department planted thousands of barrels of clean oyster shells in key areas. Yet the prices received and the demand for oysters were tied to a declining economy. Even the quality of the oysters seemed affected. The 1927–28 season was one of the best (Apalachicola had sixteen seafood and packing plants operating in full force); the 1930–31 season was one of the worst.[16]

Saint George Island remained virtually uninhabited save for a few goats and hogs and the cattle grazed and owned by J. S. Hathcock, Jr. Occasionally, the turpentine leasee made his rounds, and during hunting season men and boys came over from the mainland to shoot doves, quail, and ducks. In October the skies were filled with white-collared Canadian geese. The handsome birds remained until March. Many groups still made Sunday outings to the island.[17] Some people even kept the fading posters that showed Popham's island dotted with homes and dominated by the rainbow hotel, but the paper representations of a nonexistent development seemed a mockery. Apalachicola was cut off, or almost cut off, from the outside world. Efforts to span Apalachicola Bay with a bridge failed for lack of money, although the Wing line of ferries provided services, and most citizens did not give up hope.[18]

There were ongoing difficulties with the Popham Trust Estate. Early in January 1927, the court ordered part of it conveyed to Apalachicola Bay Seafoods, Inc., an enterprise organized for that pur-

15. Apalachicola *Times*, Apr. 20, 1929; Apr. 12, Oct. 4, 1930; Mar. 7, 1931.
16. Ibid., Oct. 6, 13, 1928; Apr. 13, 20, 1929; Mar. 30, 1930.
17. Author's interview with Homer Marks; Apalachicola *Times*, Mar. 26, June 11, 1927; July 28, 1928; June 15, 1929.
18. Promotional brochures by Johnston in Hodges papers; for Hathcock's exclusive grazing privileges see Franklin County Deed Book AA, 412–13. Before the Gorrie Bridge was opened in 1935, the most notable ferry line serving Apalachicola and Eastpoint was that of Capt. A. L. Wing. "Captain Andy" began operations in 1886 and continued to 1929. See Apalachicola *Times*, Feb. 16, May 11, 1929.

pose. Then in 1928, an attempt was made to give Mabel Osborne power of attorney to restructure the entire estate. She would appoint a new trustee (or trustees) who would appraise the properties and survey them. Then the various investors would receive land based on the amount of money they had paid in. The response was a strong endorsement from the investors. A young attorney, later a U.S. senator and still later U.S. congressman, disagreed. Claude Pepper, then a lawyer in Perry, agreed to handle the proceedings but pointed out the legal obstacles involved. The whole matter was abandoned.[19]

Greene Johnston remained in charge of the estate. In 1929, for example, he sold H. G. Fannin and his associates over nine thousand acres on the mainland.[20] Yet try as he might, Johnston was unable to keep the estate from declining, and tax sales of island lots remained slow. In the summer of 1932, an attempt was made to appoint three trustees who would in turn liquidate the holdings as best they could. Acting on orders from Judge E. C. Love, Johnston made an escrow agreement and executed a trustee's deed to a group of Apalachicola seafood men. The depleted estate, which had sold for $675,000 in the heady days of 1926, brought only $10,000 in the depression year of 1932.[21]

The new owners were H. L. Oliver and S. E. Montgomery, already trustees of the Acme Packing Company; S. E. and R. R. Rice of Rice Brothers Packing Company; and P. H. Ploeger, Popham's old adversary, of Sea Food Products Company. By mutual consent, and no doubt from economic necessity, the three companies had merged in March 1931. Attempting to sell the estate at a profit proved impossible for the men. Finally, having held the property less than three months, Oliver and Montgomery (acting with the consent of the others) sold the estate. In October 1932, they exe-

19. Claude Pepper to Mable L. Osborne, Dec. 10, 1928, Hodges papers. See also scattered references, ibid.

20. Apalachicola *Times*, July 27, 1929. Although "no plans for development of the property have been announced by the new owners," the *Times* called it "a deal of great importance to Apalachicola and the immediate territory."

21. Franklin County Deed Book CC, 1, 396–99. The deceased C. L. Shephard had been a partner in the Acme Packing Company, and the deceased S. Castorina had been a partner with Ploeger.

cuted a trustee's deed for ten dollars to the Cultivated Oyster Farms Corporation, a Florida company.[22]

At the time the people of Franklin County were not overly concerned with the latest transfer of ownership of Saint George Island and the estate. As had happened during Reconstruction after the Civil War, they were self-absorbed, trying to make ends meet. The Cultivated Oyster Farms Corporation sounded worthy of a name Popham might have dreamed up in his heyday. When news got around that it actually was a Popham concoction, the citizens had a sense of déjà vu.

Incarceration in a federal penitentiary would be unlikely to produce in anyone a feeling of gratification. Yet more than most sufferers of that fate, Popham, who entered prison on November 27, 1926, had been able to cope. It has not been established that he sold any lots on Saint George Island to his fellow inmates, but according to local legend, he served as prison librarian. It is certain that he polished his dormant literary talents. Within a few months William Lee published a slim volume of verse entitled *Prison Poems*. Among the twenty-six entries were "First Month of Prison a Hundred Years," "Love's Pen," "A Prisoner Waits," "Dear Daddy, Please Come Home," "By-Gone, Brighter Days," "The Letter That Made Me Sad," "A Prisoner's Meditation," and "My Little Boy's Hand." If the titles were excruciating and trite, the circumstances that produced them were painfully real. The book, published at Apalachicola in 1927, was priced at ten cents, but even at that modest sum the softcover edition sold only a few copies.[23]

William Lee was a model prisoner, and he was paroled after serving less than two years of his four-year sentence. While her husband was in jail, Maude remained at home, visited from time to time by friends and kin. She and Clara kept up their voter registration (and their pride) and were good citizens. With few exceptions, there was no social ostracism of the Popham family in Apalachicola.[24]

22. Ibid., 393–95.

23. Popham planned to write a book of verse every month and have young boys serve as salesmen and carriers on a commission basis. Printing costs and limited sales prevented him from following through.

24. Author's interviews with Tilla Sheally and Tessie Mecoen, George Core, and Alice Hodges.

Released on June 30, 1928, Popham returned home in July. When the former island promoter got off Captain M. L. Wing's *Jessie Mae* at the ferry landing in Apalachicola, a crowd was on hand to welcome him. Hardly visible in the throng was eight-year-old William Lee, Jr. Yet the moment remained vivid with him. "It was in the early evening," he reminisced as a mature man, "when crowds began to gather, until by the time the 'Jessie Mae' . . . was pulling alongside the dock . . . it seemed that every man, woman, and child in that little town of Apalachicola was gathered there in that moon-lit Florida night to 'Welcome him home'!" [25] In reporting his arrival, the Apalachicola *Times* tactfully remarked that Popham had been on "an extended stay in Atlanta." [26]

William Lee's financial affairs were in a shambles, but his mother mortgaged property that he had transferred to her. Using these funds, Popham attempted a comeback. "I finally decided," he wrote, "that I was Divinely led to re-enter the field in which I had formerly lost, under a new Corporate identity." [27] He still dreamed of planting oysters in Apalachicola Bay, and, as always, Saint George Island would be part of his plans.

Popham was not dismayed by the failure of *Prison Poems* to sell. Given the subject matter and the tenor of the times, the book was not likely to attract many buyers. Popham had not lost his flair for writing, and his desperate need for money caused him to resume his literary efforts. He soon produced a book of verse which he titled *Heart Poems*. Before the volume could be circulated and before he could advertise its merits, Popham would have to get the mail fraud order of 1923 revoked. In 1929, he appealed to Post Office officials in Washington, promising that never in the future would he engage in questionable business activities. Popham's request proceeded through the proper channels and was closely scru-

25. William Lee Parker to author, Jan. 31, 1982.

26. Apalachicola *Times*, July 7, 1928; William Noonan, Jr., executive assistant to the warden, United States Department of Justice, Bureau of Prisons, United States Penitentiary, Atlanta, Georgia, to author, Dec. 8, 1977.

27. For Clara's support see, for example, Franklin County Mortgage Book M, 18–19, when in October 1930, she mortagaged town lots and an additional two hundred acres in Franklin County to J. W. Griffin. For Popham's strong vow to start over, see William Lee Popham to Arthur C. Popham, June 23, 1934, Popham-Shoelles papers.

tinized, but on October 12, 1929, Postmaster General Walter F. Brown lifted the restriction. Popham was free to use the mails.[28] He soon discovered that *Heart Poems* was not the answer to his economic woes. The volume had a limited sale, faring little better than *Prison Poems* had.

Since his young manhood, Popham had known and enjoyed attention and praise. Now it was 1930 and the former celebrity was a forty-five-year-old has-been; worse, his failure was stigmatized by a prison record. Popham had written too many poems of uplift and too many books calculated to inspire and delivered too many speeches and sermons about keeping the faith to give up. Yet he was as unsettled as the Popham estate (where lots on Saint George Island and on the mainland, many of them in Clara Popham's name, went unclaimed even when auctioned for unpaid taxes).[29] Popham achieved some stability by keeping Apalachicola as his base. Maude continued her daily strolls, Clara kept busy making trips to and from Kentucky, and William Lee, Jr., was a popular student at Chapman High School. Popham himself was restless— he ranged as far north and west as Saint Louis and lived briefly at Panama City, Florida.[30] Somehow, he had to reestablish himself. Popham wrote his lawyer that "They have had me for the past few years where I could not do much fighting, but with the assistance of the Good Lord and able attorneys, I am going to win this fight and then these Conspirators will know who is the owner of St. George Island."[31]

Popham's major effort to achieve his former glory was through the Cultivated Oyster Farms Corporation. An estimated $10,000 was involved when the company gained control of the Popham estate in October 1932. The new enterprise was an outgrowth of the Modern Oyster Farms Corporation, which Popham had organized in 1931. That company was granted lease number 339 from the

28. Memorandum, Horace J. Donnelly to Walter F. Brown, Oct. 10, 1928; Walter F. Brown, Order no. 0472, Oct. 12, 1928; Record Group 28, National Archives.

29. Apalachicola *Times*, June 7, 1930; July 4, 1931.

30. Ibid., May 10, 24, June 4, Aug. 6, Oct. 4, 11, 1930.

31. William Lee Popham to John H. Carter, Aug. 4, 1931, Popham-Shoelles papers.

state, which entitled it to five hundred acres of water bottoms in Apalachicola Bay. By early 1931, the corporation was granted a state permit to gather a hundred thousand barrels of unculled oysters from Franklin County's natural reefs for transplanting onto lease 339. For undeclared reasons, in early 1931 Popham formed a new corporation by simply substituting the word "Cultivated" for the word "Modern." He was also instrumental in the formation of Whatley Farms Corporation (an oyster-producing operation) in 1932, and William Lee Popham Corporation (designed to deal in real estate) in 1933.[32] But most of his time and attention were devoted to the Cultivated Oyster Farms Corporation, and for a while one of his associates was William A. McRae, former state commissioner of agriculture.

"This is no get-rich-quick proposition, and we neither know nor estimate what the harvest or income will be," the rejuvenated ex-prisoner wrote in a promotional pamphlet. In truth, his claims were scarcely less modest than those of the 1920s. An investor was treated to some attractive mathematics: 90 percent profit on the oysters, guaranteed royalty of 50 cents per barrel on oysters, and 90 percent of the net profits from other seafoods. The oysters would come from seven thousand acres of the state's natural beds and from thirty-five thousand acres of water bottoms leased from the State Board of Conservation. All of the labor and equipment necessary for the enterprise would be furnished by the corporation. Saint George Island was mentioned as a major asset, but its specific role was not defined.[33]

The large acreage claimed for the oyster beds was legitimate but never realized. Yet in the years 1932 and 1933, the Cultivated Oyster Farms Corporation signed sixty-five separate leases, one from a private individual and the remainder from the state.[34] All one had to do to take advantage of the proposal was to become a

32. United States of America v. William Lee Popham, Maude Miller Popham, and William A. McRae. The various materials relating to the case are on file at the Federal Records Center, East Point, Georgia. (Hereinafter cited as US v. Popham.)

33. Brochure in Sawyer Collection; promotional pamphlet in Popham-Shoelles papers.

34. For typical examples of a private lease and of a state lease see Franklin County Deed Book CC, 262–63; DD, 35–37.

"unit holder" in the corporation. A unit consisted of ten barrels of seed oysters that would be propagated on four seedbeds. The annual increase would go to the unit holder, and then be replanted on one acre of suitable oyster bottom. The price was a hundred dollars per unit with a 5 percent discount for cash. Popham claimed that ten thousand people subscribed $1 million to the corporation.[35] By April 1933, the Apalachicola *Times* announced that Popham's company planned to purchase and consolidate all of the larger oyster and seafood factories and canning plants in Apalachicola and the vicinity.[36] The sensational proposal was never carried out.

With various partners, Popham formed two new companies in 1934: World-Wyde Products, Incorporated, and Florida Oyster Farms, Incorporated. Their purpose was to capitalize on some of Popham's most original, although impractical, ideas. Popham planned to build some three thousand Oyster Huts and Seafood Restaurants that would handle the corporation's products exclusively. The $6 million investment had provisions to permit thirty thousand independent restaurants to sign contracts. The various Oyster Huts would use Popham's new process of reducing oysters, as well as clams and other seafoods, to powdered form. The powdered products, known as World-Wyde Oyster Puree, could also be packaged as cubes and tablets. They would be put in paper-fiber containers of different sizes and shipped by truck, freight, express, and parcel post. Popham also developed a drink known as Oyster Nip, which, drunk hot or cold, would sell for five cents a glass. Unlike beverages such as Coca-Cola,™ Oyster Nip, according to Popham's aims, was nutritional as well as tasty. The plans were never put into effect, but they were not preposterous. Variations of Popham's ideas would be applied by thousands of "quick food" restaurants in later decades. His drink was surely close related to

35. Brochure in Sawyer Collection; promotional pamphlet in Popham-Shoelles papers.

36. Apalachicola *Times*, Apr. 22, 1933. On July 15, 1933, the *Times* reported that the corporation had purchased historic Lanark Inn and thirty-five hundred acres of adjoining land fronting the Gulf.

many liquid health products that were developed in the last decades of the twentieth century.[37]

The proliferation of companies founded or fostered by Popham increased in 1935 when he incorporated Florida Sunland Farms (it succeeded his Florida Sunland Company, Unincorporated, which he had founded a few months earlier). Popham's idea was to sell five-acre farms all over the state, especially in DeSoto County, which lay in South Florida and where he was negotiating purchases. Florida Sunland Farms had the ironic motto of "Our Success Is Our Recommendation," a slogan Popham had used earlier. Sales in Florida's "Kingdom of the Sun" were aimed at small investors who could pay sixty dollars for five-acre farms. Popham sought out persons "earnestly desiring to flee from the hardships of depression, unemployment, hot Summers, cold Winters, floods, dust-storms, drought, 'Hard Times,' and financial lack."[38] In 1935, Popham wrote his son about the progress of Florida Sunland Farms: "Our land proposition is going like wild fire, as I predicted; and is going to be, and in fact already is, a tremendous success, with very bright prospects in the future for unlimited business."[39]

Popham promoted all of the companies, but he concentrated on the Cultivated Oyster Farms Corporation. The operation benefited from legislation passed in 1933 that permitted the kind of oyster production he proposed and allowed the leasing of bottomland to nonresidents as well as Floridians.[40] From 1931 through 1935, Popham traveled throughout Florida. Headquarters for the Cultivated Oyster Farms Corporation were in the Trout Building on East Bay Street in Jacksonville, although there were branch offices in Tampa, Tallahassee, Miami, and elsewhere. Prospective clients were bombarded with handbills, circular and personal letters,

37. US v. Popham; brochure in Sawyer Collection; promotional pamphlet in Popham-Shoelles papers.

38. US v. Popham; brochure in Popham-Shoelles papers.

39. William Lee Popham to William Lee Popham, Jr., May 17, 1935, Popham-Shoelles papers.

40. Popham's advertising took advantage of the statutes' provisions. See *Laws of Florida* 1933: 531, 531–32.

folders, cards, maps, blueprints, plans, and photographs. Later, his son reflected, "I still remember while in my 'teens, standing on the street corners in Jacksonville, passing out circulars with him, announcing his . . . promotion of Florida oyster culture . . . oyster farming off the shores of Saint George Island in the Apalachicola Bay."[41]

Popham even produced a talking movie that touted his ventures. He would show the film (advertised as a free movie) and then play gramaphone records over loudspeakers. Hoping that the audience was in a receptive mood, William Lee then explained his oyster farms. But hard cash was scarce in the thirties. Subscriptions were taken but allowed to lapse. Seeking new investors, Popham visited small towns in Georgia and the Carolinas. With his assistant, Alvin M. Sayers, Popham went by truck to out-of-the-way county seats showing his movie, playing records, and making speeches. The curious audiences watched and listened politely, but few among them had money to invest.[42]

Any significant success for Popham was dependent on conditions in Apalachicola and Franklin County. Poor even before the depression struck, the people there had a difficult time. Several agencies of the New Deal brought relief and made Franklin D. Roosevelt a folk hero in Franklin County. People who had at least some money were reassured when they saw evidence of membership in the new Federal Deposit Insurance Corporation posted in bank windows. Federal Emergency Relief Administration (FERA) funds were used to open a mattress factory in Carrabelle and to build an airport at Apalachicola in 1934. There was irony in the conversion of the Rice Brothers Packing Plant into a beef-canning plant. The conversion lasted only a year, but the FERA project temporarily helped solve the labor problem. Money supplied in part from the Works Progress Administration (WPA) and the Public Works Administration (PWA) greatly boosted the economy. Federal funds aided in the construction of a new courthouse (opened in 1940).

In 1937, there were forty-six young men from Franklin County

41. William Lee Parker to author, Jan. 31, 1982.
42. US v. Popham.

enrolled in the Civilian Conservation Corps (CCC). By 1938 Franklin County had 125 people working on federal projects and another 281 who were part-time employees. The single most dramatic event for the county was the opening of the John Gorrie Bridge in November 1935. After more than a century of isolation and many years of frustrating efforts, Apalachicolans now had a bridge that connected them with Eastpoint and beyond. Funded by PWA and state and local appropriations, the bridge became a symbol of hope. The opening was celebrated in grand style and was attended by thousands of people. Dignitaries made speeches and, for the moment, citizens forgot their problems.[43]

It was pleasant to go to Barnett's Circus, which came to Apalachicola in 1934, or to drive across the glistening six and a half miles of John Gorrie Bridge that spanned the bay. On special occasions there were dances with music supplied by the newly formed Pair-O-Dice Pals. The eight-piece orchestra was novel in that it was composed of men and women. Yet the hard facts were that Franklin County was suffering. Diversions were welcome, but poverty was ever present, and hardest hit was the oyster industry.

The drought that created the Dust Bowl of the Great Plains had a damaging effect on Apalachicola Bay. An extreme dry spell in the Apalachicola River valley in 1935 created a shortage of fresh water in the bay. The unusual increase in salinity resulted in the appearance of the oyster leach or wafer. Attaching themselves to the shells, the leaches decimated several major oyster bars. Oyster shipments for the season were cut almost in half. It was a bitter truth that soon Chesapeake Bay oysters were arriving from Baltimore for sale in Florida. By 1937, Apalachicola had only six seafood plants operating. Remedial action was taken as state and federal moneys were used to create a marine laboratory at Indian Pass and oyster bars were dredged and replanted. In a few seasons the leach was controlled and production returned to normal.[44] Yet future relief was no consolation to people whose economic mainstay had been drastically reduced.

43. Every issue of the Apalachicola *Times* in the 1930s contained articles about the depression. No attempt is made to cite specific stories, but for the bridge see the issues of Sept. 14, Oct. 26, Nov. 2, 1935.

44. Ibid., Jan. 12, 19, Feb. 9, 16, Mar. 23, May 4, June 15, 1935.

The infestation of oyster leaches could not have come at a worse time for Popham. By hard work he had overcome some obstacles, not the least being his credibility. In this he was aided by a Florida politician named Jerry W. Carter. Serving as state insurance commissioner in the 1920s, Carter had known Popham. Now in the 1930s he and an associate in Tallahassee opened a branch office of the Cultivated Oyster Farms Corporation. In large newspaper advertisements, Carter, who even then was becoming something of a legend, advised potential customers that Popham was a man of honor. He declared his belief that Popham had been falsely accused and imprisoned. Carter even printed affidavits from jurors who claimed they had convicted the oyster king because of misinformation and regretted their votes. "While I have not enjoyed a close friendship with William Lee Popham, for few indeed are close to him," Carter wrote, "I have carefully followed his career and activities." Carter was proud to be Popham's business associate because "he is a real human being, without horns, and is on the job every working hour of every working day, in the biggest comeback ever accorded the persecuted."[45]

By 1935, Popham was not only having difficulty making sales, he was limited in what he had to sell. As his income declined, he kept up an outward appearance of confidence. He was constantly on the move—to Jacksonville, to Orlando, and further south. At home in Apalachicola, his family lived frugally. Popham faithfully sent money to his mother even when it meant he had little himself and even when it meant reducing the already low salary of his employee Sayers. Maude was aided by a faithful, talented, and largely unpaid cook named Vene. They kept the house going and looked after Maude's brother Jim. William Lee, Jr., graduated from Chapman High School in 1935 and enrolled that fall at the University of Florida. Popham's sister lived in Gainesville and was the wife of Dr. Clarence Tillman, a physician and doctor for the university. Relieved about his son's well-being, Popham was beset by other problems. At one point in the summer of 1935, he had to rent his boat to pay the light and water bill. After meeting his payroll, he had

45. See advertisements in Tallahassee *Daily Democrat*, July 9, 1933; Tampa *Tribune*, Jan. 21, 1934.

eighty-seven cents on hand and still owed forty-four dollars in office rent.[46]

Popham was hopelessly in debt. In 1935, he engaged in a number of corporative maneuvers and turned as a last resort to Saint George Island. In January he got three associates to form the Florida Goat, Sheep, and Turkey Farms, Incorporated. Then the Cultivated Oyster Farms Corporation made two moves simultaneously. It deeded Saint George Island to the new corporation and it transferred the remainder of the estate to Popham personally.[47]

Property juggling could not solve Popham's monetary woes, but he hoped that Saint George Island would. In December 1935, the Florida Goat, Sheep, and Turkey Farm, Incorporated, borrowed $5,000 from George M. Counts, a prominent timber and turpentine man of Apalachicola. For security, Popham mortgaged Saint George Island.[48] A native South Carolinian, Counts had moved to Franklin County in 1906 when he was a young man of nineteen.[49] Before dealing with Popham, Counts had bought several tax certificates against the island in 1933.[50] According to Florida law, land upon which taxes went unpaid could be acquired by an outside party who followed specified legal procedures and paid the taxes. If the owner failed to redeem his land within a certain period, it became the property of the person holding the tax certificates.

Counts secured still another interest in the island, an interest that brought forward a colorful man named Clifford C. Land. In December 1935, Counts obtained a naval stores lease for five years from the Florida Goat, Sheep, and Turkey Farms, Incorporated. The "cup system" was to be used in turpentining, and the rent was two cents per face or turpentine box. In turn, Counts subleased the contract to Land.[51] A native of Wewahitchka, Florida, Land had

46. William Lee Popham to Alvin M. Sayers, July 19, 1935, Popham-Shoelles papers. See also Apalachicola *Times,* July 20, 1935; Aug. 22, 29, 1936.

47. Franklin County Deed Book DD, 231–32; 232–33; each transaction involved the sum of ten dollars.

48. Franklin County Mortgage Deed Record M, 418–20.

49. Author's interview with George M. Counts, Sr.

50. Franklin County Record of Land Sold for Taxes, Book 5, 41–42, 93–94; author's interview with George M. Counts, Sr.

51. Franklin County Deed Book DD, 417–19; ibid., 419–21, mentions that Counts got the lease from the William Lee Popham Corporation.

lived in Franklin County for nineteen years. His home, on the eastern outskirts of Eastpoint on the way to Carrabelle, looked across Apalachicola Bay to Saint George Island.

As a man interested in turpentine and cattle, Land had a special feeling for the island. He ranged some 250 to 300 head of cattle (there was also the usual scattering of hogs and goats). At various times Land sold some of his cows. He and his workers rounded up the cattle and ferried them across the bay on barges to the mainland. There they were waded or swum ashore and staged on property adjacent to Land's home. As for the other work, Land sent a crew of men over by the week (a black cook named Acey provided for them), and, as he said, "The timber we turpentined covered the entire island and we chipped and dipped gum and grist and regrist all over the island." Land paid Counts twenty cents on the dollar for the turpentine and provided him with 117 head of cattle free of charge.[52]

Neither Land nor Counts realized much profit from the cattle or turpentine on Saint George Island. Not only were the times depressed, but, as Counts said later, "I never was a money maker. I was too lenient with labor. I couldn't abuse labor like I saw some people do."[53]

Popham had returned from prison firmly resolved to salvage his reputation. He engaged in several ventures, but even a man of his resources and inventiveness could not accomplish a triumph in the troubled America of the 1930s. Finally, he turned in desperation to Saint George Island as the means for survival. Few men labored more diligently to achieve success, but as Popham was about to discover, his efforts had once again incurred the wrath of the legal system.

52. Author's interview with Clifford C. Land. From Dec. 29, 1940, to Jan. 1, 1941, Land leased the turpentine rights from the new owner, the St. George Island Club, Inc., for one dollar a year. In turn Land subleased those rights to the Peninsular Lumber Company of Duval County for one dollar. See Franklin County Deed Book FF, 420, 422. See also Action to Quiet Title 1 and 2.
53. Author's interview with George M. Counts, Sr.

16

"You Can't Help Wondering . . ."

P OPHAM went to Washington in 1936 to face a fraud hearing before officials of the Post Office Department. Shortly afterward, postal officials and the Federal Securities Commission obtained a federal court order banning Popham's business literature from the mails. Popham denied the charges, claiming there was a conspiracy against him by his opponents. He declared himself innocent and mentioned the injustice of his previous conviction. "But I've made the best comeback you ever heard of from an ex-convict," he said.[1]

Yet it took no clairvoyance for the oyster king to know that the next step would be an indictment by a federal grand jury. He even knew that he would be charged with having violated Section 215 of the U.S. Penal Code. The ordeal that he had endured in 1925 was about to be repeated. If the circumstances were similar, there still were differences. This time Popham was more vulnerable and less confident, although he managed to hide his fears if not his bitterness.

The grand jury handed down the anticipated indictment on September 5, 1936. William Lee and Maude as well as William A. McRae were charged with fraudulent use of the U.S. mails. Although Clara was also named as one of the participants, Popham's mother was never arrested or tried. At the time, Popham was in

---

1. Jacksonville *Journal*, Feb. 1, 1936.

Houston, Texas, on a quixotic venture to get rich quick by purchasing gold and silver mines. Acting on the request of Herbert S. Phillips, U.S. district attorney in Jacksonville, H. H. Black, a postal inspector, made the arrest. Surrendering to Black, Popham declared that he had been "framed by business competitors" and "railroaded by government agents." [2] He believed that quick exoneration would follow and promised that "if free I will pay back every cent to my investors." He informed a reporter that the money would come from his Texas mines, which, properly operated, "would make 100 men wealthy." [3]

Deputy U.S. Marshall C. V. Kern brought William Lee to Jacksonville, and on September 21, he and Maude (McRae was absent because of illness) were arraigned before Judge Louis W. Strum in the U.S. District Court for the Southern District of Florida. Bond was set for Popham at $10,000, while McRae was required to post the smaller amount of $2,500. Maude was permitted to remain in the custody of her counsel until $2,500 was raised for her bond. McRae got his total reduced to $1,500, obtained the necessary sureties, and was released on September 21. Popham was able to raise bond for Maude but not for himself. Because the term of court was set for October 5, the time interval did not seem burdensome nor the amounts of the bonds excessive. It was clear that the trial would be complex and take a long time to conclude. Over sixty people had been arraigned before Judge Strum on other charges, and he faced a crowded docket. Left with little choice, the judge postponed Popham's trial until the January 1937 term. Popham faced the discomfort and indignity of waiting in jail for three months. [4]

Finally, in December, Popham asked that his bond be reduced to $5,000, an amount he could obtain. The request was granted, and Samuel B. Roggins and Mrs. Annie Mae Ferrell, both of Tallahassee, made bond for Popham. During his incarceration Popham had secured the services of some outstanding lawyers: Clyde A. Atkin-

2. Jacksonville *Florida Times-Union*, Sept. 8, 1936.
3. Tallahassee *Tribune*, Sept. 12, 1936. See also Jacksonville *Journal*, Sept. 5, 11, 1936.
4. Jacksonville *Florida Times-Union*, Sept. 22, 1936; US v. Popham, no pagination.

son of Tallahassee; State Senator Edgar W. Waybright and his son, Roger J. Waybright, of Jacksonville; and State Senator William C. Hodges of Tallahassee. While preparing the case, the lawyers visited Popham in jail. Atkinson noted that he was still a master of words. Over the years William Lee had grown heavier and more bald, but he had a commanding presence and did not doubt that the government's case would fail.[5] An acquaintance remarked that Popham "had wind enough to last a thousand years."[6]

The defendant's lawyers had him file a sworn affidavit of his indigence, and he became entitled to call witnesses at the expense of the government. By taking advantage of the *in forma pauperis* statute, they hoped to counter the many witnesses summoned by the prosecution. William Lee and Maude were penniless, and they subsisted on fifteen dollars a week supplied by Popham's brother. No less than ninety witnesses were called. Over twenty came from Apalachicola and many others from across Florida, including Nathan Mayo, commissioner of agriculture, and George W. Davis, commissioner of conservation. Also receiving subpoenas were people from Washington, D.C., Ohio, Utah, New York, California, Georgia, Mississippi, and North Carolina.[7]

The trial began Monday morning, January 4, 1937. The Pophams had their lawyers, McRae was present with his, and the government was represented by two assistant district attorneys, Damon O. Yerkes and William A. Paisley. Demurrers by the defense had already been overruled, and after the jury was selected and legal preliminaries dispensed with, Paisley and Yerkes plunged into a confusing jungle of charters, deeds, letters,, and memoranda. Specific dates of events, supplied for the sake of clarity, had the opposite effect. A Jacksonville reporter called the trial "one of the most involved and technical criminal cases to be conducted in the United States District Court here in a number of years."[8]

The jurors were to decide if the defendants had, as charged,

5. Author's interview with Clyde A. Atkinson, July 27, 1977; US vs. Popham.

6. Author's interview with George M. Counts, Sr.

7. US v. Popham; Tallahassee *Daily Democrat*, Jan. 17, 1937; Jacksonville *Journal*, Jan. 14, 1937.

8. Jacksonville *Florida Times-Union*, Jan. 5, 1937; see ibid., Dec. 31, 1936; Jan. 4, 1937; and Jacksonville *Journal*, Jan. 4–5, 1937.

made six misrepresentations. The government claimed: (1) their venture was not backed by 10,000 unit holders who had sub-scribed $1 million to develop oyster bottoms; (2) Popham and his associates were not building the world's largest cultivated oyster farm and seafood corporation at Apalachicola (another misrepre-sentation was similar to the second and denied Popham's claims of the number of acres planted); (3) they had not purchased the fac-tories that they claimed; (4) their planting operations and pre-dicted future operations wre untruthfully advertised; (5) their oyster barrels were smaller than legal size, thus preventing an hon-est count of production and affecting the correct amount of royal-ties due to the investors; (6) at the time they claimed rights to oyster bottoms, December 9, 1931, the state had issued no permits or leases to them. The most important charge—that Popham and the others had entered a conspiracy to violate Rule 215 of the U.S. Penal Code—was thrown out.[9]

The case marked the first time in a federal court in Florida that motion pictures were exhibited as evidence. When the government sought permission to issue four reels of Popham's advertising films, neither he nor his lawyers objected. McRae was opposed, but Judge Strum allowed the showing. After a week of testimony from a stream of witnesses, the jurors welcomed the showing of the half-silent, half-talking movies. When the court recessed for the week-end, only one witness for the government remained to be heard.[10]

By the time Yerkes rested the government's case on Monday, U.S. District Attorney Herbert S. Phillips was on hand to assist in the trial. The prosecution had gone into all of the six charges and pro-duced letters specifically relating to each accusation. Next, McRae asked for a directed verdict of not guilty. His lawyer claimed that the government had offered no evidence connecting McRae with the mail fraud charges. In fact, the former commissioner of agri-culture had severed his connections with Popham before any of the cited letters were written. Judge Strum decided to withhold a de-

9. US v. Popham.

10. Jacksonville *Florida Times-Union*, Jan. 7–9, 11, 1937; Tallahassee *Daily Democrat*, Jan 8, 1937; Jacksonville *Journal*, Jan. 8, 1937.

cision on the motion for a directed verdict until all the evidence was in.[11]

During the course of the trial three witnesses testified in behalf of McRae, and the former state official testified in his own behalf. Popham was determined not to repeat the strategic mistake of his earlier trial. This time he would take the stand. His lawyers agreed and contented themselves with reading to the jury letters attesting to William Lee's good character. One strong endorsement came from former governor Doyle E. Carlton. Instead of calling witnesses, the defense attorneys asked that Popham be sworn.[12]

For most of an entire day Popham was subjected to direct examination. The next day the accused summoned his old evangelistic energy and underwent cross-examination. His lawyers' strategy, which Popham executed brilliantly, was to claim that he and everyone connected with him had acted in good faith. Projecting an air of scientific objectivity, itself an act of impressive theatricality, Popham calmly stated that he had made no claims for oyster production that had not been made in official government publications. The statistics used to advertise the Cultivated Oyster Farms Corporation were taken directly from data published by the U.S. Government Printing Office.

Popham gave a classic performance. He lectured the jury on the habits of oysters. Calling on reservoirs of skill, William Lee explained the intricacies of promoting land and shellfish. Enjoying himself, Popham was reluctant to stop talking. "Now I want to take time to explain another feature of this splendid organization," he remarked, long after the jurors had heard more than they could possibly comprehend and long after the government lawyers were beside themselves. When the oyster king finished, the prosecution was unable to offer any rebuttal.[13]

The government's most serious charge, the existence of a conspiracy, had been thrown out. Popham had so many ventures that

11. Jacksonville *Florida Times-Union*, Jan. 16, 1937.

12. US v. Popham; Jacksonville *Journal*, Jan. 12, 1937.

13. Jacksonville *Journal*, Jan. 14, 1937; author's interview with Clyde A. Atkinson; US v. Popham.

it was impossible for all of them to have been part of a single scheme to defraud. The defense attorneys showed further that the letters offered in evidence often had been written before the related corporation was formed. How could a company be guilty when it had not even been organized?[14] That the enterprises failed was due to the Great Depression, a catastrophe for which Popham could not be held personally or criminally responsible. Few in the courtroom were unaware of a cruel paradox: oyster production, of all businesses, should have been impervious to a drought. Yet the prolonged dry spell had been of major significance in ruining Popham's ventures.

The trial ended on Friday, January 15. Judge Strum then declined to give a directed verdict to McRae. The jury would decide his guilt or innocence. Next, Judge Strum said that he saw nothing in the evidence to show "purposeful participation" by Maude in any of the promotions. That being so, he directed the jury to find her not guilty. In his charge to the jury, the judge selected his words carefully. Whatever the verdict, neither Popham nor McRae could claim unfair treatment.[15]

While the jury was deliberating, Atkinson asked his client how he would react to a verdict of guilty. The poet-promoter replied that such a decision would be acceptable to him. He would use the time to complete some books he had been writing. Beyond that, jail was a good place in which to rest.[16] Three and a half hours later, the jury returned to the courtroom. It was late in the afternoon when Foreman W. A. Evans rose to announce that the jury had found the defendants not guilty on all counts.[17]

Popham was free, but he had no means of paying his attorneys their fees. As usual, he relied on Saint George Island. In November 1936, the Florida Goat, Sheep, and Turkey Farms, Incorporated, executed a mortgage to the senior Waybright, Hodges, and Atkinson for the island (and other property as well) to secure an indebt-

14. US v. Popham.
15. Ibid.
16. Author's interview with Clyde A. Atkinson.
17. US v. Popham; Jacksonville *Florida Times-Union*, Jan. 16, 1937; Jacksonville *Journal*, Jan. 15–16, 1937.

edness of $12,000.[18] The amount clearly represented the lawyers' charges for defending William Lee and Maude. Then in September 1937, Waybright assigned all of his interest in the mortgage to his son, Roger.[19]

Earlier, in March 1937, Popham's corporation had mortgaged the island a second time. Alphonse Pichard of Tallahassee loaned $2,000 to the Florida Goat, Sheep, and Turkey Farms, Incorporated, and the island was offered as security.[20] A few weeks later, in April, title to Saint George Island was transferred to Florida Sunland Farms, Incorporated, a ploy that made sense only to Popham.[21] The last transfer had no meaning since Sunland Farms never attempted to exercise possession, claim ownership, or pay taxes on the island.

As time passed and Popham made no payments to his lawyers, Waybright, Hodges, and Atkinson filed a bill of complaint in the Circuit Court, Second Judicial Circuit of Florida, on March 10, 1938. The defendants were the Florida Goat, Sheep, and Turkey Farms, Incorporated, Popham and his wife, William Lee, Jr., and Alphonse Pichard. The final decree of foreclosure on August 23, 1938, forced the defendants to yield Saint George Island and other property.[22] It is doubtful that Pichard, whose claim was considered inferior, ever recovered the $2,000 he had loaned Popham's firm in March. On October 19, 1938, W. D. Hopkins, special master in chancery, carried out the court's decree and turned the island over to Waybright, Hodges, and Atkinson.[23]

Counts, who held a mortgage on Saint George Island dating back to 1935, as well as tax certificates, was less than pleased. In August 1939, he filed a bill of complaint in the Circuit Court, Second Judicial Circuit of Florida, against the three new owners and the Florida Goat, Sheep, and Turkey Farms, Incorporated. His case was simple: $7,388.97 was due him. The final decree in chancery

18. Franklin County Mortgage Deed Record M, 519–22.
19. Ibid., 542–46.
20. Franklin County Mortgage and Lien Assignment Record B, 67.
21. Franklin County Deed Book EE, 78–79.
22. Franklin County Chancery Order Book H, 276–78.
23. Ibid., 278; Franklin County Deed Book E, 536–38.

came in February 1940; it declared that unless the corporation paid Counts, the island would be sold at public outcry to the highest bidder.[24]

Counts did not retain control. The bill of complaint that ended in his favor in February became the basis of negotiations between him and William H. Wilson, the brother-in-law of William C. Hodges. A Tallahassee businessman, Wilson, along with Atkinson, would be a key figure in shaping the future of Saint George Island. On April 1, 1940, Counts assigned his right to the final decree, together with mortgage notes and his tax certificates, to Wilson.[25] The two men reached a separate financial agreement. Wilson paid Counts approximately $8,000.[26] The next day, Clyde and Elizabeth Atkinson, Margaret W. Hodges (as executrix of William C. Hodges's last will and testament), and Roger J. and Evelyn Waybright conveyed their claim to the island to Wilson. No money, other than a nominal ten dollars, was involved.[27] As of April 1940, William H. Wilson was the sole owner of Saint George Island. No one at any level issued an official pronouncement, but a new era had begun.

After being declared innocent, Popham said that he had no intention of returning to the business of oyster culture.[28] He tried to retain control of the island but failed. There was little left for him and his family at Apalachicola and Franklin County, although conditions in the area were improving. The town and county were woefully short of money, but oyster production was increasing. Both the shrimp and crabmeat industries were expanding, and there was pressure to make a permanent cut through Saint George Island. If Congress provided the money and the U.S. Army Corps of Engineers the labor, the shrimp boats and others seeking deepwater fish would greatly benefit. Hope for the future was evidenced

24. Franklin County Chancery Order Book H, 329–33. The Cultivated Oyster Farms Corporation was dissolved in December 1937, and the Florida Sunland Farms, Incorporated, in 1940.

25. Franklin County Mortgage and Lien Assignment Record B, 88–89.

26. Author's interview with George M. Counts, Sr.

27. Franklin County Deed Book FF, 232–34. For Hodges's will see ibid., 267. The will was made June 28, 1937, and recorded July 11, 1940.

28. Jacksonville *Florida Times-Union,* Jan. 16, 1937.

by the celebration of Mardi Gras. The event was so successful in 1938 that Apalachicolans repeated it the following year.[29]

At Carrabelle the channel was deepened to twenty-five feet. That meant a partial revival of the old and profitable lumber industry. By 1938 the L. B. Buck Lumber Company was making shipments from Carrabelle's deep-water port, a facility that Apalachicola had tried unsuccessfully to secure. As world events crowded in, another lumber company at Carrabelle entered into a "cash and carry" contract with the British government in 1940. The pine and cypress poles furnished by Franklin County were used in constructing barbed-wire entanglements on the Maginot Line in France.[30] Closer to home, in the summer of 1940, Apalachicola's National Guard unit, Company E of the 106th Engineers, joined other units of the Third Army for three weeks of maneuvers in Louisiana.[31]

True to form, Saint George Island went from one owner to another and back again. But in 1942 the U.S. government took over the island for the duration of World War II. It became important for gunnery practice by the Army Air Corps and for training in amphibious warfare. In the postwar years, the island became the storm center of a classic struggle between private developers and environmentalists. Local, state, and national governments, and inevitably politics, became involved. That story will be told in a subsequent study.

It seems logical to conclude with the departure of William Lee Popham from the scene and with the advent of World War II. Evaluating Popham requires that one accept his impractical, romantic side. He was extroverted, flamboyant, a grandstand performer, a teller of tall tales. The unrealistic evangelist loved the trappings of power, and his ego craved attention. He invented a utopian world. For him, the excitement of watching a circus was the proper emotional level at which to live every day. Success was elusive but worth the pursuit, and Popham was sure that he would attain it. All he had to do was experiment until he found the right formula. Then

---

29. Apalachicola *Times*, Feb. 26, Mar. 5, Apr. 19, June 6, 24, 1938; Feb. 17, 24, Apr. 21, July 7, 28, Aug. 25, Dec. 5, 1939; Feb. 16, May 24, 1940.

30. Ibid., Apr. 4, July 22, Sept. 2, 1938; Jan. 12, 1940.

31. Ibid., July 26, Aug. 23, 1940.

fiction would become fact, phantasy would become reality. William Lee was a part-time charlatan and mountebank, and much that he proposed was pure humbug.

To his credit, Popham was imaginative and innovative and his resiliency and fortitude were striking. The evangelist-promoter was incapable of carrying a grudge, not even against Shell Fish Commissioner Hodges. A blanket of emotional serenity and self-assurance protected him. Popham had been prepared for a verdict of guilty in his second trial, and he even managed to view his first prison term as a positive experience. After he was released in 1928, Popham told a young man of Apalachicola that being in jail had given him the opportunity to catch up on his reading.[32] Popham had almost irresistible charm and was a kind and loyal friend. People who knew the oyster king, including sworn enemies, never forgot him. He wrote and spoke and promoted both day and night. That the basic moral tenets of Southern Protestantism were deeply embedded in him is not to be doubted. That he was scrupulously honest is subject to considerable debate. Yet he was genuinely shocked at the vociferousness of his accusers. How, the tireless promoter wondered and asked, could they have so misjudged his motives? Such was his invariable reaction whether the evidence against him was flimsy or incontrovertibly true.

After his acquittal, Popham must have reflected about the first trial. If he had testified in his own behalf the criminal proceedings might have resulted in a different verdict. A North Florida jury so hardened as to resist Popham's mellifluous oratory is difficult to imagine. Whatever his musings, the oyster king was not a man to waste time on self-pity. Even so, in 1938, Popham probably did not disagree with a *Times* editorial suggesting that Saint George Island be made into a state park.[33] That way the island he had worked so hard to obtain and develop would belong to everybody.

Shortly after the trial ended, Clara Popham died. Popham and his family left Florida. At first Popham went to Detroit, but the midwestern city yielded few if any opportunities. He moved on to

32. Author's interview with Judge John Hodges, Aug. 14, 1976; John Hodges to author, Oct. 3, 1977. Judge Hodges lives in Tampa, Florida.
33. Apalachicola *Times*, June 4, 1938.

Ely, Nevada, to investigate mining claims that he knew about. Gold was a possibility. Yet, following his penchant for seeking something different, Popham investigated the potential of carborundum, a trade name for a hard, abrasive compound prepared from sand and carbon. The difficulty, as in Detroit, was his lack of investment capital. Popham finally moved to Los Angeles, California, and became a realtor. William Lee, Jr., also settled down in California, married, and raised a family.[34]

Popham never forgot Saint George Island and his efforts to combine island property and oyster culture into a profitable enterprise. According to his son, Popham "was always promotional minded, always planning what he continually referred to as his 'comeback'."[35] The comeback never occurred. Popham died on August 22, 1953, in Los Angeles. The sixty-eight-year-old Popham had a number of health problems, but uremia was the major cause of his death. He was buried in Valhalla Cemetery. Maude remained in California, outliving William Lee by many years. She died in 1980 at the age of ninety-three and was also buried in Los Angeles.[36]

Even with his far-fetched paper schemes, William Lee was a man in advance of his times. A number of people would have agreed with Ward Green, who interviewed him for the Atlanta *Journal* in 1919. "You can't help wondering," Green wrote, "if the world wouldn't be a good deal better off if we had more Pophams in it."[37] But, then, maybe one was enough.

34. William Lee Parker to author, Jan. 31, 1982. Popham and Maude approved when their son changed his last name to Parker. His new wife and most of their friends in California had difficulty pronouncing and spelling Popham, and Parker was substituted to end the confusion.

35. Ibid.

36. The death certificates for William Lee and Maude are on file at the California Department of Health Services, Office of the State Registrar of Vital Statistics, Sacramento.

37. Atlanta *Journal Sunday Magazine*, July 13, 1919.

Bibliography

Primary Sources

Manuscripts

Hodges, Joseph Harper. Papers. In possession of Alice Hodges, Apalachicola.
Kimball Lumber Company, Apalachicola. Ledger Book 1888–89. Special Collections Room, University of West Florida Library, Pensacola.
Love-Scarborough papers. Florida State University, Tallahassee.
Milton, John. Letterbook, 1861–63, 1863–65. Florida Department of Archives, History, and Records Management, Tallahassee.
Miscellaneous letters. P. K. Yonge Collection, University of Florida, Gainesville.
Popham-Shoelles papers. In possession of Ruth Shoelles, Apalachicola.
Ralstad, Royce. Papers. In possession of Ralstad family, Apalachicola.
Sawyer, Fred, Sr. Scrapbook. In possession of Dorothy Sawyer Matthews, Apalachicola.

Documents, General and Federal, Published and Unpublished

Adjutant General, Office of. *Records.* Record Group 94, National Archives.
Apalachicola Land Co. *Annual Report,* 1838–39, 1841–42. New York.
_____. *Articles of Agreement and Association.* New York, 1835.
_____. *Extract from a Report to the Trustees.* New York, 1837.
Brice, John J. "The Fish and Fisheries of the Coastal Waters of Florida." *Annual Report of the U.S. Fish Commission for 1896,* Part 22.
Carter, Clarence E., ed. *The Territorial Papers of the United States, Florida Territory,* vols. 22–26. Washington, 1956–62.
Cobb, John N. "Possibilities for an Increased Development of Florida Fishery Resources." *Bulletin of the United States Fish Commission.* 17 (1897).

Final Report of the United States de Soto Expedition. Washington, 1939.

Fraud Order Case Files. No. 4113. Record Group 28, National Archives.

Kappler, Charles J. *Indian Affairs Laws and Treaties.* 5 vols. Washington, 1904.

Miscellaneous materials relating to Saint George Island and lighthouses. Record Group 26, National Archives.

Official Records of the Union and Confederate Navies in the War of the Rebellion. 30 vols. Washington, 1894–1927.

Peters, Richard, ed. *Reports of Cases Argued and Adjudged in the Supreme Court of the United States.* Vol. 9. New York: Banks and Brothers, 1884.

Quartermaster General, Office of. *Records.* Record Group 92, National Archives.

Swift, Franklin, Lieutenant. "Report of a Survey of the Oyster Regions of St. Vincent Sound, Apalachicola Bay, and St. George Sound, Florida." In *Annual Report of the U.S. Fish Commission for 1896,* Part 22, 187–217.

U.S. Army. Records of the Continental Commands. Record Group 393, National Archives.

U.S. Census (unpublished), 1850, 1860, 1870, 1880.

U.S. Census, 1860, 1900.

U.S. Circuit Court of Appeals Fifth Circuit. No. 4698, William Lee Popham, Appellant v. United States, Appellee Transcript and Brief.

U.S. Congress. House. *Report No. 19.* 23d Cong., 2d sess.

_____. *Document No. 129.* 54th Cong., 2d sess.

_____. *Documents Nos. 622, 834.* 63d Cong., 2d sess.

U.S. District Court, Northern District of Florida at Pensacola. Criminal Minute Book U. East Point Records Center, National Archives.

U.S. Fish Commission. *Bulletin 6* (1886).

United States of America v. William Lee Popham, East Point Records Center, National Archives.

U.S. Reports, 1926.

U.S. Statutes at Large. Vols. 4, 5, 9.

War of the Rebellion: A Compilation of the Official Records of the Union and Confederate Armies. 127 vols. Washington, 1880–1901.

Documents, State, Published and Unpublished

California. State Registrar of Vital Statistics, Sacramento. Certificates of Death for Maude Miller Estes Popham and William Lee Popham, Sept. 12, 1980.

Census of Apalachicola, Florida, June 1, 1884–May 31, 1885. Special Collections Room, University of West Florida Library, Pensacola.

Convention of the People of Florida at a Called Session, Begun and Held at the Capitol, in the City of Tallahassee, on Tuesday, January 14, 1862. *Journal.* Tallahassee, 1862.

Convention of the People of Florida Convened Third Day of January 1861. Florida Department of Archives, History, and Records Management, Tallahassee.

Florida Department of Agriculture. *Seventeenth Biennial Report.* Part 1, 1921–22. Tallahassee, 1922.

Florida Department of Agriculture. Shell Fish Division. *Second Bi-Ennial Report,* 1915–16. Tallahassee, 1916.

Florida General Assembly. *Acts and Resolutions,* 1847–51, 1859–61, 1868, 1870, 1872, 1879, 1881, 1884–87, 1889, 1891, 1893, 1895, 1901, 1905, 1913, 1915, 1919–21, 1933.

Florida Master Site File. Historic Site Data Sheet. Florida Department of Archives, History, and Records Management, Tallahassee.

Florida Reports. Vol. 86 (1923).

Florida. Senate. *Journal,* 1862.

Florida, Territory of. Legislative Council. *Acts,* 1823, 1825, 1827–32, 1836, 1840.

Georgia. General Assembly. *Acts,* 1823, 1827–28, 1853–54.

Manuscript election returns. October 1, 1860. Florida Department of Archives, History, and Records Management.

Morris, Allen, comp. *The Florida Handbook 1981–1982.* Tallahassee: Peninsular Publishing Co., 1983.

Soldiers of Florida, Civil War 1861–65, 1. Typescript. Florida Department of Archives, History, and Records Management.

Documents, County, Unpublished

FRANKLIN COUNTY

Book of Probates. Vol. 1, 1833–44; Vol. 3, 1867–1903.

Chancery Order Book, G, H.

Circuit Court File. William H. Neel v. H. N. Humphries et al.

Commissioners' Minutes, Book 2–3, 1898–1915.

Commissioners' Record Book, 1876–77.

Deed Book, A–M, R–Z, AA–FF, U2. Franklin County Courthouse, Apalachicola.

Incorporation Book, A, B.

Les Pendens Record Book, A.

Marriage Record Book 3, 1919–22.

Mortgage and Lien Assignment, Record B.

Mortgage and Lien Satisfactions, Book C.

Mortgage Deed Record Book, A, E, G, J, K, L, M.

Primary Election Records, 1914–21, 1914–42. Supervisor of Elections, Franklin County Courthouse.

Record of Land Sold for Taxes, Book 5.

Record of Leases, Book 2.

Record of Liens, Book A, B.

Record of Wills, 1846–1894.

GADSDEN COUNTY

Deed Book A. Gadsden County Courthouse, Quincy.

BIBLIOGRAPHY

HENRY COUNTY, GEORGIA

Marriage Record, 1903–27. Probate Office, County Courthouse, McDonough, Georgia.

LEON COUNTY

Deed Book E, MM, K. Leon County Courthouse, Tallahassee.
Chancery Order Book 1.

LIBERTY COUNTY

Deed Book, A, B, T. Liberty County Courthouse, Bristol.

MUSCOGEE COUNTY

Charter Record, Book 1, 227–29.
Deed Book KK, 455–57; LL, 554–56. Muscogee County Courthouse, Columbus, Georgia.

Newspapers and Magazines

Apalachicola *Advertiser,* 1839–44.
Apalachicola *Commercial Advertiser,* 1843–47, 1849, 1856, 1858.
Apalachicola *Courier,* 1839.
Apalachicola *Florida Journal,* 1840, 1844.
Apalachicola *Gazette,* 1836–39.
Apalachicola *Oyster Farm News,* 1922.
Apalachicola *Star of the West,* 1844.
Apalachicola *Times,* 1898, 1900–1931, 1933, 1935–36, 1938–41, 1943–44, 1946, 1948, 1952–53, 1957, 1961, 1966–67, 1973, 1976–79.
Apalachicola *Watchman of the Gulf,* 1843.
Apalachicolan, 1840.
Atlanta *Journal Sunday Magazine,* 1919.
Bainbridge [Georgia] *Argus,* 1856–57.
Bainbridge *Southern Georgian,* 1858–59.
Bainbridge *Southern Spy,* 1829.
Bainbridge *Southern Sun,* 1871.
Jacksonville *Florida Times-Union,* 1919, 1923–25, 1936–37.
Jacksonville *Journal,* 1936–37.
Mobile [Alabama] *Commercial Advertiser,* 1835.
New Orleans *Daily Picayune,* 1840, 1843, 1856.
New Orleans *Times-Picayune,* 1873.
Niles' Weekly Register, 1819, 1822, 1834–35, 1840–41.
North & South [Louisville, Kentucky], 1909. Records of the Bureau of Plant Industry, Soils, and Agricultural Engineering, Record Group 54, National Archives.
Pensacola *Gazette,* 1835.
Pensacola *Gazette and West Florida Advertiser,* 1825.

St. Joseph *Times*, 1838, 1840.
Tallahassee *Daily Democrat*, 1921–24, 1933, 1937.
Tallahassee *Dispatch*, 1923.
Tallahassee *Florida Journal*, 1842.
Tallahassee *Florida Sentinel*, 1851, 1861, 1863.
Tallahassee *Floridian*, 1837, 1839, 1851, 1871, 1873, 1883, 1892.
Tallahassee *Floridian and Journal*, 1860.
Tallahassee *Star*, 1839.
Tallahassee *Tribune*, 1936.
Tallahassee *Weekly Floridian*, 1873, 1892.
Tallahassee *Weekly Sentinel*, 1863.
Tallahassee *Weekly Tallahasseean*, 1899.
Tampa *Tribune*, 1916, 1921, 1925, 1934.
Thomasville [Georgia] *Times*, 1883, 1887–88.

Books

Bandelier, Fanny, trans. *The Narrative of Álvar Núñez Cabeza de Vaca*. Barre, Mass.: Imprint Society, 1972.
Boggs, W. R. *Military Reminiscences of General William R. Boggs, C.S.A.* Durham: Seeman Printery, 1913.
Brinton, Daniel Garrison. *A Guide-Book of Florida and the South, for Tourists, Invalids, and Emigrants*. Philadelphia: G. Maclean, 1869.
Cohen, M. M. *Notices of Florida and the Campaigns*. New York, 1936. Facsimile reproduction of the 1836 edition. Gainesville: University of Florida Press, 1964.
Estes, Maude Miller. *Love Poems and the Boyhood of Kentucky's Poet, Being the Life-Story of William Lee Popham*. Louisville: n.p., 1910.
Forbes, James Grant. *Sketches, Historical and Topographical of the Floridas; More Particularly of East Florida*. New York, 1821. Facsimile reproduction of the 1821 edition. Gainesville: University of Florida Press, 1964.
Griffith, Mrs., trans. *The Shipwreck and Adventures of Monsieur Pierre Viaud, A Native of Bordeaux, and Captain of a Ship*. London: T. Davis, 1771.
Hallenbeck, Cleve. *Alvár Nuñez Cabeza de Vaca—The Journey and Route of the First European to Cross the Continent of North America, 1534–1535*. Glendale: Arthur H. Clark Co., 1940.
Kelley, Oliver H. *Origin and Progress of the Order of the Patrons of Husbandry in the United States; A History from 1866 to 1873*. Philadelphia: J. A. Wagenseller, 1875.
Lanier, Sidney. *Florida: Its Scenery, Climate, and History*. Philadelphia, 1875. Facsimile reproduction of the 1875 edition. Gainesville: University of Florida Press, 1973.
Lewis, Theodore H. "The Narrative of the Expedition of Hernando de Soto by the Gentlemen of Elvas." In *Spanish Explorers of the Southern United States*. New York: Charles Scribner's Sons, 1907.

Long, Richard C. *Florida Portrayed: Its Sections, Climate, Productions, Resources, etc.* London: South Publishing Co., 1885[?].

Martin, Edward Winslow. *History of the Grange Movement* . . . . Philadelphia: National Publishers Co., 1873.

Merwin, J. W. *Roster and Monograph: 161st Reg't N.Y.S. Volunteer Infantry. Rebellion 1861–1865.* N.p., n.d.

Moore, Frank, ed. *The Rebellion Record: A Diary of American Events, with Documents, Narratives, Illustrative Incidents, Poetry, etc.; with an Introductory Address by Edward Everett.* 11 vols. New York: G. P. Putnam's Sons, 1861–68.

Popham, William Lee. *The Garden of the Gods Romance.* Louisville: World Supply Co., 1911.

_____. *Grand Canyon of Arizona Romance.* Louisville: World Supply Co., 1913.

_____. *Heart Poems.* Apalachicola: n.p., 1927.

_____. *Love's Rainbow Dream.* Louisville: W. L. Popham, 1910.

_____. *The Mammoth Cave Romance.* Louisville: World Supply Co., 1911.

_____. *The Natural Bridge Romance.* Louisville: World Supply Co., 1911.

_____. *The Niagara Falls Romance.* Louisville: World Supply Co., 1911.

_____. *Nutshells of Truth.* New York: Broadway Publishing Co., 1910.

_____. *Poems of Truth, Love and Power.* New York: Broadway Publishing Co., 1910.

_____. *Prison Poems.* Apalachicola: n.p., 1927.

_____. *The Road to Success: The Best Book in the World.* Murray, Kentucky: William L. Popham, 1905.

_____. *She Dared to Win.* Louisville: Westerfield-Bonte Co., 1910.

_____. *Silver Gems in Seas of Gold.* New York: Broadway Publishing Co., 1910.

_____. *A Tramp's Love.* Louisville: n.p., 1910.

_____. *The Valley of Love.* Louisville: Westerfield-Bonte Co., 1910.

_____. *The Village by the Sea.* Louisville: Westerfield-Bonte Co., 1910.

_____. *The Washington Monument Romance.* Louisville: World Supply Co., 1911.

_____. *The Yellowstone Park Romance.* Louisville: World Supply Co., 1911.

_____. *The Yosemite Valley Romance.* Louisville: World Supply Co., 1911.

Richardson, Simon Peter. *The Lights and Shadows of Itinerant Life.* Nashville: Publishing House of the Methodist Episcopal Church, 1900.

Roberts, William. *An Account of the First Discovery, and Natural History of Florida.* London, 1763. Facsimile reprint of the 1763 edition. Gainesville: University of Florida Press, 1976.

Romans, Bernard. *A Concise Natural History of East and West Florida.* New York: n.p., 1775.

Scharf, J. Thomas. *History of the Confederate States Navy from Its Organization to the Surrender of Its Last Vessel.* New York: Rodgers & Sherwood, 1887.

Sprague, John T. *The Origin, Progress and Conclusion of the Florida War.* New

York, 1848. Facsimile reprint of the 1848 edition. Gainesville: University of Florida Press, 1964.

Wakefield, George Norton. *A Florida Sandpiper, or, A Fool Rushed in Where Angels Fear to Tread.* Gainesville: Storter Publishing Co., 1982.

Walker, Jonathan. *Trial and Imprisonment of Jonathan Walker, at Pensacola, Florida, for Aiding Slaves to Escape from Bondage.* Boston, 1848. Facsimile reprint of the 1848 edition. Gainesville: University of Florida Press, 1974.

Wilson, John A. *Adventures of Alf. Wilson: A Thrilling Episode of the Dark Days of the Rebellion.* Washington: National Tribune, 1897.

Interviews

Atkinson, Clyde A., Tallahassee, July 27, 1977.

Ausley, Susan, Tallahassee, October 7, 1977.

Brown, Charley, Apalachicola, June 29, 1977.

Brown, Gene, Tallahassee, July 18, 1983.

Brown, Herbert G., Eastpoint, December 28, 1982.

Brown, Rebecca, Eastpoint, December 28, 1982.

Core, George, Apalachicola, March 1, 1980.

Counts, George M., Sr., Winter Haven, July 28, 1978.

Cummings, Harry, Apalachicola, August 25, 1977.

Hance, Leo, Carrabelle, January 5, 1983.

Hays, Pat, Apalachicola, November 24, 1976.

Hodges, Alice, Apalachicola, August 18, 1981.

Hodges, John, Apalachicola, October 3, 1977.

Howell, Robert L., December 30, 1982.

Land, Clifford C., Eastpoint, August 5, 1977.

Lovett, Francis, Apalachicola, August 25, 1977.

Marks, Homer, Apalachicola, July 7, 1978.

Marshall, Pearl Porter, Apalachicola, September 1, 1981.

Mecoen, Tessie, Apalachicola, June 29, 1981.

Moore, John H., Tallahassee, July 19, 1982.

Proctor, Palmer, Tallahassee, August 31, 1977.

Proctor, Sarah Ball, Tallahassee, August 31, 1977.

Ralstad, Royce, Apalachicola, September 11, 1977.

Roux, Audrey, Apalachicola, October 8, 1981.

Sawyer, Frederick, Jr., Apalachicola, November 24, 1976.

Sheally, Tilla, Apalachicola, June 29, 1981.

Stanton, Claire Tillman, Orlando, October 3, 1977.

Taranto, Anthony, Apalachicola, May 11, 1983.

Williams, Leland, Apalachicola, August 18, 1981.

Williams, Lily Mae, Apalachicola, August 18, 1981.

Secondary Works

Albion, Robert G. *The Rise of the Port of New York, 1815–1860.* New York: Charles Scribner's Sons, 1939.

Bacon, Mary Ellen. *Albany on the Flint: Indians to Industry, 1836–1936.* [Albany?]: Albany Town Committee of the Colonial Dames of America in the State of Georgia, 1970.

Bearss, Edwin C. "Civil War Operations in and around Pensacola." *Florida Historical Quarterly* 36 (October, 1957), 125–65; 39 (January, 1961), 231–35; (April, 1961), 330–53.

_____. "Federal Expedition against Saint Marks Ends at Natural Bridge." *Florida Historical Quarterly* 45 (April, 1967), 369–90.

Bell, Harold W. *Glimpses of the Panhandle.* Chicago: Adams Press, 1961.

Bishop, Morris. *The Odyssey of Cabeza de Vaca.* New York: Century Co., 1933.

Blum, Daniel. *A New Pictorial History of the Talkies.* New York: G. P. Putnam's Sons, 1958.

Boyd, Mark F. "The Battle of Marianna." *Florida Historical Quarterly* 29 (April, 1951), 225–42.

_____. "The Federal Campaign of 1864 in East Florida." *Florida Historical Quarterly* 29 (July, 1950), 3–37.

Boyd, Mark F., Hale G. Smith, and John W. Griffin. *Here They Once Stood: The Tragic End of the Apalachee Missions.* Gainesville: University of Florida Press, 1951.

Boynton, Walter Raymond. "Energy Basis of a Coastal Region: Franklin County and Apalachicola, Florida." Ph.D. diss., University of Florida, 1975.

Bradburby, Alford G., and E. Story Hallock. *A Chronicle of Florida Post Offices.* N.p.: Florida Federation of Stamp Clubs, 1962.

Brooks, William K. *The Oyster.* Baltimore: Johns Hopkins University Press, 1905.

Bryan, T. Conn. *Confederate Georgia.* Athens: University of Georgia Press, 1953.

Burns, Thomas J. "The Catholic Church in West Florida, 1783–1850." Master's thesis, Florida State University, 1962.

Carse, Robert. *Keepers of the Lights: A History of American Lighthouses.* New York: Charles Scribner's Sons, 1969.

Castelnau, Compte de. "Essay on Middle Florida, 1837–1838." *Florida Historical Quarterly* 26 (January, 1948), 199–255.

Castleberry, A. J., and David L. Cipra. *Lighthouses and Lightships of the Northern Gulf of Mexico.* Washington: n.p., n.d.

Caughey, John W. *McGillivray of the Creeks.* Norman: University of Oklahoma Press, 1938.

Clubbs, Occie. "Pensacola in Retrospect, 1870–1890." *Florida Historical Quarterly* 37 (January–April, 1959), 377–96.

Coker, William S., and Thomas D. Watson. *Indian Traders of the Southeastern Spanish Borderlands: Panton, Leslie and Company and John Forbes and Company, 1783–1847.* Pensacola: University of West Florida Press, 1985.

Comnenos, Carolina Johnson. "Florida's Sponge Industry: A Cultural and Economic History." Ph.D. diss., University of Florida, 1982.

Cushman, Joseph D., Jr. *A Goodly Heritage: The Episcopal Church in Florida, 1821–1892*. Gainesville: University of Florida Press, 1965.

_____. "The Blockade and Fall of Apalachicola, 1861–1862." *Florida Historical Quarterly* 41 (July, 1962), 38–46.

Davis, Frederick T. "Florida's Part in the War with Mexico." *Florida Historical Quarterly* 20 (January, 1942), 235–59.

_____. "Pioneer Florida: The First Railroads." *Florida Historical Quarterly* 23 (January, 1945), 177–83.

Davis, William Watson. *The Civil War and Reconstruction in Florida*. New York: Columbia University Press, 1913.

Debo, Angie. *The Road to Disappearance*. Norman: University of Oklahoma Press, 1941.

Dodd, Dorothy. "Horse Racing in Middle Florida, 1820–1843." *Apalachee* 3 (1948–50), 20–29.

_____. "The Secessionist Movement in Florida, 1850–1861." *Florida Historical Quarterly* 30 (July, 1933), 3–24, 45–66.

_____. "Railroad Projects in Territorial Florida." Master's thesis, Florida State College for Women, 1929.

Dodd, William G. "Theatrical Entertainment in Early Florida." *Florida Historical Quarterly* 25 (October, 1946), 121–74.

Doherty, Herbert J., Jr. *Richard Keith Call, Southern Unionist*. Gainesville: University of Florida Press, 1961.

Doster, James F. *The Creek Indians and Their Florida Lands, 1740–1823*. 2 vols. New York: Garland Publishing Co., 1974.

Dovell, J. E. Written with the assistance of J. G. Richardson. *History of Banking in Florida, 1828–1954*. Orlando: Florida Bankers Association, 1955.

Dunham, Audrey. "Tales of Tate's Hell." *Geojourney* 1 (October, 1980), 8–9.

Flynt, Wayne. *Cracker Messiah: Governor Sidney J. Catts of Florida*. Baton Rouge: Louisiana State University Press, 1977.

_____. *Duncan Upshaw Fletcher, Dixie's Reluctant Progressive*. Tallahassee: Florida State University Press, 1971.

Foreman, Grant. *Indian Removal: The Emigration of the Five Civilized Tribes of Indians*. Norman: University of Oklahoma Press, 1953.

Frantzis, George T. *The Story of the Sponges of Tarpon Springs: Strangers at Ithaca*. St. Petersburg: Great Outdoors Publishing Co., 1962.

Gammon, William Lamar. "Governor John Milton of Florida, Confederate States of America." Master's thesis, University of Florida, 1948.

Gannon, Michael V. *The Cross in the Sand: The Early Catholic Church in Florida, 1513–1870*. Gainesville: University of Florida Press, 1965.

Garvin, Russell. "The Free Negro in Florida before the Civil War." *Florida Historical Quarterly* 46 (July, 1967), 1–17.

Garwood, Saunders B. "Florida State Grange." *Florida Historical Quarterly* 47 (October, 1968), 165–79.

Gold, Robert L. *Borderland Empires in Transition: The Triple-Nation Transfer of Florida.* Carbondale: University of Southern Illinois Press, 1969.

Gonatos, John M. *The Story of the Sponge.* Tarpon Springs, Fla.: n.p., 1946.

Green, V. H. H. *A History of Oxford University.* London: B. T. Batsford, Ltd., 1974.

Groene, Bertram H. *Ante-Bellum Tallahassee.* Tallahassee: Florida Heritage Foundation, 1971.

Hadd, Donald R. "The Irony of Secession." *Florida Historical Quarterly* 41 (July, 1962), 22–28.

Hornaday, William T. *A Mon-O-Graph on St. Vincent's Game Preserve.* Buffalo, N.Y.: Illustrated Buffalo Express, 1909.

Hoskins, F. W., ed. "A St. Joseph Diary of 1839." *Florida Historical Quarterly* 17 (October, 1938), 132–51.

Hudson, Charles M. *The Southeastern Indians.* Knoxville: University of Tennessee Press, 1976.

Ingle, Robert M., and William K. Whitfield, Jr. *Oyster Culture in Florida.* Tallahassee: State of Florida Board of Conservation, 1968.

Itkin, Stanley L. "Operations of the East Gulf Blockade Squadron in the Blockade of Florida, 1862–1865." Master's thesis, Florida State University, 1962.

Jackson, Jesse J. "The Negro and the Law in Florida, 1821–1921." Master's thesis, Florida State University, 1960.

Jahoda, Gloria. *The Other Florida.* New York: Charles Scribner's Sons, 1967.

Johns, John E. *Florida During the Civil War.* Gainesville: University of Florida Press, 1963.

Johnson, Dudley Sady. "The Railroads of Florida, 1865–1900." Ph.D. diss., Florida State University, 1965.

Joiner, Edward Earl. *A History of Florida Baptists.* Jacksonville: Convention Press, 1972.

Jones, Frank S. *History of Decatur County* [Georgia]. Spartanburg: Reprint Co., 1980.

Jones, James P., and William Warren Rogers. "The Surrender of Tallahassee." *Apalachee* 6 (1963–67), 103–10.

Jones, James Pickett. *Yankee Blitzkrieg: Wilson's Raid through Alabama and Georgia.* Athens: University of Georgia Press, 1976.

Joyce, Edwin A., Jr., and Bonnie Eldred. *The Florida Shrimping Industry.* St. Petersburg: State of Florida Board of Conservation, 1966.

Key, Alexander. *Island Light.* Indianapolis: Bobbs-Merrill, 1950.

———. *The Wrath and the Wind.* Indianapolis: Bobbs-Merrill, 1949.

Knauss, James O. *Florida Territorial Journalism.* DeLand: Florida State Historical Society, 1936.

———. "St. Joseph, An Episode of the Economic and Political History of Florida." Part 1. *Florida Historical Quarterly* 5 (April, 1926–27), 177–95. Part 2, (1927–28), 3–20.

Koenig, Louis W. *Bryan: A Political Biography of William Jennings Bryan.* New York: G. P. Putnam's Sons, 1971.

BIBLIOGRAPHY

Leonard, Irving A. *Spanish Approach to Pensacola, 1689–1693.* Albuquerque: Quivira Society, 1939.

Livingston, Robert J. *Resource Atlas of the Apalachicola Estuary.* Tallahassee: Florida Sea Grant College Program, 1983.

Lonn, Ella. *Salt as a Factor in the Confederacy.* New York: Walter Neale, 1933.

_____. "The Extent and Importance of Federal Naval Raids on Salt Making in Florida." *Florida Historical Quarterly* 10 (April, 1932), 167–84.

Marchetta, Beverly. "Florida's Part in the Mexican War." Honors thesis, Florida State University, 1962.

Martin, John H., comp. *Columbus, Geo., from Its Selection as a "Trading Town" in 1827, to Its Partial Destruction by Wilson's Raid, in 1865. History—Incident—Personality.* Columbus: Tho. Gilbert Book Printers, 1874.

Massey, Richard W., Jr. "A History of the Lumber Industry in Alabama and West Florida, 1880–1914." Ph.D. diss., Vanderbilt University, 1960.

Miles, Robley M. "Analysis of the 'Trash Fish' of Shrimp Trawlers Operating in Apalachicola Bay and the Adjacent Gulf of Mexico." Master's thesis, Florida State University, 1951.

Miller, William. "The Battle of Natural Bridge." *Apalachee* 4 (1950–56), 76–86.

Montgomery, Horace. *Howell Cobb's Confederate Career.* Tuscaloosa: Confederate Publishing Co., 1959.

Nichols, James L. *Confederate Engineers.* Tuscaloosa: Confederate Publishing Co., 1957.

Nichy, Fred Eugene. "The Effect of Predators on the Mortality of Oysters in a High Salinity Area in Florida." Master's thesis, Florida State University, 1956.

Nixon, Eugene L. "A Doctor and an Island." *Journal of the Florida Medical Association* 61 (August, 1972), 45–53.

Owens, Harry P. "Port of Apalachicola." *Florida Historical Quarterly* 58 (July, 1969), 1–25.

_____. "Sail and Steam Vessels Serving the Apalachicola-Chattahoochee Valley." *Alabama Review* 21 (July, 1968), 195–210.

_____. "Apalachicola before 1861." Ph.D. diss., Florida State University, 1966.

Pacetti, Derald, Jr. "Shrimping at Fernandina, Florida, before 1920: Industry Development, Fisheries Regulation, Wartime Maturation." Master's thesis, Florida State University, 1980.

Parker, Daisy. "John Milton, Governor of Florida; a Loyal Confederate." *Florida Historical Quarterly* 20 (April, 1942), 346–61.

Pertrof, Vasil. "A Study of the Florida Natural Sponge Industry with Special Emphasis on Its Marketing Problems." Ph.D. diss., University of Florida, 1967.

Porter, Louise M. *The Chronological History of the Lives of St. Joseph, Written, Assembled, and Edited . . . .* Chattanooga: Great American, 1975.

Price, Marcus W. "Ships That Tested the Blockade of the Gulf Ports, 1861–1865." *American Neptune* 11 (November, 1952), 304–90; 12 (January, 1953), 52–59; (April, 1953), 154–61; (July, 1953), 229–36.

Rerick, Rowland H. *Memoirs of Florida.* Vol. 2. Atlanta: Southern Historical Association, 1902.

Rhyne, Janie Smith. *Our Yesterdays.* N.p. 1968.

Rogers, William Warren. *Thomas County, 1865–1900.* Tallahassee: Florida State University Press, 1973.

Rowsome, Frank, Jr. *The Verse by the Side of the Road.* New York: E. P. Dutton, 1966.

Ruge, John G. "The Canning Industry in the South." In *A History of the Canning Industry by Its Most Prominent Men,* edited by Arthur L. Judge. Baltimore: The Canning Trade, 1914.

Schellings, William J., ed. "On Blockade Duty in Florida Waters; Excerpts from a Union Naval Officer's Diary." *Tequesta* 15 (1955), 55–72.

Sherlock, John V. "Panton, Leslie and Company." Master's thesis, Florida State University, 1948.

Sherlock, V[ivian] M. *The Fever Man: A Biography of Dr. John Gorrie.* Tallahassee: Medallion Press, 1982.

Sherlock, Vivian M. "Medical Practices in the Port of Apalachicola, 1830–1850." *Apalachee* 9 (1980–83), 97–104.

Shofner, Jerrell H. *Nor Is It Over Yet: Florida in the Era of Reconstruction, 1863–1877.* Gainesville: University of Florida Press, 1974.

Simmons, William H. "Journal of Dr. W. H. Simmons, Commissioner to Locate the Seat of Government of the Territory of Florida." *Florida Historical Quarterly* 1 (April, 1908), 28–36.

Smith, Gene. "St. Vincent Island." *Florida Wildlife* (September, 1969), 10–15; (October, 1969), 12–17.

Smith, Julia Floyd. *Slavery and Plantation Growth in Antebellum Florida, 1821–1860.* Gainesville: University of Florida Press, 1973.

Standard, Diffie W. *Columbus, Georgia in the Confederacy.* New York: William Frederick Press, 1953.

Stanley, J. Randall. *History of Gadsden County.* Quincy: Gadsden County Historical Commission, 1948.

_____. *History of Jackson County.* [Marianna]: Jackson County Historical Society, 1950.

Strickland, Alice. "Blockade Runners." *Florida Historical Quarterly* 36 (Oct., 1957), 85–93.

Swanton, John R. *Early History of the Creek Indians and Their Neighbors.* Washington: Government Printing Office, 1922.

Thronateeska Chapter, Daughters of the American Revolution, comps. *History and Reminiscences of Dougherty County, Georgia.* Albany: Thronateeska Chapter, 1924.

Thurston, William N. "A Study of Maritime Activity in Florida in the Nineteenth Century." Ph.D. diss., Florida State University, 1972.

Tressler, Donald K. *Marine Products of Commerce: Their Acquisition, Handling, Biological Aspects, and the Science and Technology of Their Preparation and Preservation.* New York: Chemical Catalog Co., 1923.

Turner, Maxine. "Naval Operations on the Apalachicola and Chattahoochee Rivers, 1861–1865." *Alabama Historical Quarterly* 36 (Fall and Winter, 1974–75), entire issue.

Unger, Frank Albert. "Some Aspects of Land Acquisition and Settlement in Territorial Florida: The St. Joseph Community." Master's thesis, Florida State University, 1974.

Upchurch, John Calhoun. "Aspects of the Development and Exploration of the Forbes Purchase." *Florida Historical Quarterly* 48 (October, 1969), 117–39.

_____. "Some Aspects of Early Exploration, Settlement, and Economic Development within the Forbes Purchase." Master's thesis, Florida State University, 1965.

Vanderhill, Burke G. "The Historic Spas of Florida." *Geographic Perspectives on Southern Development* 20 (June, 1973), 59–77.

Walker, Anne Kendrick. *Backtracking in Barbour County.* Richmond: Dietz Press, 1941.

Whiddon, Juanita. "David Saunders Johnston, The Man and His Times." In *Collections of Early County* [Georgia] *Historical Society* 2 (1979), 136–45.

White, David H. "The John Forbes Company: Heir to the Florida Indian Trade: 1801–1809." Ph.D. diss., University of Alabama, 1973.

Williams, John Lee. "Journal of John Lee Williams, Commissioner to Locate the Seat of Government of the Territory of Florida." *Florida Historical Quarterly* 1 (April, 1908), 37–44; (July, 1908): 18–30.

Womack, Miles Kenan, Jr. *Gadsden: A Florida County in Word and Picture.* Quincy: Gadsden County Bicentennial Committee, 1976.

Wood, Virginia Steele. *Live Oaking Southern Timber for Tall Ships.* Boston: Northeastern University Press, 1982.

Woodman, Harold D. *King Cotton and His Retainers: Financing and Marketing the Cotton Crop of the South, 1800–1925.* Lexington: University of Kentucky Press, 1968.

Wooster, Ralph A. "The Florida Secession Convention." *Florida Historical Quarterly* 36 (April, 1958), 373–85.

Worsley, Etta Blanchard. *Columbus on the Chattahoochee.* Columbus: Columbus Office Supply Co., 1951.

Wright, J. Leitch, Jr. *William Augustus Bowles: Director General of the Creek Nation.* Athens: University of Georgia Press, 1976.

_____. *The Only Land They Knew: The Tragic Story of the American Indians in the Old South.* New York: Free Press, 1981.

Yonge, C. M. *Oysters.* London: Collins, 1960.

Young, Mary E. *Redskins, Ruffleshirts, and Rednecks: Indian Allotments in Alabama and Mississippi, 1830–1860.* Norman: University of Oklahoma Press, 1961.

Zahendra, Peter. "Spanish West Florida, 1781–1821." Ph.D. diss., University of Michigan, 1976.

Index

INDEX

INDEX

Taken on the Spot June 1837 by H.A.Norris, Civil Engr.

P.A.Mesier &

CITY OF APA